Organizations and Technology for Sustainability

Editors

Elisabetta Magnaghi

Deputy Director General and Dean
KEDGE Business School
France

Eleonora Veglianti

Associate Professor
Management Department
KEDGE Business School
France

CRC Press
Taylor & Francis Group
Boca Raton London New York

CRC Press is an imprint of the
Taylor & Francis Group, an **informa** business
A SCIENCE PUBLISHERS BOOK

Cover credit: Image created by Prof. Eleonora Veglianti.

First edition published 2025
by CRC Press
2385 NW Executive Center Drive, Suite 320, Boca Raton FL 33431

and by CRC Press
4 Park Square, Milton Park, Abingdon, Oxon, OX14 4RN

CRC Press is an imprint of Taylor & Francis Group, LLC

Library of Congress Cataloging-in-Publication Data (applied for)

ISBN: 978-1-032-59824-6 (hbk)
ISBN: 978-1-032-59825-3 (pbk)
ISBN: 978-1-003-45644-5 (ebk)

DOI: 10.1201/9781003456445

Typeset in Times New Roman
by Prime Publishing Services

Preface

In the today's environment, organizations cannot be indifferent to the huge transformative change pushed by digital technologies which creates new challenges as well as new opportunities for the overall society. We can identify a new path that requires a focus on the role of sustainability between the interplay of organizations and technological tools. Interest among academics and practitioners has grown around IT-based solutions considering different organizational contexts with a strong focus on sustainability issues. Moreover, recent unexpected events, such as the COVID-19 pandemic, has enhanced the use of technology. The latter provides additional insights on the importance of Sustainable Development Goals (SDGs).

Publications and discussions raise on these themes which aim at defining the concepts, the recurring elements as well as the innovative features. In other words, several disciplines, as the management one, contribute to this vivid and critical debate to advance the knowledge and to better manage this important revolution.

The present book is a response to this digital transition providing a multidisciplinary perspective with various contributions coming from different management perspectives. Thus, this book focuses on interplay many managerial aspects such as organizational, financial, environmental and social to improve the organizations' effectiveness. This book is of interest for a large audience, from all disciplines interested in organizations, information and communication technology (ICT) and sustainability. In this book, you will find insights to develop and implement organizational and technological capabilities within our entities to enlarge the need for a more sustainable business-oriented approach.

Elisabetta Magnaghi
Eleonora Veglianti

Acknowledgments

We would like to thank the keynote speakers, presenters and participants to our Interdisciplinary Conference on Management, Information Technology and Computer Sciences, which took place in Lille, on 25–26 May 2023. They provided a scientific debate and interesting contributions which are included in some chapters of this book.

Contents

CHAPTER 1

Tools and Methods of Efficient Judicial Proceedings
A Comprehensive Framework from a Literature Review

Silvia Di Varano, *Kamran Khan* and *Daniela Mancini**

1. Introduction

In recent years, the administration of justice has assumed an important role in Italian political, economic and social debates. An efficient, effective and fair judicial system is fundamental for a country's economic and social progress in terms of contributing to business development and opportunities (Bianco and Gaicomelli 2004, La Porta et al. 1996, Masciandaro 2000, Zingales et al. 1999). The European Council, in its annual recommendations, has constantly urged Italy to "reduce the length of civil trials at all levels of judgment" and to "increase the effectiveness of the prevention and repression of corruption by reducing the duration of criminal trials and implementing the new anti-corruption framework" (PNRR 2021, p. 28).

Furthermore, in Italy, the National Recovery and Resilience Plan (PNRR) planned a "complete and coherent package of reforms and investments" (PNRR 2021/2022) of the Italian government to access the financial resources made available by the European Union (EU) as part of the Next Generation EU strategy. The reform of the judicial system included measures aimed at speeding up the progress of trials

Department of Law, University of Teramo, Italy, Via Renato Balzarini.
Emails: sdivarano@unit.it; kamran.khan0722@gmail.com
* Corresponding author: dmancini@unite.it

and specific allocations for the digitization of judicial proceedings for managing the previous load of civil and criminal cases and the efficiency of judicial buildings (Civini 2021). The PNRR's set of measures should lead to a significant reduction in the backlog and duration of civil, criminal and administrative trials. The PNRR intends to reduce trial times through the following objectives: (a) implementing the Process Office; (b) strengthening the administrative capacity of the judicial system; (c) enhancing digital infrastructures; (d) constructing efficient and modern building structures; and (e) reducing recidivism through re-education and social reintegration of prisoners (PNRR 2021, p. 54). Therefore, in Italy, as in other geographical contexts, the efficiency of the judicial system is perceived as an urgent and relevant problem to address.

Various studies have proposed a range of techniques, tools and methods for making lawsuits, courts and, in general, the judicial system faster and more reactive in terms of efficiency, effectiveness and productivity (Contini and Viapiana 2020). Scholars have shown how several tools and methods, such as machine learning (ML), convolutional neural network (CNN) architecture, the long short-term memory (LSTM) bidirectional network, the text classification of legal documents, the bag-of-word (BoW) model and linear support vector machine (LSVM) classifiers, can help predict the sentence of a case (Luz de Araujo et al. 2022), the legal area (Sulea et al. 2017) or the date of issuing a sentence, making the judicial system more efficient and effective. Researchers have investigated various phases of the proceedings, particularly filing, since it is slower and could cause a backlog (Undavia et al. 2018, Luz de Araujo et al. 2020). Other studies have highlighted the lack of digitization or the limited use of information and communication technologies (ICT) in the judicial system and underlined the need to speed up the time of court cases (Baranenko et al. 2022).

Discussing the efficiency and effectiveness of legal systems is difficult and elusive in many respects. Studies have investigated the efficiency, effectiveness and productivity of law courts and have suggested technological tools and organizational mechanisms to resolve legal backwardness and slowness. Regardless of its geographical context, the difficulties encountered by judicial systems are always the same. Studies discussing the efficiency and effectiveness of the judicial system mainly emphasize the role of ICT but neglect classification methods and organizational solutions. Furthermore, the literature is still scarce and gives a fragmented overview of problems related to the judicial system and potential solutions. There is a need to systematize the current literature and provide an all-encompassing overview of the problems related to efficiency, effectiveness and productivity in the judicial system to identify solutions to these issues, in terms of tools and methods.

Considering the above-mentioned PNRR reforms in Italian judicial management, the Italian judicial offices face problems and challenges in implementing the required reform, so additional research is needed. This study presents a literature review to connect the administrative problems facing judicial offices to develop tools to improve their efficiency and effectiveness. In addition, it provides a taxonomy of problems and related subcases of courts and tribunals currently being analyzed in national and international studies to better identify a future research agenda.

This paper is structured into the following sections: Section 2 describes the methodology, Section 3 the findings, Section 4 presents the discussion and Section 5 concludes the study.

2. Methodology

The authors performed a systematic literature review, which identifies and critically appraises relevant research and analyzes its data (Liberati et al. 2009). Given the particularity of the theme, a lot of time was spent identifying the right keywords and filter criteria to be used in the Web of Science search engine. In this phase, the PNRR, various scientific articles from the Italian journal *Azienda Pubblica* and some others focused on legal themes were examined to identify the recurring keywords related to our objectives. Selecting the keywords first occurred through a preliminary brainstorming session between the authors to identify, based on their experience, some useful scientific studies on the topic based on personal experiences. Subsequently, a careful reading of these scientific articles was carried out to isolate keywords. A preliminary search for these keywords on Google Scholar and a discussion with legal research and legal affairs experts to refine and complete the selection were performed.

The research's second phase consisted of selecting and reading the articles. Selecting the articles was based on relevance to the investigated topic. The systematic search approach of the literature review ensures a transparent, accurate and replicable process and reduces search bias. The keywords used for selecting the relevant materials were "case", "case management", "classification", "court", "efficient judicial process" and "effective judicial system". With these keywords, we identified 118 articles from the Web of Science database. After reading the titles and abstracts of the articles, we chose 40 articles for further analysis. We then read the full articles and selected the 20 most relevant to our research objective. Figure 1 indicates the steps for selecting the articles. The selected articles met our

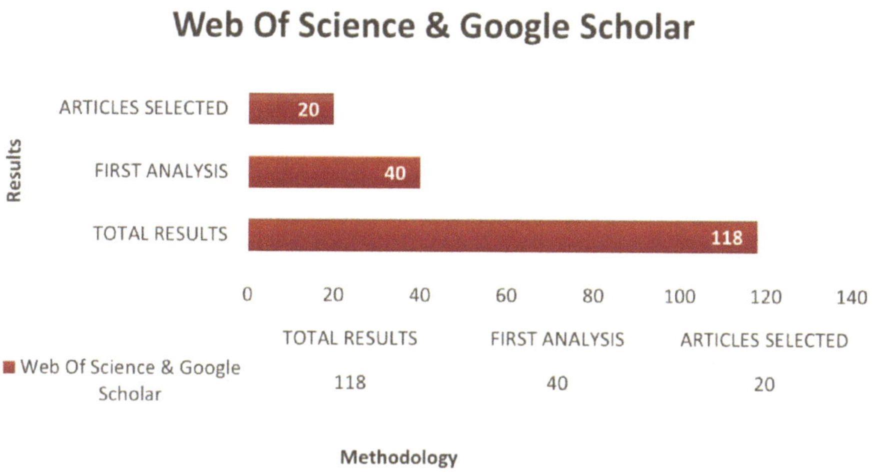

Figure 1. Steps for selecting the articles.

research objective, while the eliminated articles did not present useful information or were irrelevant to our research objectives. The first column of Table 1 shows the articles selected.

The structured literature review proposes a comprehensive efficiency and effectiveness scheme to identify problems in judicial organizations and solutions to help courts and justice office managers improve the speed of lawsuit proceedings.

3. Findings

Twenty articles were selected and analyzed in a systematic and indepth manner. The articles highlight issues related to improving the judicial system's performance and decreasing time to sentence and legal backlog. Furthermore, they underline that justice delayed is justice denied. Long legal delays threaten the legitimacy of a country's judicial and political systems (Wei et al. 2022). The articles cover the period 2009 to 2022, except for one article published in 1997. The articles were published in scientific journals in the legal, medical and computer science fields; most were published in *Azienda Pubblica* and *The International Journal of Computer Science and Network Security*. The articles examine different geographical areas and contexts. They concern the Brazilian Supreme Court, the French Supreme Court, the American Supreme Court, the Singapore Supreme Court and other European and Asian courts. The sample deals with different legal contexts ranging from first-instance to second-instance appeals and their filing. We analyzed each article regarding its research scope and methods. Many papers conducted case studies for implementing and introducing machine learning techniques (Luz de Araujo et al. 2020, Luz de Araujo et al. 2022, Sulea et al. 2017, Undavia et al. 2018). Some were descriptive studies (Baranenko et al. 2022, Demchenko et al. 2022). After a preliminary review of the articles, we developed a deep manual content analysis to identify the problems they found with the judicial system and/or offices and the tools designed or tested to find solutions. This analysis is summarized in Table 1.

The Brazilian legal system suffers from an unreasonably large number of lawsuits due to the time it takes to process them (Luz de Araujo et al. 2020). In the Brazilian Supreme Court, court employees spend thousands of hours analyzing legal documents and classifying cases (Luz de Araujo et al. 2022). In this context, various authors observe that using multimodal CNNs, which combine features extracted from texts and images, helps classify the pages of legal documents, reduce the backlog and facilitate the classification of the cases. The use of natural language processing (NLP) and ML techniques is fundamental to reducing the number of lawsuits at the Supreme Court of Brazil (Supremo Tribunal Federal or STF) (Luz de Araujo et al. 2020).

Combining textual features with visual features extracted from separately trained CNNs on image and text data allows each page in the expanded corpus to be stored in at least one of the two formats. The text data is first extracted through optical character recognition (Smith 2007) with additional preprocessing steps. In this case, the tools are the best and most effective solution. The classification of judicial years represents another problem related to the concepts of efficiency and effectiveness, which are present in the Supreme Court of the United States (SCOTUS), and in this case, the supreme court classifier (SCC) was used. This system applies ConvNet,

Table 1. Classification of the articles selected concerning efficiency and effectiveness issues, and tools.

N.	References	Problems	Tools and Methods
1	Afonso et al. 2020	To improve the financing and operation of the Brazilian health system through regulations and legal practices.	Epi Info 6 software analysing lawsuits filed against healthcare professionals.
2	Agrifoglio et al. 2010	To support court performance measurement and the managers' planning and control activities.	The balanced scorecard.
3	Arena and Ferris 2018	To explore how national factors affect litigation risk.	A probit analysis.
4	Baranenko et al. 2022	To analyse through information technology the dimension of the delimitation of the jurisdiction of the courts.	Historical, comparative-juridical, formal-logical, empirical, analogy, synthesis, analysis and systematic methods.
5	Bussetti and Vecchi 2018	To improve the management of judicial offices in Italy.	PT, which is a qualitative method that uses Bayesian reasoning to improve the accuracy of within-case inferences.
6	Luz de Araujo et al. 2020	To reduce the unreasonably large number of lawsuits in the Brazilian legal system.	NLP and ML techniques.
7	Luz de Araujo et al. 2022	To manage many paper legal documents.	Multimodal combination methods and sequential learning methods.
8	Demchenko et al. 2022	To ensure the right to a fair trial in civil and commercial proceedings during the era of information technology development.	System, historical, comparative-legal, legal-formal, logical-legal, alternative, analysis and generalization methods.
9	Gomes et al. 2014	To reduce the backlog of lawsuits in the medical and pharmaceutical fields and their growth.	PASW statistics software, IDUS, the unified table of the SUS, SIA and SIH tables for the analysis of the judicial action
10	Howe et al. 2019	To classify judgments in legal areas of the American Supreme Court.	NLP methods.
11	Jung et al. 2018	To prepare surgical personnel to avoid preventable medical litigation and backlogs.	Data analysis software.
12	Lai and Che 2009	To better manage patent-related litigation.	BPNN.
13	Lepore 2009	To make judicial administrations more efficient and cost-effective.	The analysis of institutional sources and legislation on the subject.
14	Morawska et al. 2019	To identify the factors influencing the functioning of the courts to reduce the excessive duration of judicial proceedings.	Historical analysis and software.

Table 1 contd. ...

...Table 1 contd.

N.	References	Problems	Tools and Methods
15	Oliveira et al. 2020	To ensure universal access to safe, effective and quality medicines at the lowest possible price for all citizens.	SPSS software for data analysis in cases related to drugs.
16	Ross 1997	To reduce lawsuits and backlogs for making appropriate decisions regarding the safety and well-being of prisoners.	Content analysis and data analysis using software of the decisions of the cases of correctional civil liability contested under Section 1983.
17	Sherman 1994	To reduce cost and delays of litigations.	Hybrid and new alternative dispute resolution (ADR) methods.
18	Sulea et al. 2017	To help legal professionals speed up their work.	The application of text classification methods to predict the area of law and the decision of the case judged through BoW and linear SVM.
19	Undavia et al. 2018	To classify documents relating to the opinion of SCOTUS.	The SCC system using a CNN.
20	Wei et al. 2022	To present online trials.	PNL, AI, SVM, BiLSTM and DNN.

recurrent neural network (RNN), support vector machine (SVM) and logistic regression methods trained on a dataset of SCOTUS cases to address the problem of classifying court opinion documents (Undavia et al. 2018).

In the Chinese context, the use of multimodal convolutional tools, such as neurolinguistic programming (NP), artificial intelligence (AI), support vector machines (SVMs), bidirectional LSTM (BiLSTM) and DotNetNuke (DNN), has proposed a full-process intelligent trial system (FITS) to provide intelligent assistance to achieve more efficient, fair and explainable procedural processes (Wei et al. 2022). Other authors (e.g., Howe et al. 2019) apply state-of-the-art NLP methods with traditional statistical models to a legal corpus. For example, all textual approaches, including the argument model, word embedding and language model classifiers, are used to classify judgments in legal areas of the Supreme Court of Singapore and make them more innovative and efficient. Furthermore, a study (Howe et al. 2019) highlighting how in the Supreme Court of Singapore, each legal case falls under one or more areas of law (legal areas) is illustrative. These areas are attorneys' shorthand for the subset of legal principles and rules governing the case. Thus, attorneys often evaluate a new case by asking whether it falls within tort, contract or other legal areas. Answering this question helps send unresolved cases to the right experts and efficiently retrieve resolved precedents (Howe et al. 2019).

Several authors have examined the application of text classification methods to predict the area of law and the decision of adjudicated cases. They investigated to what extent it is possible to automatically identify argumentative propositions in the legal text, together with their function and argumentative structure (Sulea et al. 2017). These authors use a corpus containing legal texts extracted from the European Court of Human Rights (ECHR) and classify argumentative and nonargumentative judgments. Such applications are developed to help legal professionals speed up their work by providing shorter summaries of long legal documents. The use of the SVM linear classifier method trained on lexical characteristics has been used to predict the area of law and the decision of the cases judged by the French Supreme Court (Sulea et al. 2017). In the American context and more specifically in the district courts, the back-propagation neural network (BPNN) has been used to build an evaluation model on patent infringement lawsuits. A BPNN was also applied to construct a patent valuation model. The 17 indicators to quantitatively describe the size of patents were the inputs, and the damages were the outputs (Lai and Che 2009).

In Brazil, there is also a backlog of lawsuits in the medical and pharmaceutical fields. The messy growth of such lawsuits in recent years imposes unexpected expenditures on city, state and federal budgets, and causes a large impact on the management of the Brazilian Unified National Health System, which can aggravate inequities. At the same time, it becomes inevitable to consider the importance of judicialization as a sign of individual and collective health needs (Gomes et al. 2014). In this case, the PASW statistics software, and data from the performance index of the unified health system, the unified table of the Brazilian Unified National Health System, the Ambulatory Information System, and Hospital Information System tables were used to analyze judicial action to make it more efficient and effective (Gomes et al. 2014).

Other important articles include studies that use more theoretical methods. In this field, the Civil Justice Reform Act of 1990 and case management as a subcategory of court administration have also become the primary administrative technique for reducing delays and costs in case processing. In fact, with their broad substantive authority and general jurisdiction, states can be fertile ground for efforts to reduce the costs and delays of litigation by making the legal process more time- and cost-efficient (Sherman 1994).

Another important concept linked to efficiency and effectiveness concerns the right to a fair trial. Various authors (e.g., Demchenko et al. 2022) highlight that the right to a fair trial is universally recognized. The rapid development of information technology is reflected in the significant transformation of the judiciary and the development of its information system. Therefore, given the significant role of ensuring the right to a fair trial in civil and commercial proceedings, it is necessary to explore the features of ensuring this right in the context of expanding digital technology, highlight key principles and address issues of a fair trial. The modern world is moving towards an information society, life is shifting more and more online, the Internet have taken a prominent place in all spheres of public relations. The judicial system has also become increasingly digitalized, which affects the right to a fair and efficient trial (Demchenko et al. 2022).

Remaining in the methodological context, one study examined 475 corporate lawsuits in developed countries, exploring how national factors influence litigation risk, market value, shareholders, the results of the lawsuits and the resolution costs. The study highlights the significant effect that country-specific institutional characteristics have on the corporate litigation experience (Arena and Ferris 2018).

In the European context, a case study conducted on 210 commercial cases (electronic payment mandate proceedings, payment mandate proceedings, enforcement proceedings and company cases) by the Gdansk Regional Court of Appeal identifies the factors influencing the functioning of Polish courts. This study also underlines the risks of legal delays in terms of the loss of legitimacy of a country's judicial and political systems (Morawska et al. 2019).

In the American context, a study performed a content analysis of sentences of correctional civil liability cases contested under the Civil Rights Statute Title 42 United States Code (U.S.C.) Section 1983 from 1970 to 1994. Using a coding tool, each case was analyzed based on a schema of information on eight aspects of the case itself, thus identifying 16 major categories of corrections in which inmates commonly bring a case under Section 1983 (Ross 1997).

Several studies (e.g., Agrifoglio et al. 2010, Bussetti and Vecchi 2018, Lepore 2009) have used different theories and methodological tools in the Italian context. Agrifoglio et al. have indicated that judicial administration in Italy is more inefficient than in other industrialized countries and even some countries in the developing world. The authors tested a tool for measuring the performance of Italian courts; the tool is based on the balanced scorecard framework. The authors believe the tool can support management's decision-making processes and help improve the courts' efficiency.

Remaining in the Italian context, Lepore explored the efficiency and cost-effectiveness of judicial administrations in Italy and how modernized they are. The management by objectives methodology used by the Italian Ministry of Justice is explored, and the court management framework is analysed with the aim of highlighting the features of the different frameworks and verifying the feasibility of applying best Court Management practices in the Italian context. The judicial administrations should be managed autonomously and responsibly, using adequate managerial tools to support decision-making and control processes.

Finally, in the Italian context, Bussetti examined how the District Court of Milan (LCM) implemented a national program for improving the management of judicial offices. The study explores how the program may have contributed to the success of the LCM in three phases: engaging leaders, providing previously inaccessible knowledge and ensuring knowledge transfer. From the National Court Management Improvement Program a framework is developed, which is tested using process tracing (PT), a qualitative method using Bayesian reasoning to improve the accuracy of within-case inferences (Bussetti and Vecchi 2018).

4. Discussion

The authors examine the problems of efficiency, effectiveness and productivity and related methods and tools in different geographical and legal contexts using several. The variety of solutions and geographical and legal contexts make it difficult to understand how all these studies could help courts and justice office managers improve the efficiency and effectiveness of lawsuit proceedings. Furthermore, the lack of a systematic and comprehensive framework of the extant literature does not support researchers; instead, it produces a fragmented view of the urgent call for efficient and effective justice services, highlighting the need for a roadmap for future research based on under investigated questions.

Starting from the literature analysis and results summarized in Table 1, we develop a taxonomy of the problems investigated by the current research and design a framework linking efficient and effective issues to specific management areas and solutions. The entire schematization is linked to the concepts of efficiency, effectiveness and productivity in the field of the judicial process.

From the critical analysis of every single article, we identified the problem and its description and related tools and methods. Based on the literature, we created a classification framework concerning the problems of efficiency, effectiveness and productivity:

- Spending excessive time (eight articles).
- Reducing disputes (seven articles).
- Classifying documents (two articles).
- Court planning and controlling (three articles).

The authors also identified different management areas indicating the general area in which one or more articles belong.

Starting from the taxonomy identified, we explain the management areas relating to one or more articles with the tools and methods used to solve the problem connected to the lack of efficiency and effectiveness discussed in each article.

4.1 Spending Excessive Time

Regarding excessive time, we selected eight articles and four management areas. We first highlighted the general problem (i.e., "spending excessive time on initial analysis and limited time for the subsequent phases of the process"). We then narrowed down the management areas to "case management and classifying of legal documents". This scheme allowed us to place the related articles within the first line and with them the related solutions in terms of tools and methods. In this case, the articles propose different solutions in different geographical contexts.

In the Brazilian context, using NLP and ML techniques is fundamental to the Supreme Court of Brazil (Supremo Tribunal Federal or STF) in reducing the number of lawsuits (Luz de Araujo et al. 2020, 2022). The use of these techniques has allowed the creation of VICTOR (Luz de Araujo et al. 2020), a dataset built from the digitized legal documents of the Supreme Court of Brazil and subsequently, and the fusion module (Luz de Araujo et al. 2022), which combines textual and visual characteristics extracted from CNNs trained separately on image and text data. Furthermore, text classification techniques are used to provide valuable assistive technology for legal practitioners to obtain guidance from large corporations of previous court decisions (Sulea et al. 2017).

In the American context, the SCC was used, that is, a system that applies ConvNet, RNNs, SVMs, and logistic regression methods trained on a dataset of

SCOTUS cases, to address the problem of classification of court opinion documents (Undavia et al. 2018).

It was possible to isolate a second line relating to excessive time: "spending excessive time resolving disputes in the medical, health, and pharmaceutical field". In this context, the identified management area is "supporting the judge with experts in the field relating to the specific dispute and use of technological tools". The solutions proposed to the problems indicated above always refer to techniques and procedures that allow the lawyer to manage the legal case and its documentation more quickly and precisely.

In the Brazilian context, the relationship between law and healthcare is complex, requiring frequent insurance coverage, reduced waiting for times and unilateral and efficient resolutions (Afonso et al. 2020). In this context, Epi Info 6 software, which is an integrated package of computer programs, manages data in questionnaire format and organizes projects and results of study in texts that can form parts of written reports. Furthermore, establishing technically sound methods and developing preventive care guidelines may be some of the few viable strategies to facilitate legal procedures and reduce the backlog (Afonso et al. 2020).

In addition, other authors (e.g., Gomes et al. 2014) use PASW statistics software to analyse the legal data for identifying critical issues in healthcare lawsuits, such as reducing waiting times between scheduling and carrying out the consultation and reducing the time for emergency treatment.

The third branch related to the problem of excessive time is "spending excessive time for the resolution of disputes in terms of guaranteeing a fair trial". In this context, the identified management area is the "managing the backlog on a theoretical basis". In this context, the right to a fair trial is a fundamental issue in the judicial procedure, which can be affected by long trials and case backlogs (Demchenko et al. 2022). The authors identify the principles of a fair trial using different theoretical methods.

To conclude, there is a fourth branch relating to the problem of excessive time: "spending excessive time on the resolution of disputes". In this context, the identified management area is "case management".

Related to this branch is an important case study conducted by the Gdansk Regional Court of Appeal (Morawska et al. 2019). The authors used historical analysis and various software to identify factors to reduce judgment time and backlog: the duration of first-instance proceedings (in particular the waiting time for the first hearing) and second-instance proceedings, re-examination time for the first-degree case, the activity of the parties during the case, the dispute amount, procedural costs, procedural complexity—measured by the number of volumes accumulated during the procedure and by the number of pages in the judgment—the organizational and juridical form of the plaintiff/defendant and the participation of experts (Morawska et al. 2019).

4.2 Reducing Disputes

The second theme is reducing disputes. We selected seven articles and two management areas. We first highlighted the general problem (i.e., reducing healthcare and pharmaceutical disputes and patent litigation). We then narrowed down the management areas to "supporting the judge with experts in the field relating to the specific dispute and use of technological tools". This scheme has allowed us to place the related articles within the management areas and with them the related solutions in terms of tools and methods. In this case, the articles propose different solutions in different geographical contexts.

In a descriptive and retrospective study regarding pending first-instance lawsuits claiming medicines in the state of Rio Grande do Norte (Oliveira et al. 2020), the data analysis was performed by SPSS software, as a solution to establish coordination between prescribers, the pharmaceutical industry and lawyers to reduce disputes in the healthcare-pharmaceutical field in terms of efficiency and effectiveness (Oliveira et al. 2020).

A study about district courts in the United States is connected to the same management area (Lai et al. 2009). The authors used BPNN to construct a patent valuation model where the 17 indicators to describe the size of patents quantitatively were the inputs, and the damages were the output. The patent valuation model was validated to be feasible using error analysis. Patent infringement lawsuits have been on the rise around the world, so an integrated evaluator for patent management is needed: a completely new concept for analysing patent infringement cases, discussing the legal values of patents and providing an integrated model for patent valuation.

Again, in the American context, another study used a coding tool to relate each case to prisoners based on eight aspects, thus allowing the identification of 16 major categories of corrections (Ross 1997). In this content analysis study, the use of software was essential to analyse which law officials should develop additional ways of resolving prisoner grievances administratively by expanding policies on grievance mechanisms. If grievance mechanisms are not in place, the agency should develop an agency-level or state-level dispute resolution system to make litigation more efficient and effective and reduce lawsuits (Ross 1997).

In the medical-legal field, Jung et al. (2018) evaluated identifying patterns in the types of accidents in the surgical departments of Korean hospitals by analysing specific litigation cases to help surgical personnel avoid preventable medical disputes. The information obtained, such as patterns in the types of medical incidents, their outcomes and defendants' negligence in the court opinion, could be used to make litigation more efficient and effective (Jung et al. 2018).

Subsequently, we isolated a second general problem (i.e., "reducing litigation costs/ligation/IT"), and we linked the second management area to it (i.e., "managing the backlog on a theoretical basis"). This scheme has allowed us to place the related articles within the second general problem and with them the related solutions in terms of tools and methods. In this case, the articles propose different solutions in different geographical contexts.

Related to this branch, it is important the analyse the Civil Justice Reform Act 1990 and case management as a subcategory of court administration, which has become the primary administrative technique for reducing delays and costs in processing cases (Sherman 1994). In this case, it is important the use hybrid and new ADR methods to measure performance on various levels to reduce the costs and delays of controversies. In other words, states must convene broad-based civil justice commissions made up of jurists, lawyers and litigants, and these groups focus on four key areas: court administration, case management techniques, alternatives to trial and early resolution incentives (Sherman 1994).

Also, a study of 475 international corporate lawsuits highlighted the significant effect that specific institutional characteristics have on corporate litigation (Arena et al. 2018). In this article, a probit analysis was used to estimate litigation risks, outcomes and factors influencing litigation costs.

Concerning the line "reducing litigation costs/ligation/IT" in the literature reviewed, it is interesting to note the peculiarities of the delimitation of the jurisdiction of commercial, civil, and administrative courts through the prism of computer measurement. Indeed, due to the specifics of information technology in resolving disputes, there are often difficulties and inconsistencies (Baranenko et al. 2022); therefore, theoretical methodologies are suggested (e.g., historical, comparative-juridical law, formal-logical method, empirical, analogy and system methods). Identifying the correct jurisdiction is important in the practice of the courts; it is necessary to distinguish information-technology disputes by jurisdiction. The courts of cassation must avoid jurisprudential differences when applying the same substantive law. It is essential to determine the jurisdiction when resolving these disputes, since each jurisdiction has its characteristics and categories (Baranenko et al. 2022).

4.3 Classifying Documents

The fourth class is the classifying documents, which includes two articles and two management areas. We first highlighted the general problems (i.e., "automatic classification of the legal judgment" and "computer classification of legal evidence of sentences"). We then narrowed down the management areas to "classifying legal judgments" and "case management". This scheme has allowed us to place one article in the first management area (classifying legal judgments) and one article in the second management area (case management) with the related solutions in terms of tools and methods. In this case, the articles propose ICT tools as the solution.

Concerning the first management area, Howe et al. (2019) used NLP methods, traditional statistical models, tested approaches, the argument model, word embedding and language model classifiers to classify judgments in legal areas of the Supreme Court of Singapore. More specifically, these tools allow the identification of law areas, and these areas are attorneys' shorthand for the subset of legal principles and rules governing the case. Thus, attorneys often evaluate a new case by asking whether it falls within tort, contract or other legal areas. Answering this question helps you route unresolved cases to the right experts and efficiently retrieve resolved precedents. Legal database providers regularly provide area-based search capabilities; courts often issue judgments categorized by area of law (Howe et al. 2019). In this context, all textual approaches, including the argument model, word embedding and language model classifiers, are used to classify judgments in legal areas of the Supreme Court of Singapore and make them more innovative and efficient (Howe et al. 2019).

Concerning the second management area, the use of multimodal convolutional tools, such as NP, AI, SVMs, BiLSTM and DNN, has allowed to propose a FITS to provide intelligent assistance to achieve more efficient, fair and explainable procedural processes (Wei et al. 2022). FITS introduces essential tasks for building an intelligent court, including information extraction, evidence classification, question generation, dialogue summarization, judgment prediction and judgment document generation, and then supports the judge in making a decision (Wei et al. 2022). These tools make litigation more efficient and effective, reducing backlogs and simplifying proceedings.

4.4 Court Planning and Controlling

Planning and controlling is the fifth problematic area, which includes three articles and one management area. We first highlighted the general problem (i.e., "court planning and controlling"), and we then narrowed down the management area to "court management". The articles related to this taxonomy propose theoretical solutions to make Italian judicial administrations more efficient and effective.

More specifically, Lepore (2009) explored the efficiency and cost-effectiveness of judicial administrations in Italy and how modernized they are. This study used analysis of institutional sources and legislation on the subject; it intended to define and specify the economic dimension of public institutions and analyse and propose management and organizational best practices that can facilitate the recovery of higher functional margins. In this context, the management by objectives approach used by the Italian Ministry of Justice and the court management framework are analysed (Lepore 2009). That is, general objectives, such as reducing judicial debt, enhancing human resources, training management, being results orientated and having strategic objectives, became measurable operational objectives that can be assigned to the various departments. These goals define executive action programs, which emphasize how creating managerial tools seems to improve profitability and efficiency margins (Lepore 2009).

Subsequently, a case study carried out in the District Court of Milan examined the implementation of a national program to improve the management of judicial offices (Bussetti and Vecchi 2018). In this case, the method used by the authors used the PT technique, which is an innovative method of making within-case inferences from a single case study; this is a qualitative method using Bayesian reasoning to improve the accuracy of the inferences within the case. This process has positively evaluated the implementation of a national program for the improvement of the management of judicial offices in providing resources for leaders' engagement and access to knowledge, the transfer and consolidation of managerial knowledge with a view to efficiency and effectiveness (Bussetti and Vecchi 2018).

Finally, an Italian study examines the problem of verifying whether and how the tool for measuring the courts' performance can be useful in planning and controlling (Agrifoglio et al. 2010). The proposed tool is based on the balanced scorecard and includes five dimensions: the traditional four (user, internal processes, economic financial, learning and innovation) and the success of information systems. Furthermore, it is believed that it can support the management's decision-making

Table 2. Comprehensive classification of problems, management areas and tools and methods.

Problems	Description	Management area	Tools and methods	References
Spending excessive time	Spending excessive time for initial analysis and limited time for the subsequent phases of the process.	Case management and classifying of legal documents.	Multimodal combination methods and sequential learning methods; CNN and the bidirectional LSTM network; BoW and linear SVM; the SCC system using a CNN.	Luz de Araujo et al. 2020, Luz de Araujo et al. 2022, Sulea et al. 2017, Undavia et al. 2018
	Spending excessive time resolving disputes in the medical, health and pharmaceutical fields.	Supporting the judge with experts in the field relating to the specific dispute and use of technological tools.	Epi Info 6 software; PASW statistics software	Afonso et al. 2020 Gomes et al. 2014
	Spending excessive time for the resolution of disputes in terms of guaranteeing a fair trial.	Managing the backlog on a theoretical basis.	System, historical, comparative-legal, legal-formal, logical-legal, alternative, analysis and the generalization methods.	Demchenko et al. 2022
	Spending excessive time on the resolution of disputes.	Case management	Historical analysis and software	Morawska et al. 2019
Reducing Disputes	Reducing healthcare and pharmaceutical disputes and patent litigation.	Supporting the judge with experts in the field relating to the specific dispute and use of technological tools.	SPSS software, BPNN, content analysis and data analysis using software.	Oliveira et al. 2020, Lai et al. 2009, Ross 1997, Jung et al. 2018
	Reducing litigation cost, ligation, IT.	Managing the backlog on a theoretical basis.	Hybrid and new ADR methods; probit analysis; and historical, comparative-juridical, formal-logical, empirical, analogy and system methods.	Sherman 1994, Arena et al. 2018, Baranenko et al. 2022
Classifying Documents	Automatic classification of the legal judgment.	Classifying legal judgments.	NLP methods.	Howe et al. 2019
	Computer classification of legal evidence of sentences.	Case management.	PNL, AI, SVM, BiLSTM, DNN.	Wei et al. 2022
Court planning and controlling	Support court management decision-making and monitor organization performance to overcome malfunctioning and inefficient judicial offices.	Court management.	Balanced scorecard, management by objectives and PT.	Agrifoglio et al. 2010, Lepore 2009, Bussetti and Vecchi 2018

processes, consequently favouring the recovery of the desired margins of efficiency, effectiveness and economy. Through the balanced scorecard, it is possible to identify the activities that define the court's mission, clarify the long-term objectives and define the indicators to measure the degree of achievement (Agrifoglio et al. 2010). The indicators included in the four typical dimension provide the court management with fundamental information about the court's ability to be effective in adequately satisfying the requests of the stakeholders (user perspective), efficient in saving resources (economic-financial perspective), timely in resolving disputes (perspective of internal processes) and capable of improving overall performance by promoting organizational processes aimed at facilitating the creation, transfer and sharing of knowledge (perspective of innovation and learning). The developed tool can undeniably be considered useful in supporting the decision-making processes of court management. Furthermore, it is assumed that a possible contribution of the telematic civil process (PCT) and information systems is in favouring individual and organizational performance. The digitization of documents and registry archives has created the conditions for a better exchange of information between the various players in the judicial system, speeding up access times and the availability of data and information (Agrifoglio et al. 2010).

Table 2 highlights the classification of problems, their description, management area and tools and methods in terms of efficiency and effectiveness found in the articles of this research.

5. Conclusion

In this study, we provide information to researchers, scholars and policymakers about tools and solutions for making judicial systems more efficient, effective and productive. The proposed framework provides a clear schematization of the general problems, the management areas and the tools and methods found in the selected articles. Our research provides critical insights for court system practitioners about the tools and methods to follow to improve judicial efficiency, including such issues as excessive time, reducing disputes, classifying documents and planning and controlling. Furthermore, this work can help judicial administrative personnel develop tools to improve the overall efficiency of the judicial system. Our research provides theoretical knowledge, tools, techniques and software that are applicable in different legal and geographical contexts. In particular, the study of case studies and various methodologies can be an excellent support tool to formulate a judgment. Drawing from different geographical contexts and different types of litigation can facilitate the judgment's formulation and the case itself.

Our study highlights some shortcomings in the literature. For example, the PNRR plans to define the duration of trials, providing for appropriate adjustment mechanisms to any specificities of the individual judicial offices. In the articles analysed, however, there is little research in this regard. Furthermore, the critical analysis shows that little research exists on the quantification of costs and benefits concerning the application of the tools analyzed in terms of a performing legal system. Moreover, in the initial research, there were no references or keywords related to ICT, but many articles have highlighted how the most efficient and effective solutions lie in information technology and digital tools. Thus, technology is important for the judicial system to improve its performance; it is necessary to exploit digital technologies. However, we must highlight that organizational issues, knowledge management criticalities, human interactions and accepting ICTs in courts and justice offices are a few under-investigated research topics.

This study has considered just 20 articles, taken from Google Scholar and WoS, and it should be noted that the study is limited to publications with specific keywords and written in English. The study is also limited to examining the content of publications found in the selected database. Therefore, there may be other journals focused on this topic that were left out of this study. In general, we hope our literature review encourages further exploration into improved models and techniques. Specifically, future research should be directed at methods or programs that measure the effectiveness and efficiency of lowering the justice backlog. In fact, in this context, the application of transfer learning could be used to train classifiers in more specific and different subdomains of the legal field.

Acknowledgments

This research was funded by the European Union—FSE/FESR. Project Code: E75F21001650007 PON GOV; Project Title: "Modelli organizzativi e innovazione digitale: il nuovo ufficio per il processo per l'efficienza del sistema giustizia".

References

Afonso, A.B.P., Menegueti, M.G., de Araujo, T.R., Chaves, L.D.P. and Laus, A.M. 2020. Private health insurance coverage-related lawsuits. Rev. Bras Enferm. 73: 1–7.

Agrifoglio, R., Lepore, L., Metallo, C. and Alvino, F. 2010. Un modello per la valutazione delle performance dei tribunali: un'analisi empirica. Azienda Pubblica 3: 391–410.

Arena, M.P. and Ferris, S.P. 2018. A global analysis of corporate litigation risk and costs. Int. Rev. Law Econ. 56: 28–41. https://doi.org/10.1016/j.irle.2018.05.003.

Baranenko, D., Stepanova, T., Pillai, A.V., Kostruba, A. and Akimenko, Y. 2022. Delimitation of jurisdiction of commercial, civil and administrative courts: IT challenges. International Journal of Computer Science and Network Security (IJCSNS) 22: 85–90. https://doi.org/10.22937/IJCSNS.2022.22.7.11.

Bianco, M. and Giacomelli, S. 2004. Efficienza della giustizia e imprenditorialità: il caso italiano. Economia e politica industriale 124: 89–113.

Busetti, S. and Vecchi, G. 2018. Process tracing change management: the reform of the Italian judiciary. International Journal of Public Sector Management 31: 566–582.

Civinini, M.G. 2021. Il nuovo ufficio per il processo, tra riforma della giustizia e PNRR. Che sia la volta buona!, Questione Giustizia 3: 1–16.

Contini, F. and Viapiana, F. 2020. Quanto costa la giustizia? I tribunali italiani tra efficacia ed efficienza. Questione Giustizia. Febbraio: 1–11.

Demchenko, S., Dryshliuk, V., Tokarchuk, L., Prytuliak, V. and Melekh, L. 2022. Ensuring the right to a fair trial in commercial and civil proceedings in the information age. International Journal of Computer Science and Network Security (IJCSNS) 22: 507–514. https://doi.org/10.22937/IJCSNS.2022.22.5.70.

Gomes, F.D.F.C., Cherchiglia, M.L., Machado, C.D., Santos, V.C.D., Acurcio, F.D.A. and Andrade, E.I.G. 2014. Access to medium and high-complexity procedures in the Brazilian Unified National Health System: a matter of judicialization. Cadernos de Saúde Pública 30(1): 31–43. https://doi.org/10.1590/0102-311X00176812.

Howe, J.S.T., Khang, L.H. and Chai, I.E. 2019. Legal area classification: a comparative study of text classifiers on Singapore Supreme Court judgments. Proceedings of the First Workshop Natural Legal Language Processing 1–11. https://doi.org/10.48550/arXiv.1904.06470.

Jung, J.Y., Kim, S.Y., Kim, D.G., Kim, C.B., Chi, K.C., Kang, W.K. et al. 2018. Analysis of lawsuit cases in the department of surgery in Korea. Annals of Surgical Treatment and Research (ASTR) 94: 113–117. https://doi.org/10.4174/astr.2018.94.3.113.

La Porta, R., Lopez-de-Silanes, F., Shleifer, A. and Vishny, R.W. 1996. Law and finance. Nber Working Paper Series w5661: 1–80.

Lai, Y.H. and Che, H.C. 2009. Evaluating patents using damage awards of infringement lawsuits: A case study. J. of Eng. and Technol. Manage. 26: 167–180. https://doi.org/10.1016/j.jengtecman.2009.06.005.

Lepore, L. 2009. Efficienza, efficacia ed equità nell'amministrazione della giustizia. Azienda Pubblica 3: 429–448.

Liberati, A., Altman, D.G., Tetzlaff, J., Mulrow, C., Gøtzsche, P.C., Ioannidis, J.P.A. et al. 2009. The PRISMA statement for reporting systematic reviews and meta analysis of studies that evaluate health care interventions: explanation and elaboration. Annals of Internal Medicine 151: W–65. https://doi.org/10.7326/0003-4819-151-4-200908180-00136.

Luz de Araujo, P.H., de Campos, T.E., Ataides Braz, F. and da Silva, C.N. 2020. VICTOR: a dataset for Brazilian legal documents classification, Proceedings of the 12th Language Resources and Evaluation Conference (LREC 2020) 1449–1458.

Luz de Araujo, P.H., de Almeida, A.P.G., Ataides Braz, F., Correia da Silva, N., de Barros Vidal, F. and de Campos, T.E. 2022. Sequence-aware multimodal page classification of Brazilian legal documents. International Journal on Document Analysis and Recognition 26(1): 33–49.

Masciandaro, D. 2000. La giustizia civile è efficiente? Primo rapporto sull'economia delle regole. Laboratorio ABI-Bocconi, Roma: Bancaria Editrice.

Morawska, S., Banasik, P. and Woźniak-Jęchorek, B. 2019. The handling of business lawsuits by common courts in Poland: identification of transaction costs. Ekonomista 3: 321–342.

OECD. 2013a. "What makes civil justice effective?" Economic Department Policy Notes No. 18, OECD, Paris.

OECD. 2013b. "Italy: the digitization of the Court of Milan." Innovation for Better Public Services. 48th Session of the Public Governance Committee, OECD, Paris, pp. 62–80.

Oliveira, Y.M.D.C., Braga, B.S.F., Farias, A.D., Pereira, S.P.D. and Ferreira, M.A.F. 2020. Judicialization of medicines: effectiveness of rights or break in public policies? Rev. Saude Publica 54: 1–10. https://doi.org/10.11606/s1518-8787.2020054002301.

PNRR. 2021/2022. Piano Nazionale di Ripresa e Resilienza #NEXTGENERATIONITALIA, https://www.italiadomani.gov.it/content/sogei-ng/it/it/home.html.

Ross, D.L. 1997. Emerging trends in correctional civil liability cases: a content analysis of federal court decisions of Title 42 United States code section 1983: 1970–1994. Journal of Criminal Justice 25: 501–515. https://doi.org/10.1016/S0047-2352(97)00035-4.

Sherman, E.F. 1994. A process model and agenda for civil justice reforms in the States. Stanford Law Review 46(6): 1553–1587.

Smith, R. 2007. An overview of the Tesseract OCR engine. *In*: Ninth International Conference on Document Analysis and Recognition (ICDAR) 2: 629–633.

Sulea, O.M., Zampieri, M., Vela, M. and Genabith, J. 2017. Predicting the law area and decisions of French Supreme Court cases. pp. 716–722. Proceedings in Recent Advances in Natural Language Processing. https://doi.org/10.26615/978-954-452-049-6_092.

Undavia, S., Meyers, A. and Ortega, J.E. 2018. A comparative study of classifying legal documents with neural networks. pp. 515–522. Proceedings of the Federated Conference on Computer Science and Information Systems (ACSIS). DOI:10.15439/2018F227.

Wei, B., Kuang, K., Sun, C., Feng, J., Zhang, Y., Zhu, X. et al. 2022. A full-process intelligent trial system for smart court. Front. Inform. Technol. Electron. Eng. 23: 186–206

Zingales, L., Rajan, R.G. and Kumar, K. 1999. What determines firm size? Cepr Discussion Paper n. 221.

CHAPTER 2

Digital and Smart Technology for People with Disability in the Tourism and Hospitality Industry

A Literature Review for Smart and Inclusive Hotels

Perna G.,[1] *Varriale L.*,[2,*] *Briganti P.*,[3] *Di Vaio A.*[4] and *Volpe T.*[5]

1. Introduction

The tourism and hospitality industry presents specific aspects which imply its uniqueness, that is this industry is more vulnerable than other industries (Brown et al. 2017, Jiang and Ritchie 2017, Duro et al. 2021, Ho et al. 2023), because tourism products and experiences are linked to natural and cultural resources (Jiang and Ritchie 2017) as well as fluctuating demand (Brown et al. 2017), and also, this industry requires relevant infrastructure investment and people's ability to be flexible (Brown et al. 2017). The tourism and hospitality industry represents a service-oriented industry with relevant aspects related to experience (Otto and Ritchie 1996), where two main approaches are considered and applied, that is the

[1] University of Naples "Parthenope", Post-Doc, Naples, Italy.
[2] University of Naples "Parthenope", Department of Economics, Law, Cybersecurity, and Sports Sciences, Nola (NA), Italy.
[3] University of Naples "Parthenope", Department of Health, Sports and Wellbeing, Naples, Italy.
[4] University of Naples "Parthenope", Department of Law, Naples, Italy.
[5] CNR-ISMed - Istituto di Studi sul Mediterraneo, Naples, Italy.
* Corresponding author: luisa.varriale@uniparthenope.it

service-dominant logic (Shaw et al. 2011), and the coproduction and cocreation service perspective for memorable experiences among travelers and hotel guests (Shaw et al. 2011, Chathoth et al. 2013).

Over the last fifty years, the tourism and hospitality industry has become a primary social priority, as besides making the economy more relevant, it is a means of knowledge and discovering new realities worldwide (Safaeva et al. 2020, Sakshi et al. 2020, Ho et al. 2023, Ramkissoon 2023). Indeed, the tourism and hospitality industry is vital for economies, livelihoods and wellbeing (Ho et al. 2023). Considering the economic perspective, the COVID-19 pandemic, in early 2020, as an exceptional disruptive event, negatively affected the overall world with effects on global health and social and economic consequences especially in the tourism and hospitality industry, which recorded an interruption of its international demand development after a ten-year period of continuous growth since the financial crisis in 2009 with the declination of international tourist arrivals by 70% in 2020, the level recorded 30 years ago (United Nation World Tourism Organization 2021). "This industry deserves increased attention because many developing nations depend on it to fast-track their development and earn valuable foreign exchange. The industry is a major GDP contributor for many countries, and numerous emerging economies rely on international travelers and tourism to survive" (Sigala 2020, Pramana et al. 2021, Ho et al. 2023: p. 835–836).

Regarding the several types of livelihoods derived from the tourism and hospitality industry, it represents the most important global employers and, consequently, "the hardest hit by the pandemic" (Krishan et al. 2020, United Nation World Tourism Organization 2021). Because of the pandemic, many hotels and restaurants were closed and events and tourist attractions shut down too (Gössling et al. 2020). Indeed, due to the pandemic, many hotel companies and travel businesses, like the Accor hotel group, Pacific World (Conference and Meetings World 2020) and Roosevelt Hotel (CNN 2020), restructured, downsized, or closed (Ho et al. 2023).

Service experience in tourism and hospitality industry can enhance well-being and quality of life (Smith and Diekmann 2017). Unfortunately, during the pandemic, all the activities stopped including travelling for leisure to live tourism experience, so people worldwide started to have health and social troubles because of the lockdowns, travel restrictions and quarantine measures (Ho et al. 2023). Some scholars outline that most people require relax and recovery through holiday for improving their mental and physical health and wellness (Chen and Petrick 2013, Smith and Diekmann 2017).

Starting from this relevant positive impact of the tourism and hospitality industry on economy, livelihoods, and well-being, during the post-pandemic times, it witnessed phenomenal growth in customer numbers (Ho et al. 2023). This relevant growth has been supported and characterized by the widespread use of technologies in customer interface and backend activities, especially adopting self-serving technologies (Dwivedi et al. 2023a). In the last five decades, especially since 2020 due to the COVID-19 pandemic acting as accelerator phenomenon, digital and smart technologies have been affecting both businesses management and customer experience in the tourism and hospitality industry (Khan et al. 2021, Agarwal et al. 2022, Varriale and Volpe 2022). Thus, the COVID-19 pandemic acted as an accelerator for the adoption and widespread of digital and smart technologies in the tourism and hospitality industry. Most recent contributions in the research and practice outline that "contactless, mobile messaging, artificial intelligence, voice activation" represent the present and future of the tourism and hospitality industry (Oracle and Skift's Report 2023).

In this direction, there is also the major need to guarantee the access and usability in practice to the tourist experience to all citizens, managing any personal, social, economic, and other conditions that should limit its enjoyment.

Therefore, tourism and hospitality, technology and accessibility represent crucial keywords as phenomena to investigate adopting an integrating perspective. Accessible tourism and hospitality can be conceived as all the set of services, facilities and infrastructures that allow people with special needs to concretize a vacation or enjoy their leisure time without obstacles.

This chapter consists of conceptual research which aims to systematize the scientific contributions on accessible and usable tourism and hospitality phenomenon through a systematic literature review to identify the main lines of research and the key determinants. Specifically, the aim is to highlight the importance and role that research can take in the field of accessible and usable tourism and hospitality, especially in relation to its multidisciplinary and complexity characteristics, but also to the recent attention it appears to receive from the academic world and the entrepreneurial ones.

2. Background

The tourism and hospitality industry is unique because of its characteristics, that is this industry presents high vulnerability compared to other industries for the effects of disasters (Brown et al. 2017, Jiang and Ritchie 2017, Duro et al. 2021), as shown from the devasting effects of the COVID-19 pandemic in early 2020 which negatively impacted on the tourism and hospitality industry, making the declination of international tourist arrivals by 70% in 2020, the level recorded 30 years in advance (United Nation World Tourism Organization 2021). High vulnerability of this industry is related to the fact that tourism products and experiences derive from natural and cultural resources by organizational and geographical boundaries (Jiang and Ritchie 2017), and in this industry it is also necessary to pay attention to heavy infrastructure investment and people's ability to be flexible and moving freely (Brown et al. 2017). Moreover, the complexity of vulnerabilities of hotels are caused from the fact that this sector is highly exposed to risks for fluctuating demand depending on the travel motivation (Brown et al. 2017). In the tourism and hospitality industry, successful operations are possible only thanks to a high degree of flexibility. The tourism and hospitality industry represents a service-oriented industry where all the aspects are experiential (Otto and Ritchie 1996). This industry adopts both a service-dominant logic approach (Shaw et al. 2011) and a co-production and co-creation service perspective where memorable experiences are crucial for travellers and hotel guests (Shaw et al. 2011, Chathoth et al. 2013). Such industry with its service nature is intangible and inseparable with the need for maximum flexibility and responsiveness (Ho et al. 2023). Because of the specific service characteristics, a multidimensional and multilevel model is necessary for ensuring high quality and performance of this industry (Wu and Ko 2013).

Furthermore, the tourism and hospitality industry generally presents a multicultural environment; consequently, managers must face culture-related issues at different levels, like "potential national cultural clashes and diverse expectations from worldwide travellers from different backgrounds, as well as potential organizational cultural conflicts between local employees and expatriate managers" (Chen et al. 2012, Ho et al. 2023: p. 837). Financial risks can affect tourism companies and hotels because this industry is capital intensive with its investment in real estate and facilities with the opportunity to sell perishable products in competitive markets (Singal 2015).

In addition, specific aptitudes in managing hotels are required because of the unique ownership structures. The hospitality industry, specifically hotels, is characterized by typical ownership structures completely different from other industries (Xiao et al. 2012). It is possible to observe brand diversification; for instance, there are hotel owners with "multiple brands in different classes and scales in different markets for diversified market exposure" (Yang et al. 2017). Other ownership structures represent franchising (Lin and Kim 2020), independent hotels, chain-affiliated hotels, or in some hotel management companies there are specific strategic operation and management techniques (Kim and Lin 2021). The management of the same brand can require facing national boundaries, likewise, managers must focus on exceedingly on one market segment or brand level (Ho et al. 2023).

All the described characteristics of the tourism and hospitality industry, that is its service-oriented and multicultural nature, its high capital needs, high exposure to demand fluctuations and financing risks, complex ownership systems and the presence of multiple stakeholders to satisfy, imply that companies must manage and face many difficulties and tensions. These difficulties and tensions concern the need to keep consistency, protect brand, and national integrity, being flexible to manage changes, to manage multiple stakeholders and different customers. Therefore, tourism and hospitality organizations must deal with several uncontrollable external forces every time, such as economic crisis, political unrest, technological advancements, shortage of manpower, to natural disasters (Ho et al. 2023). For example, the COVID-19 pandemic represents one unique threat (Amankwah-Amoah et al. 2021). The scenario created by the COVID-19 pandemic, because of social distancing, travel prohibitions and mobility restrictions for all people, highlighted the need for the tourism and hospitality industry to be extra vigilant and be ready for facing the negative impact of unexpected events on the industry. Thus, environmental uncertainty related to limited information, especially regarding external factors, characterizes this industry (Duncan 1972, Lee et al. 2013).

In this direction, some authors developed a holistic resilience framework for organizations in the tourism and hospitality industry for facing uncertain environments, e.g., related to the COVID-19 pandemic, through a large review of the literature on organizational resilience and strategic leadership (Ho et al. 2023).

Other studies in the tourism and hospitality industry mostly focus on operational-level strategies and tactics (Sahebjamnia et al. 2018, Gursoy and Chi 2020, Hao et al. 2020, Lai and Wong 2020), as well as on the efficacy of strategic frameworks to face challenges like social distancing because of COVID-19 pandemic through customer management tactics and the adoption and widespread of digital and smart technologies, including contactless technology, but they are still limited. Strategic studies in the tourism and hospitality industry consist primarily of quantitative surveys (Alonso et al. 2020, Filimonau et al. 2020), online databases (Heinonen and Strandvik 2020), reflective reviews (Jones and Comfort 2020) and the published literature (Jiang and Wen 2020).

Regarding the increasing adoption and widespread of technologies in the tourism and hospitality industry, also thanks to the COVID-19 pandemic acting as accelerator, most recent contributions in the research and practice outline that "contactless, mobile messaging, artificial intelligence, voice activation" represent the main needed technologies for the present and the future of the industry; in particular, contactless is considered by both guests and hotels as king (Oracle and Skift's Report 2023, Dwivedi et al. 2023a).

Otherwise, during the post pandemic times the significant growth in customer numbers in the tourism and hospitality tourism has been also supported and accompanied by the adoption and widespread of technologies in customer interface and backend activities (Dwivedi et al. 2023a). According to the Tourism and Hospitality Market Forecast (2023), this industry is expected to grow by 3% during 2022–2027 reaching US $9tn by 2027.

In this direction, an increasing number of contributions in the research and practice have been focusing on this phenomenon, going to investigate the existing practices, implications and challenges related to the adoption and widespread of technologies (Neuhofer et al. 2015, Ercan 2019, Buhalis et al. 2019, Abdelmoaty and Soliman 2020, Pencarelli 2020, Bezvesilnaya et al. 2020, Çeltek 2022), especially generative artificial intelligence (AI), such as ChatGPT, and other similar tools in the tourism and hospitality industry (Pandey and Srivastava 2013, Leung and Law 2013, Abdelmoaty et al. 2020, Dwivedi et al. 2023a, Dogru et al. 2023a, 2023b, Law et al. 2023, Calvillo 2023, Ozdemir et al. 2023, Buhalis et al. 2023, Wang 2024).

Otherwise, because the tourism and hospitality industry, especially hotels, given its nature as part of the service sector (Pandey and Srivastava 2013, Leung and Law 2013, Buhalis et al. 2023, Ozdemir et al. 2023), "where people, processes and physical evidence are critical for success" (Dwivedi et al. 2023a: p. 5), is traditionally conservative in adopting technology, indeed customers should be hesitant to interact with technologies, especially Gen AI like chatbots or robotics (Dwivedi et al. 2023a).

Although the service nature of the industry is based on physical and direct interactions customers/employees, mostly hotel workers, the use of digital and smart technologies is somehow limited, but the scenario is rapidly changing. Above all the same technologies should make the service and products much more effective, also in terms of promoting inclusion for specific categories of people, that is customers with disability and special needs (Varriale and Volpe 2020).

Technologies, especially Gen AI, can provide relevant opportunities in the tourism and hospitality industry with concern of "operations, design, marketing, destination management, human resources, revenue management, accounting and finance, strategic management, and beyond" (Dogru et al. 2023a: p. 5), otherwise the adoption of advanced technologies require ethical, legal, social, and economic considerations (Dogru et al. 2023a). In this direction, scholars tend to largely investigate the potential challenges and opportunities of advanced technologies in the tourism and hospitality industry which is experiencing new advancements and challenges because of the rapidly evolving technological phenomenon (Carvalho and Ivanov 2023, Dwivedi et al. 2023a, 2023b, Mich and Garigliano 2023, Dogru et al. 2023a). Digital and smart technologies, mostly Gen AI like ChatGPT, can be seen as a double-edged sword, where the found solution to old problems can be the source of new ones (Zhuo et al. 2023). Numerous problems already occur in terms of "privacy and security concerns, intellectual property rights violations, and liability and accountability issues" (Dogru et al. 2023a).

The focus on the adoption of digital and smart technologies in the tourism and hospitality industry leans to definition of the large research topic represented by 'smartness' in the tourism and hospitality industry (Stylos et al. 2021).

Smart tourism is the most popular and contemporary topics investigated in the tourism and hospitality management research (Li et al. 2017, Chang et al. 2020, Stylos et al. 2021), adopting not only a technological capabilities viewpoint (i.e., advanced interconnectivity and interoperability of industry 4.0 technologies) (Buhalis and Leung 2018, Buhalis 2020, Stylos et al. 2021, Buhalis 2022).

Nevertheless, empirical research on smart hospitality is still limited (Leung 2019), although there are numerous smart hotel applications in use, such as speech recognition for smart room control.

According to previous studies (Gretzel et al. 2015, Neuhofer et al. 2015, Li et al. 2017, Femenia-Serra and Neuhofer 2018), smart technologies used in the hotel industry can improve the holiday and accommodation experiences of guests. Several typologies of technologies and applications have been using at hotels including "wireless communication technologies, virtual reality, internet of things, virtual tours, intranet, and food production technologies, central reservation systems, hotel automation systems, and specifically mobile applications and personalized services" (Neuhofer et al. 2015, p. 243, Sigala 2018), involving several organizational areas, such as reception, reservations, guest relations, food, and beverage services (Ercan 2019, 2020).

Hence, the expression "smart hotel" has been introduced (Leonidis et al. 2013, Petrevska et al. 2016, Jaremen et al. 2016, Lai and Hung 2017, 2018) and variously defined (Varriale and Volpe 2020: p. 5). Considering different definitions, the smart hotel can be conceived as an intelligent hotel, hence as "the accommodation business where the activities of the hotel business are implemented by adapting smart technologies and these technologies are used in harmony together" (Ercan 2019, p. 538).

Nevertheless, significant changes specifically concern the hotel industry. On one side, hotels face new and increasing challenges because of the continuous and constant implementation of technologies (Berry et al. 2006, Dörner et al. 2011), but research on the topic is still scarce (Orwskiliko 2000, Lamb and Kling 2003). On the other side, the hotel industry also faces the relevant challenge related to the need to be accessible and usable in practice for satisfying the specific needs of people with disability and special needs (Varriale and Volpe 2020). In fact, guests with mobility, vision, hearing, cognitive, and developmental disabilities, or special needs require specific services and facilities (Darcy 2010), and these guests can be considered as a significant emerging market and an issue still to manage for the overall tourism industry, especially the hotel industry (Varriale and Volpe 2020). Even if there are numerous studies focused on experiences of hotels with accessible facilities and services (Zhang and Cole 2016, Tutuncu 2017, Abdelraouf et al. 2018, Piramanayagam et al. 2019), accessibility and usability of hotels and all their services and facilities remain a significant challenge to face (Varriale and Volpe 2020).

This chapter aims to fill the still existing research gap regarding the smartness of tourism and hospitality industry also looking at the accessibility and usability of them for people with disability and special needs.

3. Methodology: Bibliometric and Network Analysis

This conceptual study provides a systematic literature review focused on the phenomena technology applications (technology innovation including digital and smart technologies) and accessibility and usability in practice (inclusiveness) in the tourism and hospitality industry. These topics have been investigated in the existing contributions in the literature combining them and trying to outline the main lens adopted till now to read them.

The systematic literature review is a secondary scientific research tool whose objective is to summarize data from primary research tools; for example, with an exhaustive review of the scientific literature relating to a given topic and with particular attention to the sources, which must be highly referenced, to identify, highlight and evaluate, in high-quality research, all the evidence relevant to a specific scientific question (Okoli and Schabram 2010, Okoli 2015).

According to Di Vaio and colleagues (2020), a systematic literature review represents a significant and useful research tool which consists of a scientific, recognized, useful, replicable and transparent process (Tranfield et al. 2003). Di Vaio and colleagues (2020: p. 285), starting from previous studies on systematic literature review, outline its main advantages, that is: "the obtaining of higher quality review process and outcomes (Danese et al. 2018, Leonidou et al. 2018); reduction of bias and errors (Abdelraouf et al. 2018); the validity of the process thanks to the replicability of the steps of the review process (Wang and Chugh 2014); the mapping of the contributions in the literature mapping with focus on specific research area and data synthesis (Kauppi et al. 2018, Witell et al. 2016); and the definition of a framework able to integrate existing knowledge for researchers and practitioners (e.g., Dada 2018, Nofal et al. 2018)."

We have conducted a systematic literature review that maps and evaluates the body of literature identifying potential research gaps, vividly showing the boundaries of managerial knowledge on the concept of accessible tourism. The systematic review is completed with an interactive process between researched literature and analysis. Systematic research aims to reduce the number of errors in the study and objectively summarize them. This method was chosen because it can give meaning to a substantial body of information, allows us to evaluate the critical aspects of the phenomenon and to answer a considerable number of questions. This method is also useful for mapping areas of uncertainty to eliminate them or to see where research is lacking to proceed with new studies. To provide a systematic review of the literature use the VOSviewer software (van Eck and Waltman 2010, 2014).

The process of identifying studies on accessible tourism phenomenon began with a search within the Web of Science database of articles published between the years 2008 and 2024. For this selection, the following search criterion was used: the presence of the keyword "tourism, technology and disability" within the title and abstract of the published works. Subsequently, all duplicates and articles irrelevant to the review were excluded and other relevant research was added instead. The final selection followed the following criteria: articles published in a journal that adopts a refereeing procedure based on peer-review as well as studies that contain qualitative or quantitative research and with a focus centred on the factors that can influence the accessible tourism phenomenon.

The use of bibliometric calculations taken from Web of Science, if on the one hand represents an effective operational method as it favours comparability, on the other hand exposes the rankings to the limits of this database (Zitt and Filliatreau 2016, Van Raan 2017):

- presence of disciplinary fields not covered (or poorly covered) by the database, or in which journal publications are not the prevalent method of publication (for example, legal, humanistic and social disciplines), with a consequent advantage for institutions focused on the so-called hard sciences;
- difficulty in weighing contributions to multiple names typical of some disciplinary areas (for example, medicine) and rare in others (for example, legal, philosophical and literary sciences);
- limited reliability for cases of homonymy of the authors, truncated names, typos, incompleteness/variability and errors in affiliations;
- disadvantage of publications not in English and therefore of disciplines whose scope of publication is mainly national.

Therefore, we have created a database in which the contributions present in the literature (giving priority to the contributions in journals on the topic of disability), mainly of an international nature, have been categorized according to specific dimensions, such as: the journal of publication (also identifying the journals of greater prestige in terms of high impact factor), year of publication, number of citations, average number of citations in the year, nature of the study (theoretical or empirical), methodology adopted.

Subsequently, the map of the literature relating to accessible tourism was created using the VOSviewer software; in this regard we used the term identification function of VOSviewer to systematically identify the key topics of the articles. Subsequently, a term occurrence threshold of 10 was applied, so that a term must be present in the title and/or abstract of at least 10 different articles to be considered as a candidate term for mapping. The threshold of 10 occurrences helps to ensure reliable placement of term relationships in the map and to remove incorrect and irrelevant word names (van Eck and Waltman 2010, 2014).

To prepare terms for mapping, VOSviewer defines the correlation of terms present in the selected articles using the strength of association measure. In particular, the degree of relatedness between the terms on the map is determined by the co-occurrence relationship between two terms compared to the degree of association that each term has with other terms present in the selected articles.

The result of this process is the identification of the terms that are present several times in the selected articles and the related frequencies, that is, the number of presences of a given word within the corpus. Furthermore, a relevance score was calculated and, based on this score, the most relevant terms were selected.

Next, the VOSviewer clustering algorithm was applied, which uses an optimization algorithm to systematically identify clusters of terms, that is, subject areas, based on their relationship patterns. The clustering algorithm maximizes the sum of the association strengths of pairs of terms belonging to the same cluster, minimizing the size of the clusters (van Eck and Waltman 2010, 2014).

To identify clusters, we used VOSviewer's default cluster resolution parameter of 1 and set a minimum cluster size of 10 terms (that is, enough terms to examine and be viewable in a map).

VOSviewer then displays the relationships between the terms in a two-dimensional map. The placement of terms on the map is determined by VOSviewer's mapping algorithm which minimizes the difference between the strength of association and the distance between pairs of terms such that, on average, the terms that tend to co-occur in the title and/or in the article abstract are closer together (van Eck and Waltman 2010, 2014). More precisely, through graphical analysis the words are grouped into a tree according to proximity measures and produce spontaneous classifications based on their proximity. The result of a visualization therefore lends itself to being interpreted as a summary of the topics covered in the text.

4. Results

The search returned 141 elements including articles, abstracts, and so on, with an h-index of 20 and an average citation per year of 9.22; these are, for the most part, studies of a theoretical nature that adopt a qualitative methodology. Furthermore, in Figure 1 it is possible to observe an important research activity over the last five years, with the greatest production in 2021, that is, in the post-pandemic year, as well as the trend of citations from which it is possible to deduce a continuous interest in the topic especially starting from 2018 with a significant peak in 2022.

The publications can then be grouped into different scientific research areas. Figure 2 shows that the scientific area relating to "Hospitality, leisure, sport and tourism" has the highest number of publications, that is, 32; the other scientific areas that are also closely involved in our research analysis, that is, those relating to management and the use of information technology present, respectively, 11 and 30 publications.

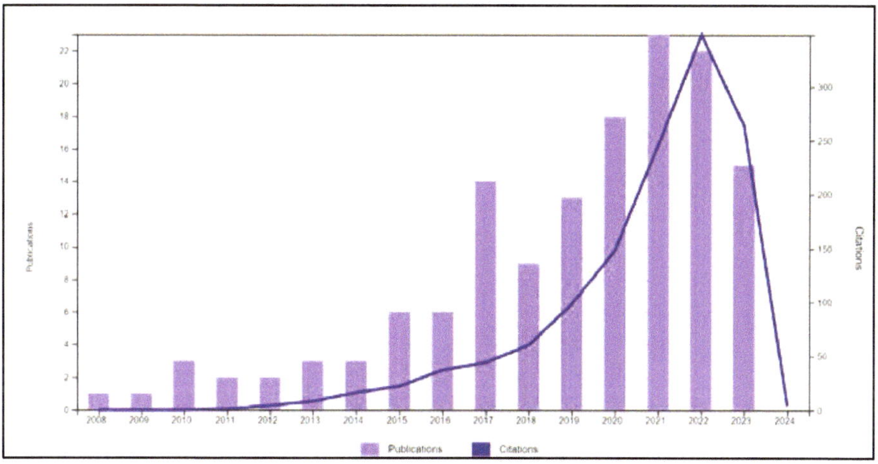

Figure 1. Publications in the years 2008–2024.

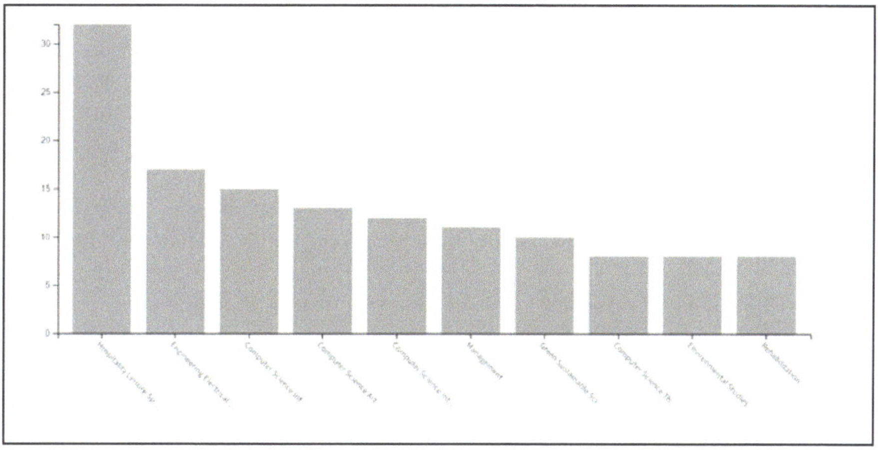

Figure 2. Scientific field to which the publications belong.

VOSviewer provides three views of the map relating to the topic we analyzed: "Network Visualization"; "Density Visualization"; "Overlay Visualization".

The Network Visualization (Figure 3) shows the two clusters based on the colour associated with it:

- cluster 1 (red colour), to identify research focused on the contribution of new technologies, mainly social media (blogs, websites, etc.), in the promotion and development of accessible tourism for people with special needs;
- cluster 2 (green colour), to identify the body of research focused on the definition of accessible tourism, understood as the products and services of the entire tourist offer designed for everyone and without barriers;

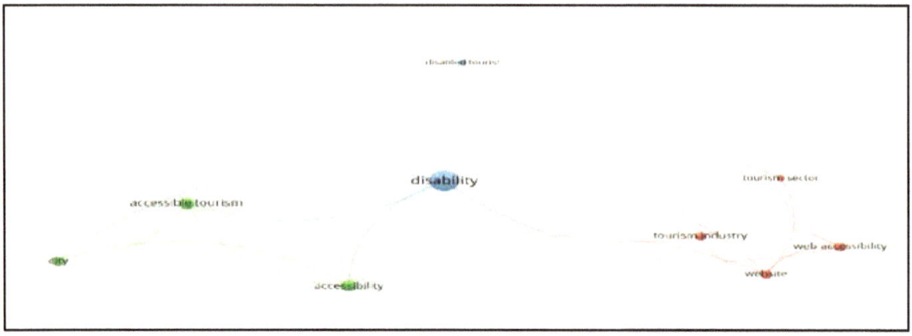

Figure 3. Network visualization.

- cluster 3 (blue colour), to identify all the research focused on the identification and definition of tourism with special needs, that is, people who require comforts and arrangements to be able to travel and take advantage of tourist opportunities.

In the density visualization (Figure 4), the colours ranging from yellow to blue indicate, based on the intensity of the colour, the number of articles associated with the topics within a given space on the map. Yellow colour indicates areas with comparatively high research intensity, while blue indicates thematic areas with comparatively lower research intensity. This map also confirms the literature's interest in accessible tourism, even if the study of the support provided by the web for the dissemination of information on the tourist experience to people with special needs is less explored.

Finally, with the overlay visualization (Figure 5) we can identify the terms present in the articles that belong to more recently published research (the period between 2008 and 2024 is always considered); specifically, the latter are represented in the map with an intense yellow colour while the topics that are present in research published in older articles are represented with cooler colours such as blue. The

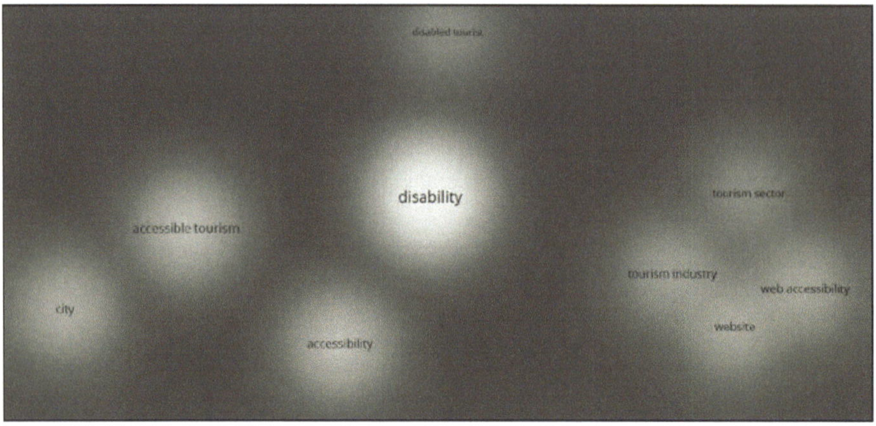

Figure 4. Density visualization.

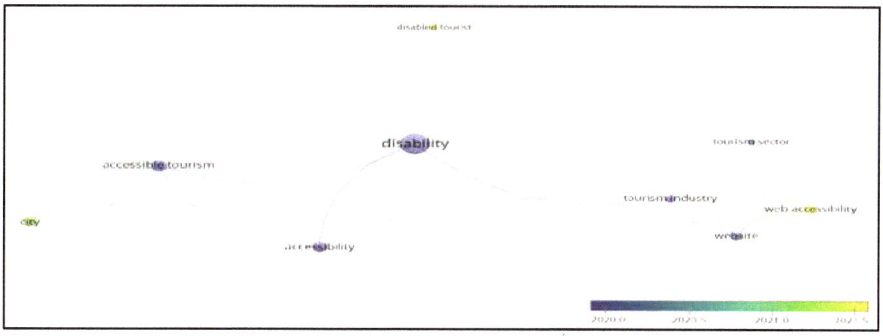

Figure 5. Overlay visualization.

result of this analysis underlines that the research activity on the relationship between technology and accessible tourism is mainly concentrated in the last five years, after the outbreak of the COVID-19 pandemic in 2020 which acted as an accelerator of the phenomenon, and which the most recent theme is represented by the web's contribution to improving the tourist experience for people with special needs.

From our research it emerged that in the panorama of the hospitality industry, the topic of the relationship between disability and technology has received relatively little attention in the literature, especially in the national one, and it is only recently that the attention of the literature has turned to web accessibility theme.

The results were processed with the narrative method which, due to the heterogeneity of the research designs, the scientific sectors of reference and the methodologies adopted by the different studies, allowed them to be analyzed, synthesized and offered a critical reading.

The current concept of accessible tourism as a set of services and facilities that allow customers with special needs to enjoy holidays and leisure without obstacles or difficulties is a concept developed over the last approximately 15 years.

Thanks to the initiatives promoted by the numerous stakeholders (businesses, public and private organizations, profit and non-profit organizations) operating in the sector, accessible tourism has become an increasingly relevant phenomenon. All of these entities understood the economic opportunity for the tourism industry and social integration for the community.

In recent decades, tourism has evolved significantly thanks to its continuous and profound diversification and has now become one of the fastest growing global economic sectors.

The various countries have adopted innovative and cutting-edge strategies to get in touch with potential customers, investing both in technology and new media, trying to make the tourist practice simpler and more accessible for everyone (Briggs 2001).

Traveling to discover new places, cultures and traditions around the world represents a growing need for people to travel, stay and enjoy the services that are now searched for on the web (Briggs 2001).

Tourism, in fact, involves the diffusion and exchange of information and the web today represents the most effective means for their distribution on a global level. The Internet is a commercial and communication channel that allows the perfect connection between service providers and consumers; through hundreds of websites, tourists can get all kinds of information to plan their trip. Thousands of destinations, flights, rooms, activities are now available with one click. The reasons for the success of tourism and the web are, in addition to the customer's easy access to the product, the variability of the price, the large availability of stock and the visibility of the brands (Corigliano et al. 2020).

The adequate use of the web allows tourist companies, but also potential consumers, to enjoy great advantages: from disintermediation on the one hand, to the possibility of booking in a simple and immediate way on the other.

The online tourist market involves both the network logic (products offered by destinations to attract tourist flows) and the package logic (products assembled by Tour Operators and offered by Travel Agencies) which have affected the redefinition of the leisure market which today includes organized tourism, do-it-yourself and new forms of disintermediation (Corigliano et al. 2020).

Nowadays, there is information and products in the market that were completely absent due to excessively high costs; today special offers, last minutes and events benefit from the timeliness of the vehicle and the reduced distribution burden. The digital revolution with new media and the transition from Web 1.0 to Web 2.0 have allowed tourists to have this large amount of information at their disposal which leads them to be increasingly attentive and looking for interesting offers (Boyd 2021).

The formula 2.0 is generally associated with the web, indicating the transition from the evolutionary state 1.0 (the source of the web) to 2.0 which dates back to 2000–2003 when social media was born. In the world of Web 2.0 the passive user becomes active in all its aspects, uses the network to produce content (User Generated Content), participates and communicates with others by spreading information. Tourism 2.0 also indicates a significant change between different time periods: from the era where travel agencies made reservations through automated systems to the era where the consumer creates their own experiences (since the late 1990s) (Lafuente and Righi 2021).

Today the web and online services are fundamental for organizing trips, both for news and for bookings, but it is true that word of mouth is a powerful tool in tourism too. Consumers take inspiration for their travels from the internet, searching for information, comparing various offers and asking friends for advice. Social networks play an important role in all phases of the journey, from choosing the destination, to the practical organization of the trip, to the sharing of material (videos, photos, etc.) and information until the return to the destination. Share what you have experienced also through reviews.

The close relationship between travelers and social media can be exploited by all tourism service providers. A structure with free connection certainly offers its customers an appreciated service but not only that, it can benefit from the resulting advertising. Tourism is therefore increasingly digitalized, given the fusion between web, mobile and the different dynamics of social networks which, in addition to the functions we know, allow us to collect feedback, attract new customers and provide responses in real time. Smartphone devices represent the main means by which travelers access web information and have features that make them adaptable to any user need. They allow you to connect to the network, they are simple to use and small in size, and for these reasons the user is always tempted to carry it with him (Cini 2019).

Especially with regards to users with disabilities, websites must be characterized by the ability to present information in an intuitive and effective way and, in general, must be easily accessible to any type of user. In these cases, we talk about "barrier-free web" to indicate a virtual world accessible to disabled people, the elderly and people with obsolete software. Unfortunately, many websites still have accessibility barriers that make it difficult if not impossible for millions of people with disabilities to navigate, understand and interact with the web (Sorci 2020).

Removing barriers is essential so that all users (with motor, physical and cognitive disabilities) can use existing technologies. The disabilities encountered by disabled users are often due to design defects in the software and content of the site which do not fully respect the design rules of devices specifically designed for disabled people such as: keyboards and mice for specific motor disabilities, Braile bar or synthesizers for the blind, Screen Reader, etc. The accessibility of the web to information and interaction plays a very important role in various fields: from educational to professional, commercial, political, and social, and therefore allows people with disabilities to be active members of social life, guaranteeing equal opportunities in different sectors (Baroni and Lazzari 2020).

Numerous international documents discuss the importance of access to information technologies for people with disabilities, so much so that this has become a central theme in the programs of the European Commission.

In general, to make websites accessible it is necessary to: use alternative texts for any type of multimedia content such as video or audio files; do not rely on just one color (the content must in fact be clear even if printed in black and white); separate the content from the presentation, use clear tables (which distinguish text and heading); specify the language used (for the Screen Reader), create reasonable pages even in the absence of scripts, avoid rapid and sudden movements of the contents, of a user interface via keyboard commands (not necessarily scripts); guarantee independence from devices (mouse, keyboard...); they do not require the use of additional technologies (e.g., pop ups, etc.); provide information for contextualization and orientation (it should be easy to understand where you are and where you can go); develop navigation mechanisms (menus, etc.) and clear and simple documents (Ranieri and Manca 2019).

Other elements capable of ensuring good web accessibility are linked to images and animations, in these cases the use of the alt attribute is required, which provides the description of each graphic element. The multimedia files must then have subtitles and transcriptions for the audio and descriptions in the case of films.

In summary, tourism promotion campaigns increasingly focus on the formulation of offers aimed at users, transforming the potential customer into a real consumer. To do this, it is no longer sufficient to distribute information on traditional media, but it is also necessary to convey it through the new channels and virtual spaces made available, such as social networks. The possibility offered by social networks to comment, interact and share allows us to guarantee continuous promotion of destinations to which users attribute credibility as witnessed by their peers. Shared memory, which consists in the diffusion and sharing of the personal tourist experience in the network of relationships, is one of the major factors that influence and direct tourist flows. Therefore, the true boundary between the "tourism of the first" and the "tourism of the future" has been and continues to be, the advent and continuous evolution of new media that elaborate, manipulate and modify the tourist imagination by creating travellers-storytellers, and increase the importance of relational dynamics.

The bibliometric analysis has therefore highlighted that, in all interventions aimed at improving accessibility, new technologies play a crucial role; it could be useful to make use of new tools to promote the elevation of people with disabilities, or of tools that allow communication and social inclusion of people with sensory disabilities. New information technologies can provide elements to make the websites of tourist facilities totally accessible.

We therefore conclude that the topic of disability represents a frontier that has not yet been sufficiently explored in the context of academic research and managerial debate and the few relevant works (which are only very recent) mainly concern foreign literature.

It should be underlined that opening up to disability requires not only overcoming any environmental, physical and, above all, cultural barrier, but also the adoption of an approach aimed at enhancing diversity, and capable of preventing or eliminating any discriminatory behavior towards of minorities.

5. Final Remarks

This chapter provides a comprehensive review of technology and disability within the tourism and hospitality industry. The technology innovation, specifically the adoption of digital and smart technologies in the tourism and hospitality industry, has been receiving an increasing attention, as shown from the conceptual study conducted through the systematic literature review, but we can observe that some related sub-topics are still under-represented, such as the implications in terms of opportunities and challenges of them regarding people with disability, specifically customers with disability or special needs. The link between technology and disability in the tourism and hospitality industry is still an emerging research area. Indeed, we observe the existing of still several gaps about the underpinnings linking these concepts, especially with concern of the hospitality context. Likewise, the findings show also that the existing contributions, although focus on technologies and disability, do not explicitly consider a sustainability perspective, where disability and inclusion can be associated to social dimension of sustainability. Otherwise, the conceptual study shows that the existing contributions mostly adopt the customers' perspective, and less attention is paid to inside the organizations in this industry, that is managers and staff and the possible implications and effects derived from technology for them in terms of performance, work processed and job design, especially considering the typical and unique service nature of this industry.

Future research can also consider sustainability topic as well as focus much more on the main inhibiting factors in adopting digital and smart technologies in hospitality, mostly associated to factors conceived already by scholars as obstacles for making the tourism and hospitality industry much more technologically innovative and also sustainable, that is technological barriers, financial barriers, attitude, and behavioral barriers, and environmental factors (Kaynak et al. 2005, Wang et al. 2016, Leung 2019, Nam et al. 2020). Likewise, future research, starting from the preliminary findings of this conceptual study, can develop a specific framework taking into account technology and disability and sustainability topics for making the tourism and hospitality industry much more innovative, inclusive and sustainable, and then in the future it should be interesting to develop a research model to empirically validate considering the double perspective, inside and outside the organizations, that is conducting a survey field study considering the point of view of managers and staff of the organizations, stakeholders and customers.

References

Abdelmoaty, G.A. and Soliman, S.A.E.M. 2020. Smart technology applications in tourism and hospitality industry of the new administrative capital, Egypt. Journal of Association of Arab Universities for Tourism and Hospitality 19(2): 102–129.

Abdelraouf, O.A.M., Shaker, A. and Allam, N.K. 2018. Novel design of plasmonic and dielectric antireflection coatings to enhance the efficiency of perovskite solar cells. Solar Energy 174: 803–814.

Agarwal, P., Swami, S. and Malhotra, S.K. 2022. Artificial intelligence adoption in the post COVID-19 new-normal and role of smart technologies in transforming business: a review. Journal of Science and Technology Policy Management XX: 2053–4620.

Alonso, A.D., Kok, S.K., Bressan, A., O'Shea, M., Sakellarios, N., Koresis, A. et al. 2020. COVID-19, aftermath, impacts, and hospitality firms: an international perspective. International Journal of Hospitality Management 91: 102654–102654.

Amankwah-Amoah, J., Khan, Z. and Wood, G. 2021. COVID-19 and business failures: the paradoxes of experience, scale, and scope for theory and practice. European Management Journal 39(2): 179–184.

Baroni, F. and Lazzari, M. 2020. Tecnologie informatiche e diritti umani per un nuovo approccio all'accessibilità. Italian Journal of Disability Studies 1(1): 79–92.

Berry, J.W., Phinney, J.S., Sam, D.L. and Vedder, P. 2006. Immigrant Youth: Acculturation, Identity, and Adaptation. Applied Psychology.

Bezvesilnaya, A.A., Shadskaja, I.G.E., Kozlova, N.A., Shelygov, A.V. and Alekseenko, E.V. 2020. Digital technology development in tourism and hospitality industry. Eurasian Journal of Biosciences 14(2).

Boyd, D. and Ellison, N. 2021. Social network sites: Definition, history, and scholarship. Journal of Computer-Mediated Communication Vol. 13, Blackwell.

Briggs, S. 2001. Successful Web Marketing for the Tourism and Leisure Sector, Kogan. Page Limited, pp. 62–65.

Brown, N.A., Rovins, J.E., Feldmann-Jensen, S., Orchiston, C. and Johnston, D. 2017. Exploring disaster resilience within the hotel sector: a systematic review of literature. Int. J. Disaster Risk Reduct.

Buhalis, D. and Leung, R. 2018. Smart hospitality—Interconnectivity and interoperability towards an ecosystem. International Journal of Hospitality Management.

Buhalis, D., Harwood, T., Bogicevic, V., Viglia, G., Beldona, S. and Hofacker, C. 2019. Technological disruptions in services: lessons from tourism and hospitality. Journal of Service Management 30(4): 484–506.

Buhalis, D. 2020. Technology in tourism-from information communication technologies to eTourism and smart tourism towards ambient intelligence tourism: a perspective article. Tourism Review 75(1): 267–272.
Buhalis, D., O'Connor, P. and Leung, R. 2023. Smart hospitality: from smart cities and smart tourism towards agile business ecosystems in networked destinations. International Journal of Contemporary Hospitality Management 35(1): 369–393. doi: 10.1108/IJCHM-04-2022-0497.
Calvillo, M. 2023. How will AI like ChatGPT change the restaurant industry? Hospitality technology. Available at: https://hospitalitytech.com/how-will-ai-chatgpt-change-restaurantindustry (Accessed 10 november 2023).
Carvalho, I. and Ivanov, S. 2023. ChatGPT for tourism: Applications, benefits and risks. Tourism Review (2023): 1–14. https://doi.org/10.1108/TR-02-2023-0088.
Çeltek, E. 2022. Smart technology trends in the tourism and hospitality industry. Smart Cities and Tourism: Co-creating Experiences, Challenges and Opportunities 14.
Chathoth, P., Altinay, L., Harrington, R.J., Okumus, F. and Chan, E.S. 2013. Co-production versus co-creation: a process-based continuum in the hotel service context. International Journal of Hospitality Management 32: 11–20.
Chen, C.C. and Petrick, J.F. 2013. Health and wellness benefits of travel experiences: a literature review. Journal of Travel Research 52(6): 709–719.
Cini, D. 2019. Web Marketing. In Dall'Ara G. (a cura di), Le nuove frontiere del marketing applicato al turismo, Franco Angeli.
CNN. 2020. New York's Roosevelt Hotel to close after nearly 100 years due to the coronavirus pandemic. 12 October.
Conference and Meetings World. 2020. Pacific World the latest casualty of pandemic as it announces departure from meetings and events. 1 September.
Corigliano, M.A. and Baggio, R. 2020. Internet & turismo 2.0. Tecnologie per operare con successo, EGEA, pp. 28–48.
Danese, P., Manfè, V. and Romano, P. 2018. A systematic literature review on recent lean research: state-of-the-art and future directions. British Journal of Management.
Di Vaio, A., Palladino, R., Hassan, R. and Escobar, O. 2020. Artificial intelligence and business models in the sustainable development goals perspective: A systematic literature review. Journal of Business Research 121: 283–314.
Dogru, T., Line, N., Mody, M., Hanks, L., Abbott, J.A., Acikgoz, F. et al. 2023a. Generative artificial intelligence in the hospitality and tourism industry: Developing a framework for future research. Journal of Hospitality & Tourism Research 10963480231188663.
Dogru, T., Line, N., Hanks, L., Acikgoz, F., Abbott, J.A., Bakir, S. et al. 2023b. The implications of generative artificial intelligence in academic research and higher education in tourism and hospitality. Tourism Economics 13548166231204065.
Donner, R.V., Small, M., Donges, J.F., Marwan, N., Zou, Y., Xiang, R. et al. 2011. Recurrence-based time series analysis by means of complex network methods. International Journal of Bifurcation and Chaos 21(04): 1019–1046.
Duncan, R.B. 1972. Characteristics of organizational environments and perceived environmental uncertainty. Administrative Science Quarterly 17(3): 313–327.
Duro, J.A., Perez-Laborda, A., Turrion-Prats, J. and Fernandez-Fernandez, M. 2021. Covid-19 and tourism vulnerability. Tourism Management Perspectives 38: 100819.
Dwivedi, Y.K., Pandey, N., Currie, W. and Micu, A. 2023a. Leveraging ChatGPT and other generative artificial intelligence (AI)-based applications in the hospitality and tourism industry: practices, challenges and research agenda. International Journal of Contemporary Hospitality Management.
Dwivedi, Y.K., Kshetri, N., Hughes, L., Slade, E.L., Jeyaraj, A., Kar, A.K. et al. 2023b. So what if ChatGPT wrote it? Multidisciplinary perspectives on opportunities, challenges and implications of generative conversational AI for research, practice and policy. International Journal of Information Management 71: 102642.
Ercan, F. 2019. Smart tourism technologies: applications in hotel business. Theory and Practice in Social Sciences 528–546.

Femenia-Serra, F. and Neuhofer, B. 2018. Smart tourism experiences: conceptualisation, key dimensions and research agenda. Investigaciones Regionales - Journal of Regional Research, Asociación Española de Ciencia Regional 42: 129–150.
Filimonau, V., Derqui, B. and Matute, J. 2020. The COVID-19 pandemic and organizational commitment of senior hotel managers. International Journal of Hospitality Management 91: 102659.
Gössling, S., Scott, D. and Hall, C.M. 2020. Pandemics, tourism and global change: a rapid assessment of COVID-19. Journal of Sustainable Tourism 29(1): 1–20.
Gretzel, U., Sigala, M., Xiang, Z. and Koo, C. 2015. Smart tourism: foundations and developments. Electron Markets 25: 179–188.
Gursoy, D. and Chi, C.G. 2020. Effects of COVID-19 pandemic on hospitality industry: review of the current situations and a research agenda. Journal of Hospitality Marketing and Management 29(5): 527–529.
Hao, F., Xiao, Q. and Chon, K. 2020. COVID-19 and China's hotel industry: impacts, a disaster management framework, and post-pandemic agenda. International Journal of Hospitality Management 90: 102636.
Heinonen, K. and Strandvik, T. 2020. Reframing service innovation: COVID-19 as a catalyst for imposed service innovation. Journal of Service Management 32(1): 101–112.
Ho, G.K., Lam, C. and Law, R. 2023. Conceptual framework of strategic leadership and organizational resilience for the hospitality and tourism industry for coping with environmental uncertainty. Journal of Hospitality and Tourism Insights 6(2): 835–852.
Jaremen, D.E., Jędrasiak, M. and Rapacz, A. 2016. The concept of smart hotels as an innovation on the hospitality industry market – Case Study of Puro Hotel in Wrocław. Ekonomiczne Problemy Turystyki 36: 65–75.
Jiang, Y. and Ritchie, B.W. 2017. Disaster collaboration in tourism: motives, impediments and success factors. Journal of Hospitality and Tourism Management 31: 70–82.
Jiang, Y. and Wen, J. 2020. Effects of COVID-19 on hotel marketing and management: a perspective article. International Journal of Contemporary Hospitality Management 32(8): 2563–2573.
Jones, P. and Comfort, D. 2020. The COVID-19 crisis and sustainability in the hospitality industry. International Journal of Contemporary Hospitality Management 32(10): 3037–3050.
Kauppi, P.E., Sandström, V. and Lipponen, A. 2018. Forest resources of nations in relation to human well-being. PLoS ONE 13(5).
Kaynak, E., Tatoglu, E. and Kula, V. 2005. An analysis of the factors affecting the adoption of electronic commerce by SMEs: Evidence from an emerging market. International Marketing Review 22(6): 623–640.
Khan, M.S., Nam, K., Dutt, C.S., Chathoth, P. and Daghfous, A. 2021. The adoption of artificial intelligence and robotics in the hotel industry: prospects and challenges. Electronic Markets 31(3): 553–574.
Kim, Y.R. and Lin, S.C. 2021. The non-linear relationship between brand diversification and hotel owner performance: the roles of ownership structure and location as moderators. Journal of Hospitality and Tourism Management 49: 235–243.
Krishan, V., Mann, R., Seitzman, N. and Wittkamp, N. 2020. Hospitality and COVID-19: how long until 'no vacancy' for US hotels? McKinsey and Company.
Lafuente, A.L. and Righi, M. 2021. Internet e Web 2.0, Utet Università.
Lai, I.K.W. and Wong, J.W.C. 2020. Comparing crisis management practices in the hotel industry between initial and pandemic stages of COVID-19. International Journal of Contemporary Hospitality Management 32(10): 3135–3136.
Lamb, R. and Kling, R. 2003. Reconceptualizing users as social actors in information systems research. MIS Quarterly 27(2): 197–235.
Law, R., Lin, K.J., Ye, H. and Fong, D.K.C. 2023. Artificial intelligence research in hospitality: a state-of-the-art review and future directions. International Journal of Contemporary Hospitality Management.
Lee, A.V., Vargo, J. and Seville, E. 2013. Developing a tool to measure and compare organizations' resilience. Natural Hazards Review 14(1): 29–41.
Leonidis, A., Korozi, M., Margetis, G., Grammenos, D. and Stephanidis, C. 2013. An intelligent hotel room. *In*: Augusto, J.C., Wichert, R., Collier, R., Keyson, D., Salah, A.A. and Tan, A.H. (eds.). Ambient Intelligence. AmI 2013. Lecture Notes in Computer Science, vol 8309. Springer, Cham.

Leonidou, L.C., Katsikeas, C.S., Samiee, S. and Aykol, B. 2018. International marketing research: a state-of-the-art review and the way forward. *In*: Leonidou, L., Katsikeas, C., Samiee, S. and Aykol, B. (eds.). Advances in Global Marketing. Springer, Cham.
Leung, R. and Law, R. 2013. Evaluation of hotel information technologies and EDI adoption: the perspective of hotel IT managers in Hong Kong. Cornell Hospitality Quarterly 54(1): 25–37.
Leung, Michael. Treatment and Spillover Effects under Network Interference (January 14, 2019). Available at SSRN: https://ssrn.com/abstract=2757313.
Li, C., Chen, Q., Zhang, X., Snyder, S.A., Gong, Z. and Lam, S.H. 2017. An integrated approach with the zebrafish model for biomonitoring of municipal wastewater effluent and receiving waters. Water Research 131: 33–44.
Lin, S.C. and Kim, Y.R. 2020. Diversification strategies and failure rates in the Texas lodging industry: franchised versus company-operated hotels. International Journal of Hospitality Management 88: 102525.
Mich, L. and Garigliano, R. 2023. ChatGPT for e-Tourism: A technological perspective. Information Technology & Tourism 25(1): 1–12. https://doi.org/10.1007/s40558-023-00248-x.
Nam, K., Baker, J., Ahmad, N. and Goo, J. 2020, Dissatisfaction, disconfirmation, and distrust: an empirical examination of value co-destruction through negative electronic word-of-mouth (eWOM). Inf. Syst. Front. 22: 113–130. https://doi.org/10.1007/s10796-018-9849-4.
Neuhofer, B., Buhalis, D. and Ladkin, A. 2015. Smart technologies for personalized experiences: a case study in the hospitality domain. Electronic Markets 25: 243–254.
Nofal, E., Elhanafi, A.M., Hameeuw, H. and Vande Moere, A. 2018. Architectural contextualization of heritage museum artifacts using augmented reality. Studies in Digital Heritage 2(1): 42–67.
Okoli, C. and Schabram, K. 2010. A guide to conducting a systematic literature review of information systems research. Sprouts: Working Papers on Information Systems 10(26). Available at: http://sprouts.aisnet.org/10-26.
Okoli, C. 2015. A guide to conducting a standalone systematic literature review. Communications of the Association for Information Systems 37.
Oracle and Skift's Hospitality Report. 2023. Industry Insights: 4 Questions with Oracle Hospitality (Access on Dec 2023: https://skift.com/2023/12/14/industry-insights-4-questions-with-oracle-hospitality/).
Orwskiliko, W.J. 2000. Using technology and constituting structures: a practice lens for studying technology in organization. Organization Science 11(4): 404–428.
Otto, J.E. and Ritchie, J.B. 1996. The service experience in tourism. Tourism Management 17(3): 165–174.
Ozdemir, O., Dogru, T., Kizildag, M. and Erkmen, E. 2023. A critical reflection on digitalization for the hospitality and tourism industry: value implications for stakeholders. International Journal of Contemporary Hospitality Management. doi: 10.1108/IJCHM-04-2022-0535.
Pandey, N. and Srivastava, V. 2013. Factors affecting tourists' intention to purchase: a study of Indian domestic tourists. International Journal of Indian Culture and Business Management 6(3): 314–329.
Pencarelli, T. 2020. The digital revolution in the travel and tourism industry. Information Technology & Tourism 22(3): 455–476.
Petrevska, B., Cingoski, V. and Gelev, S. 2016. From smart rooms to smart hotels. Zbornik radova sa XXI međunarodnog naučno-stručnog skupa Informacione tehnologije-sadašnjost i budućnost, Žabljak. 201–204.
Piramanayagam, S., Pritam, P. and More, B.A. 2019. Inclusive hotel design in India: A user perspective. Journal of Accessibility and Design for All 9(1): 41–65.
Pramana, S., Paramartha, D.Y., Ermawan, G.Y., Deli, N.F. and Srimulyani, W. 2021 Impact of COVID-19 pandemic on tourism in Indonesia. Current Issues in Tourism 2021: 1–21.
Ramkissoon, H. 2023. Perceived social impacts of tourism and quality-of-life: A new conceptual model. Journal of Sustainable Tourism 31(2): 442–459.
Ranieri, M. and Manca, S. 2019. I social network nell'educazione. Basi teoriche, modelli applicativi, linee guida, pp. 89–91.
Safaeva, S.R., Alieva, M.T., Abdukhalilova, L.T., Alimkhodjaeva, N.E. and Konovalova, E.E. 2020. Organizational and economic aspects of the development of the international tourism and hospitality industry. Journal of Environmental Management and Tourism 11(4): 913–919.

Sahebjamnia, N., Torabi, S.A. and Mansouri, S.A. 2018. Building organizational resilience in the face of multiple disruptions. International Journal of Production Economics 197: 63–83.

Sakshi, Shashi, Cerchione, R. and Bansal, H. 2020. Measuring the impact of sustainability policy and practices in tourism and hospitality industry. Business Strategy and the Environment 29(3): 1109–1126.

Shaw, G., Bailey, A. and Williams, A. 2011. Aspects of service-dominant logic and its implications for tourism management: examples from the hotel industry. Tourism Management 32(2): 207–214.

Sigala, M. 2020. Tourism and COVID-19: impacts and implications for advancing and resetting industry and research. Journal of Business Research 117: 312–321.

Singal, M. 2015. How is the hospitality and tourism industry different? An empirical test of some structural characteristics. International Journal of Hospitality Management 47: 116–119.

SKIFT and ORACLE HOSPITALITY Report. 2023. Hospitality in 2025: Automated, Intelligent... and More Personal. Available at https://www.oracle.com/hospitality/hospitality-in-2025-report/ (Accessed on December 15 2023).

Smith, M.K. and Diekmann, A. 2017. Tourism and wellbeing. Annals of Tourism Research 66: 1–13.

Sorci, P. 2020. Il comportamento del consumatore turista. In Dall'Ara G. (a cura di), Le nuove frontiere del marketing applicato al turismo, Franco Angeli.

Stylos, N., Fotiadis, A.K., Shin, D.D. and Huan, T.C.T. 2021. Beyond smart systems adoption: Enabling diffusion and assimilation of smartness in hospitality. International Journal of Hospitality Management 98: 103042.

Tourism and Hospitality Market Forecast. 2023. Global Tourism and Hospitality Market. Market Data Forecast (Access on Dec 2023: https://www.marketdataforecast.com/market-reports/tourism-and-hospitality-market).

Tranfield, D., Denyer, D. and Smart, P. 2003. Towards a methodology for developing evidence-informed management knowledge by means of systematic review. British Journal of Management.

Tutuncu, O. 2017. Investigating the accessibility factors affecting hotel satisfaction of people with physical disabilities. International Journal of Hospitality Management 65: 29–36.

United Nation World Tourism Organization. 2021. Impact assessment of the COVID-19 outbreak on international tourism. Updated December 2020.

van Eck, N.J. and Waltman, L. 2010. Software survey: VOSviewer, a computer program for bibliometric mapping. Scientometrics 84: 523–538.

van Eck, N.J. and Waltman, L. 2014. Visualizing bibliometric networks. pp. 285–320. *In*: Ding, Y., Rousseau, R. and Wolfram, D. (eds.). Measuring Scholarly Impact. Springer.

Van Raan, A. 2017. Patent citations analysis and its value in research evaluation: a review and a new approach to map technology-relevant research. Journal of Data and Information Science.

Varriale, L. and Volpe, T. 2022. Industry 4.0 in the tourism and hospitality business: Insights and challenges for 'smart inclusive hotels'. pp. 139–168. In Tourism, Hospitality and Culture 4.0: Shifting towards the Metaverse. McGraw-Hill Education.

Wang, C.L. and Chugh, H. 2014. Entrepreneurial learning: Past research and future challenges. International Journal of Management Reviews 16(1): 24–61.

Wang, P.Q. 2024. Personalizing guest experience with generative AI in the hotel industry: there's more to it than meets a Kiwi's eye. Current Issues in Tourism 1–18.

Wang, Z., Sharma, P.N. and Cao, J. 2016. From knowledge sharing to firm performance: A predictive model comparison, Journal of Business Research October 2016, 69(10): 4650–4658.

Witell, L., Snyder, H., Gustafsson, A., Fombelle, P. and Kristensson, P. 2016. Defining service innovation: A review and synthesis. Journal of Business Research.

Wu, H.C. and Ko, Y.J. 2013. Assessment of service quality in the hotel industry. Journal of Quality Assurance in Hospitality and Tourism 14(3): 218–244.

Xiao, Q., O'Neill, J.W. and Mattila, A.S. 2012. The role of hotel owners: the influence of corporate strategies on hotel performance. International Journal of Contemporary Hospitality Management.

Yang, Y., Cao, Y. and Yang, L.T.G. 2017. Product diversification and property performance in the urban lodging market: the relationship and its moderators. Tourism Management 59: 363–375.

Zhang, Y. and Cole, S. 2016. Dimensions of lodging guest satisfaction among guests with mobility challenges: A mixed-method analysis of web-based texts, Tourism Management.

Zhuo, Y.T., Huang, Y., Chen, C. and Xing, Z. 2023. Exploring AI ethics of ChatGPT: A diagnostic analysis. arXiv preprint arXiv:2301.12867. https://doi.org/10.48550/arXiv.2301.12867.

Zitt, M. and Filliatreau, G. 2016. Big Is (Made) beautiful – some comments about shanghai-ranking of world-class universities. *In*: Sadlak, J. and Liu Nian Cai (eds.). The World-Class University and Ranking: Aiming Beyond Status. UNESCO-CEPES, Shanghai Jiao Tong University, Cluj University Press.

Chapter 3

Revolutionizing Accounting with RPA and Alternative Data Sources

A Real Estate Market Case Study

Fabian Altendorfer,[1] *Susanne Leitner-Hanetseder*[1,*] and *Lisa Perkhofer*[2]

1. Introduction

The field of accounting is currently undergoing significant digital transformation, driven largely by automation and the availability of big data (Green et al. 2018, Leitner-Hanetseder et al. 2021). In particular, publicly available websites are a vast and rich source (Mahlendorf et al. 2022), offering a wealth of data, such as market trends (Kościelniak and Puto 2015), economic outlooks, price developments (Macias et al. 2023) and stats on competitors, which have the potential to influence decision-making in accounting (Khder 2021).

However, utilizing these data from websites, is not an easy task (Bumblauskas et al. 2017, Wamba et al. 2015). Consequently, companies that use Big Data Analytics for decision-making often turn to more dynamic approaches such as programmatic methods, such as web scraping (Boegershausen et al. 2021). Therefore, the exploration of web-based information allows for the collection of data beyond conventional data sources (e.g., financial statements), which is increasingly gaining importance in

[1] University of Applied Sciences Upper Austria, Faculty for Business and Management, Wehrgrabengasse 1 – 3, 4400 Steyr, Austria.
[2] MCI Management Center Innsbruck, Universitätsstraße 15, 6020 Innsbruck, Austria.
Emails: fabian.altendorfer@fh-steyr.at; lisa.perkhofer@mci.edu
* Corresponding author: susanne.leitner-hanetseder@fh-steyr.at

accounting. The added significance of the methods is not only seen within the realm of business, but also in the academic context (Anand et al. 2020, Grybauskas et al. 2021, Polidoro et al. 2015).

Web scraping is a technique concerned with the extraction and transformation of semi- or unstructured data, typically in the form of HTML documents, into a structured format that can be easily organized, stored and analyzed in databases or spreadsheets (Mauro et al. 2018, Vargiu and Urru 2012). The transformation of semi- or unstructured data into structured data is a crucial aspect of web scraping, as it enables the valuable information from websites to be used and incorporated into the decision-making process (Ciampi et al. 2021). For this purpose, various possibilities for web scraping are available—from the Robotic Process Automation (RPA) software offering options in low-code (Microsoft Power Automate, UiPath) (Mishra et al. 2022) to sophisticated code solutions offering code building blocks in R or Python using libraries (Anand et al. 2020).

With our target audience working in accounting, we assume high domain knowledge, but restricted expertise in programming languages (Apostolou et al. 2019, Appelbaum et al. 2017). Thus, this study focuses on the low-code option RPA for data extraction from websites and demonstrates its procedure based on a use case for comprehensibility. We believe that the low-code approach has the potential to allow non-IT experts to trigger and execute data collection from websites themselves (Huang and Vasarhelyi 2019). This can support the ongoing digitalization and allow for a first and straightforward step in the field of digital accounting, taking away caution and fear by automating an otherwise annoying task (data cleaning and collection).

In doing so, we first address the question of applicability of web scraping in the domain of accounting, second, we demonstrate a possible implementation process based on our case "real estate data". Of course, as with any method that reduces complexity, trade-offs must be considered. Thus, restrictions on web scraping using RPA with respect to proxy rotation and parallel processing have been identified, which limit its applicability especially with respect to larger web scraping endeavors. Nonetheless, we highlight its possible opportunities in accounting, but we also complement chances by the restraints of this method and compare RPA with respect to more sophisticated approaches of data collection, such as, using R or Python.

The paper is structured as follows: First, in section two, we discuss web scraping techniques in detail. In section three, we demonstrate a comprehensive workflow to web scrape data and demonstrate a sample workflow using an RPA-generated bot and highlight the benefits and limitations, as well as potential problems, associated with it. Finally, in Section 4, we summarize the key findings and particularly focus on the skills required by accountants to use internet data with web scraping techniques for decision-making and conclude with future research questions that would help us to further develop our web scraping solution.

2. Background

Web scraping refers to the creation and use of program code for automatic Internet data collection, storage and analysis (Boegershausen et al. 2021, Mauro et al. 2018,

Mitchell 2018). The idea of searching the Internet for and extracting specific data is not new (Vargiu and Urru 2012). Back in 1993, MIT student Matthew Gray developed the World Wide Web Wanderer, which is now considered the first web scraper in history (Knoblock 1997). Web scraping, which involves the use of computer programs to search for and index web-based information, has been a long-standing practice (Vargiu and Urru 2012).

Today, web scraping has become a widely used technique by both, external institutions such as OECD or Statista, with the core function of being an information provider (Da Diniz Silva et al. unpublished data, Kühnemann 2021), as well as individual companies, to enable them to address specific business management questions such as market price determinations, trend analyses for brands and products (Mahlendorf et al. 2022, Vording 2021), sales forecasts (Mahlendorf et al. 2022) and financial market analyses (Khder 2021, Lin and Yang 2022). Consequently, its potential impact on decision-making is significant.

To achieve this ongoing success, web scraping has been supported by a variety of techniques, which we divided into three main groups: partial tools, complete web scraping tools and libraries and frameworks (Nigam and Biswas 2021, Raj et al. 2021). While partial tools include third-party plug-ins and browser add-ons that make it possible to extract data from tables such as the price of a product (Nigam and Biswas 2021, Raj et al. 2021), complete web scraping tools are often proprietary software, developed and sold by commercial vendors. These tools include complete web scraping solutions that allow efficient and automated data collection (Mohapatra et al. 2023). Third, libraries and frameworks are software components typically written in general-purpose programming languages (Nigam and Biswas 2021). These components enable access to websites and facilitate the extraction of web content while preserving the characteristics of the HTTP protocol.

The selection of an appropriate technique is crucial for the success of a scraping project. Figure 1 provides an overview of the web scrapping techniques and lays out the level of IT expertise that is required for their application. A detailed description of each group is provided below.

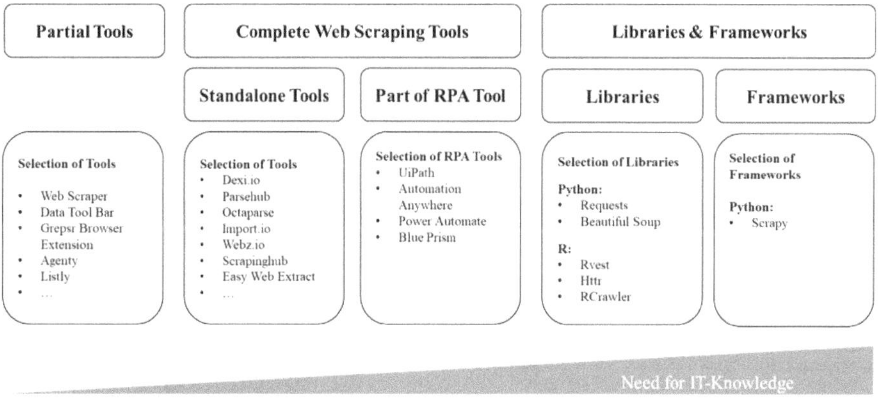

Figure 1. Overview of web scraping techniques related to needed IT-knowledge (source: authors).

2.1 Partial Tools

Partial tools, such as plugins and browser add-ons, facilitate the extraction of data from tables and assist users with various web scraping tasks, while browsing the internet (Nigam and Biswas 2021, Raj et al. 2021). Frequently used options include the web scraper, data tool bar and Grepsr browser extension. They are usually only suitable for small web scraping projects in which a limited amount of data, especially from data tables, is extracted from the internet at a single point in time (Nigam and Biswas 2021). Partial tools are not recommended for projects that require the extraction of large datasets that are not stored in a table. Additionally, the functionality of a database for self-updating is not supported by partial tools.

2.2 Complete Tools for Web Scraping

With respect to tool-options and for a better differentiation between all possible offers, we divided solutions into *standalone complete web scraping tools* and web scraping tools, which are part of a *Robotic Process Automation (RPA)* software. While tools such as Dexi.io, Parsehub, Octoparse and Easy Web Extract offer user-friendly interfaces to extract all available data from websites such as text, images and video (Raj et al. 2021), extracting information is their sole purpose. They support the user by incorporating features such as a robust graphical user interface, computer vision-enabled visual scraping utilities, query capturing and recording functionality, APIs (Application Programming Interfaces) and audit dashboards (Nigam and Biswas 2021). With these features, even users who are unfamiliar with programming languages can develop reliable web scraping solutions.

RPA on the other hand, enables the use of a software bot that can log in to a website, extract data, transform the data into a structured format and store it in a database. In other words, you instruct a virtual assistant to do your work in the same way that a human would perform the task. However, in contrast to an Excel VBA, it can also work across multiple software applications (Cooper et al. 2019, Langmann and Turi 2023, Li et al. 2023) and therefore look up information on the internet and transfer data into a database. This is a huge advantage of RPA software used in web scraping, because how the process is constructed does not differ in the IT application with respect to a worker performing the task in real life.

In addition, RPA has a user-friendly interface and non-intrusive functionalities (e.g., it uses a recorder for variable definitions). With a basic understanding of Microsoft tools (Microsoft 365) especially for bots generated with Microsoft Power Automate, a user should be able to work with the program in a few days' time, as it is easy to follow and hands on tutorials available online targeted at users with limited knowledge in IT.[1] When applying RPA, companies can reduce their reliance on human resources for repetitive, time-consuming and error-prone tasks (Mohapatra et al. 2023) and due to their domain knowledge, accountants can build a web scrawler themselves. Thus, the use of RPA in accounting has become popular in recent years (Langmann and Turi 2023).

[1] For example, the Youtube-Channels Anders Jensen or Pragmatic Works.

In the context of web scraping, several software tools are available for RPA, including UiPath, Automation Anywhere, Microsoft Power Automate and Blue Prism, which are some of the most widely used tools (Gartner Research 2022). However, with all reductions in complexity comes a price, and thus negative aspects worth mentioning. First, for the full set of functionalities, license fees must be paid, and second, for particular types of websites, RPA is restricted and unfortunately error prone. In particular, if a large dataset must be loaded from websites and if you want to repeat the scraping process based on a certain time interval (weekly, monthly, yearly), we recommend working with other solutions such as R or Python. These programs, however, require the user to be familiar with a specific language. Therefore, we advise that these projects collaborate closely with IT experts.

2.3 Libraries

Developing all functions required for web scraping can be time-consuming and unproductive, and for this reason, software developers often rely on libraries that have already been created for scripting (El Asikri et al. 2020). Libraries are collections of code bricks that allow for the rapid implementation of functions in new projects (Krueger 1992). Many programming languages offer their own web scraping libraries, including Python, R, Java, PHP and Ruby (Glez-Peña et al. 2014). However, Python and R are the preferred programming languages for many web scraping projects (Khder 2021, Krotov and Tennyson 2018) thus, only these two languages are discussed in further detail.

Requests and Beautiful Soup are the two most important *Python* libraries for web scraping (Patel 2020). Requests is a library that allows sending HTTP requests and receiving responses to retrieve web content. The library manages cookies and redirects, thus making network interaction easier for the programmer (Hajba 2018). Beautiful Soup provides a convenient and easily understandable interface for traversing Document Object Model (DOM) structures, ensuring high flexibility in processing various types of documents (Patel 2020). In combination, Requests and Beautiful Soup offer a powerful and straightforward solution for web scraping tasks, enabling the retrieval of web content and the subsequent search and extraction of data (Patel 2020).

However, it is not only Python which offers libraries for web scraping. *R* also provides libraries, such as rvest and httr, which allow for the parsing of HTML and XML documents and the sending and processing of HTTP requests and responses (Bradley and James 2019). RCrawler is another popular web scraping library in R, which enables the parallel crawling of multiple websites and detects broken links or network issues, while also bypassing websites security measures (Khalil and Fakir 2017).

Which program or language to use is highly dependent on the coder's preferences. In the context of web scraping, both R and Python offer robust and versatile solutions using a variety of available libraries and tools. Python, with its extensive ecosystem of libraries such as BeautifulSoup and Scrapy, is often favored for its simplicity and readability, making it a popular choice for web scraping tasks and applications in business informatics. On the other hand, R, with packages such as rvest and httr, has a strong appeal for those already familiar with its syntax and capabilities, particularly among statisticians and data scientists. Ultimately, the choice between R and Python for web scraping boils down to the coder's familiarity with the language, specific requirements of the project and desired level of customization and flexibility.

Libraries, regardless of their programming language, are modular pieces of code designed for use in specific contexts. Modifying these code modules is generally discouraged, and the incorporation of additional functionality may be limited. If the built-in features of a library are insufficient, and other libraries also fail to provide the desired functionality, a programmer might consider using a framework instead, which typically offers a more comprehensive set of tools and features for building applications.

2.4 Frameworks

Frameworks are software packages that offer pre-built code to execute specific functionalities, typically providing a more comprehensive solution for the entire web scraping process. Scrapy is a well-known Python framework for web scraping, which allows spiders to crawl websites and process data directly, circumventing restrictions on data access (Raj et al. 2021). To construct a viable and sustainable web scraper in Python or R, it is necessary to overcome various obstacles and establish certain prerequisites. These factors can be either internal and customized, such as the programmer's level of expertise and the requisite computational resources (Kühnemann 2021), or external, such as circumventing IP address blocking or evading detection of the scraping operation via browser history tracking (Milev 2017).

In the next chapter, we will discuss the applicability, and reasons for as well as reasons against using the above-described techniques. As our project requires the extraction of a large dataset that is not stored in a table, the option of partial tools was not applied. In addition, as our target audience is based in accounting, and we focus on limited IT requirements, we abstain from a detailed description of using libraries and frameworks.

3. Case Study: Web Scraping of Real Estate Data from a Real Estate Platform

In this section, we introduce our case study. We first demonstrate the relevance of real estate data, and in which scenarios the extracted information can be used from an accounting perspective. Second, we lay out the process of web scraping in general and describe how this relates to our sample website – the real estate platform "willhaben". Finally, we will show how to work with the RPA tool "Microsoft Power Automate". By discussing skills and requirements, as well as the results of the web scraping process, we can argue for an implementation given some identified restrictions.

Please note that especially for the third part, although no programming skills are required, the reader is expected to have basic knowledge of the creation of RPA processes and the use of Microsoft Power Automate. *The bot exclusively scrapes data related to the purchase of houses as displayed on the discussed website.*

3.1 The Relevance of Real Estate Data for Accounting

The real estate market is highly contested and has always generated interest in investment and sales opportunities. There are different data sources for information about the respective real estate market, some of which are not freely accessible. Based on the real estate market in Austria, Kainz (2017) suggests that the land register, published data collections from financial institutions (Higgins et al. 2022) and applications of real estate agents should be considered (Kainz 2017). While the land register offers only limited and expensive information, data from real estate agents is of varying quality.

An additional source of information, that is often overlooked, is data from real estate platforms (Kainz 2017). Platforms allow for the use of publicly available information, offering the potential do describe supply and demand in the real estate market (Beręsewicz 2015, Bricongne et al. 2023). However, the efficient and effective extraction of publicly available data has not yet been fully explored or tested. Therefore, scraping real estate data from online marketplaces is a good starting point for improving decision-making for market participants or other interested parties such as banks (for collateralization) and a useful case study demonstrating real life problems for our research agenda.

Even though the scraped prices represent asking prices rather than actual selling prices, and not all available properties are listed on online real estate marketplaces such as willhaben.at, the data obtained through web scraping can serve as a valuable indicator of potential trends in the overall real estate market or specific regions. This knowledge about trends in the market, for instance, can be particularly beneficial for IFRS accountants who are required to estimate the Expected Credit Loss (ECL) components of IFRS 9 (Financial Instruments), specifically the Loss Given Default (LGD) or for plausibility checks of the fair value in the context of IAS 40 (Investment Properties) (Gabriel 2021).

3.2 The Process of Web Scraping

How a web scraping project should be set up is described by Persson (2019). According to him, the web scraping process encompasses three main phases: (1) fetching the data from the website, (2) defining and extracting the relevant variables from the website, and (3) transforming the obtained data in a usable format to store it in a database (see Figure 2). All three stages as well as how we managed to finalize each stage, is presented in the next paragraphs.

Phase 1 – Fetching: In this phase, the web scraper sends HTTP requests to the target website, requesting it to return the website's content. The website's server then responds with the requested content, which may include text, images or other types of data (Persson 2019).

In our case, we extracted real estate data from a popular Austrian online marketplace for real estate (willhaben.at). The aim of the scenario is to extract all

Figure 2. Visualization of the comprehensive workflow for web scraping use case (source: authors).

available data on real estate in the category "house purchase" for the province of Upper Austria. At the time of the case study, there were 1,900 properties available in this category, restricted to Upper Austria.

From our perspective, the benefits of using RPA for web scraping tasks lie in its ability to seamlessly process websites with JavaScript elements. By simulating user interactions, such as scrolling, the RPA solution effectively navigates and retrieves data from websites without requiring explicit handling of the JavaScript components. With the utilization of RPA, the fetching process can be accomplished with relatively minimal effort.

Phase 2 – Extraction: Once the website content has been fetched, the web scraper analyzes it to identify and extract relevant data. This is usually done using techniques such as Regular Expressions (RegEx), XPath queries or HTML parsing (Persson 2019).

In this phase, we must define which of the possible variables must be used in the data collection process. The online marketplace provides numerous variables for these residential properties, that can vary for each property. These variables include the living area in square meters, number of rooms, type of property, type of heating, availability of the property, presence of a carport, presence of a parking space, presence of a garden, presence of a terrace, presence of a storage room, property description, energy certificate of the property, information about the location, information about any special equipment, additional information and further information depending on the type of property.

Phase 3 – Transformation: In this phase, the extracted data must be transformed into a structured format that can be used for analysis or further processing. This step may involve cleaning, normalization or reformatting of the data, depending on the original format of the data source (Persson 2019).

In the case of our real estate data, some of the transformation processes necessary to store the data in a useful format converted the original data types into varchar types. The programmer can further adjust the scraped data and cut out unnecessary symbols.

After successfully scraping the available data, they were structured and saved in a relational MS-SQL database. As illustrated in Figure 2, the data scraping workflow involves several key steps.

3.3 Scraping Data with "Microsoft Power Automate"

This study seeks to offer an in-depth understanding of the application of RPA in web scraping tasks, and to serve as a basis for comparison with other technologies. The focus is on the implementation of RPA through Microsoft Power Automate, a software tool that belongs to the Microsoft Power Platform suite, which includes Power Apps, Power Virtual Agents and Power BI, among others. According to a recent study by Gartner Research (2022), Microsoft Power Automate is considered to be one of the leading RPA applications in 2022. This finding is in line with the author's experience and expectations in research and education, where Microsoft's automation products have been increasingly established as effective solutions for automating business processes and routine tasks.

To enhance comprehensibility and ease of tracing, the web scraping process was divided into two workflows. The first component, called "main workflow", involves opening and closing the SQL connection and browser instance, as well as launching the sub-process. The second is a sub-workflow, labeled "scraping_houses_to_purchase", encompasses the actual web scraping process. This separation into main and sub-workflow serves several purposes, including facilitating the understanding of individual process steps and enabling the integration of additional tasks into the same process without significant modifications to the existing main process. For example, in a web scraping scenario for real estate data, it would be possible to integrate additional categories of the illhaben.at website such as data for renting a house, or for including other real estate marketplaces (other websites) into the scraping process by the time it takes to click a mouse.

Another advantage of dividing the web scraping process into two parts, from our perspective, is the clear separation of tasks between IT-related topics (setup of the database and the connection of the database with the web scraping tool) and domain specific content (defining which properties and which variables to be scraped and

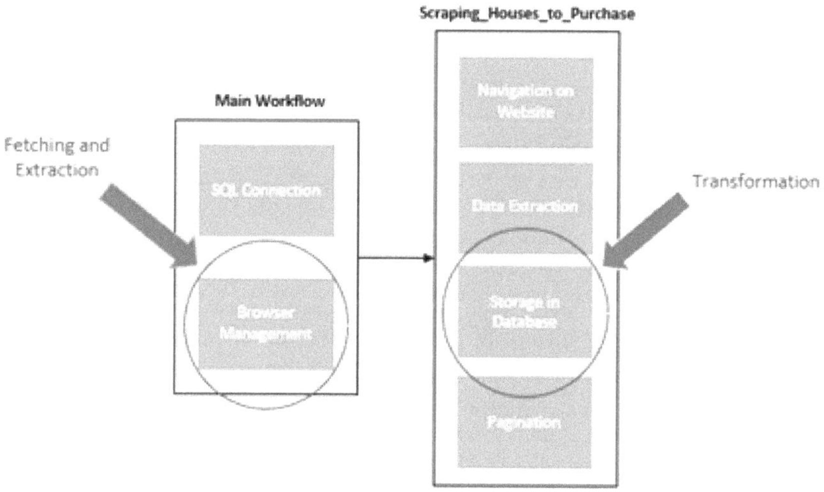

Figure 3. Visualization of the RPA web scraping process (source: authors).

downloaded in which quality). In this way the more technical main workflow is ideally managed by the IT department, whereas the domain-specific sub-flows are administered by the respective accounting specialist.

The *main workflow* starts with an Open SQL connection, which establishes a link to a pre-created SQL database in the MS SQL Server relational database management system. To establish a successful connection, information about the SQL database and the server used must be provided in the action parameter "connection string". In Microsoft Power Automate, actions are the building blocks that can be combined and configured to create automated workflows, which are sequences of steps that are executed in a specific order. The connection is necessary for storing the data obtained in the sub-process in the database, which is discussed later in the process.

Once the SQL connection has been successfully established, a new browser instance is opened, using the action "launch new Microsoft edge" specifying the website for web scraping. In our application, this refers to the real estate search engine of willhaben.at, specifically https://www.willhaben.at/iad/immobilien. The action also involves fetching and extraction of the content by simply opening a browser window and using the functions provided by the browser-application. The creator of the RPA-process doesn't necessarily need to be familiar with concepts such as fetching and extraction, as the application automatically applies all the necessary steps. The user only needs to input the website and select the desired data elements for extraction.

After this initial phase, the *subprocess* "scraping_houses_to_purchase" is started automatically, as in our case study we do not use triggers, that need to be initiated by the user. The subprocess "scraping_houses_to_purchase" encapsulates the actual web scraping procedure, comprising two nested loops. The first loop is dedicated to handling pagination, whereas the second loop focuses on extracting information for each property and subsequently storing the data in the database. The section "*navigation on website*" comprises all actions responsible for guiding the RPA bot to the destination containing the desired data. This includes pagination and computation of available pages. In other words, the user needs to tell the bot where to click and what to select to load the right information for the data collection process.

As this subprocess is at the heart of the application, these steps are discussed in further detail. In the first part of the subflow, additional steps are applied on the website to subsequently navigate to the target page containing the offers with the desired data. This initial part of the process is optional, as the information could also be captured in the URL, thus bypassing this interaction with the Graphical User Interface (GUI), which is common in web scraping using programming languages. In a "Set drop-down list value on webpage" action, the search category is selected using the German term "Haus kaufen" (englisch: houses to purchase). Subsequently, using three actions, the geographical search area is narrowed down to "Oberösterreich" (englisch: The Austrian province of Upper Austria). Finally, with the last action in this process segment, the "Press button on web page", the button "show objects" on the website is clicked, which loads the offers on the page. Next, the number of available objects should be calculated, for which we need to extract the first content of the website.

The second loop is responsible for gathering the information from the websites. With the "Extract data from webpage" action, it is possible to read the total number of offered properties, which is displayed on this part of the website. The result of this action is the storage of the extracted data in a string variable named "amount_of_objects_raw". A string is an ordered sequence of characters used to represent text in programming. Thus, the RPA bot is highly dependent on the website's loading behavior, which is why a slow internet connection may cause the website not to load in time. To counteract this, a repetition structure has been implemented to accommodate these requirements. By storing the total number of objects in the variable as a string, it cannot be used for calculations.

Thus, strings need to be converted using the following procedure: First, the thousands separator, commonly used on willhaben.at, must be removed using the action "replace text". Then, the "Convert text to number" action can be used to convert the value to an integer, which can then be used for calculations. In a "Set variable" action, the total number of available properties, converted to an integer, is used to calculate the number of offer pages by dividing the total number of objects by the number of objects per page. In a "Truncate number" action, the calculated value is rounded to a whole number, providing the process with the number of available offer pages.

Finally, necessary counter variables for loops are created using several "set variable" actions. These counter variables are used to control the loops. In the next step, the first loop of the process is implemented, iterating through all the offer pages. The loop, which is integrated into the process with a loop condition, first extracts the URL of the current address using the action "get details of web page" but only if it is the first page. This is checked using an If element. The address of the first page is required later to access the subsequent pages. At this point in the process, the goal is to extract the URLs of the offer detail pages (so-called "href" HTML elements).

Because willhaben.at uses JavaScript elements on the offer overview page, not all 30 href attributes can be scraped from the website at once. Due to the JavaScript elements, the website responds to user activities, which is why the RPA bot must scroll to the end of the page to scrape all 30 href attributes. Microsoft Power Automate does not provide a ready-made solution for this, so the author created a scrolling function using "Run JavaScript function on web page" actions. These elements enable the integration of JavaScript code, which is used to implement a simple scrolling function on the website.

To enable a gradual loading of the href attributes, four JavaScript actions were employed. The process reaches the end of the website after executing these four elements. The href attributes can now be extracted using the action "extract data from webpage". The results are stored in the list variable "listofobjects", which now contains all offer detail pages for the properties on the respective offer overview page. To conclude the "Navigation on Website" section, a "set variable" action is used to define the counter variable "counter_objects", which is necessary for the loop in the next part of the process.

The sections "data extraction" and "storage in database" both take place in another loop, which is nested in the loop responsible for pagination and forms

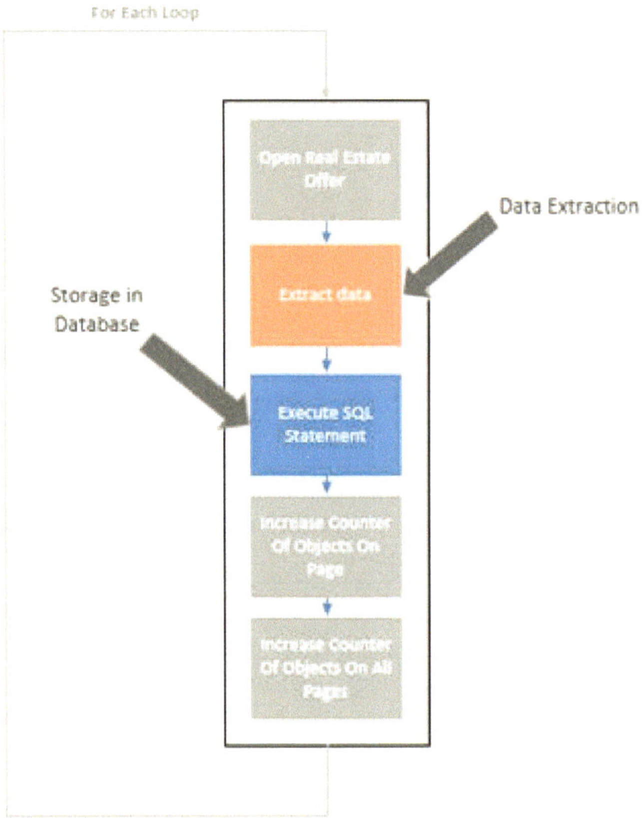

Figure 4. Visualization of the loop for data extraction and storage (source: authors).

the main component of the subprocess. For a better understanding, the process is illustrated in Figure 4.

The loop is executed for each element in the list stored in the variable "listofobjects" and starts with the invocation of the respective offer detail page through the Action "Go to web page". This action, like all relevant elements of the process, is equipped with an exception handling procedure for any errors that may occur. The actual web scraping takes place in the following action, "Extract data from web page". At this point, the process is on the offer detail page. In the "Extract data from web page" action, all elements to be extracted by the process can be easily selected using the Recorder, which is one of the most significant strengths of RPA web scraping solutions. The recorder allows us to track user activity, but also generates UI automation of the tracked activity. After all selected elements have been extracted, the obtained data is saved in the database using the Action "Execute SQL Statement". For this purpose, the values for each element are passed on to the stored procedure "dbo.realestate_raw" within the action. A stored procedure is an SQL script stored in the RDBMS, which can be executed repeatedly. Using a stored procedure has the advantage that the web scraper does not have to provide the data types for each value with every object and can instead rely on the values stored once in the stored procedure. In addition to data types, the stored procedure also specifies the database and table where the data should be stored.

At the end of the loop, the variables "counter_objects" and "counter_objects_global" must be incremented to allow the processing of the next element. This has been implemented in the process using two "Increase variable" actions. The outer loop, and thus the subflow, concludes with the Action "Go to web page", which directs the process to the next page of the offer overview. This loop is repeated as long as the value of the counter variable "counter_pages" is smaller than the value in the variable "number_pages".

After all offer overview pages have been searched for offers and their data has been extracted, the RPA bot closes all windows opened during the process, using the previously explained "Close" actions in the main process, and the RPA process is terminated. In the event of error messages that cannot be resolved by predefined exception handling, the process would come to a standstill at the problematic point, and the windows would not close.

4. Conclusion

Using Big Data for decision-making in accounting presents a new challenge. The importance of the resource "data" has undergone a drastic boost in recent years (Lev 2019); however, there is no clear guidance for users with high domain knowledge combined with limited IT expertise such as accountants, on which methods works best for data extraction from the highly versatile data source "website". One of the most used methods is web scraping, which has been employed for decades by search engines such as Google and Bing to index billions of websites and furnish users with pertinent results (Knoblock 1997, Mirtaheri et al. 2013). Consequently, there is a need to establish efficient web scraping techniques and processes for decision making in the accounting domain.

In this study we attempt to evaluate whether web scraping is a useful addition to the accounting toolset. This process involves the use of software tools and techniques to parse and extract relevant information from HTML documents and convert this information into a structured format that can be easily organized, analyzed and used in the decision-making process. To do so, we assess a software-based web scraping technique, more precisely RPA using "Microsoft Power Automate", which is associated with a low need for IT related expertise in a case study environment, dealing with real estate data. We want to specify the highest possible output (high quality and quantity data) using the lowest possible input (demand for IT competences) and assess the areas of application and limitations of the method. Furthermore, we discuss the strengths and weaknesses of RPA and compare it to other approaches such as libraries or frameworks available for web scraping in R or Python.

4.1 Discussion on RPA in Accounting

In conclusion we want to answer two specific questions: How does the process of web scraping look like and can an accountant perform the process using a software tool?

Do results from a software tool reach the critical quality criteria for data inclusion in the process of decision-making and what are the limitations of the method compared to other tools in this regard?

How does the Process of Web Scraping Look Like and What Do Accountants Need to Perform the Process using an RPA Tool?

Web scraping involves the selection of appropriate tools for data acquisition, which can be challenging for accountants with limited IT skills. Thus, user-friendly applications, such as RPA solutions, are often the only option available to a target audience with limited IT expertise. These solutions adhere to the citizen developer concept of RPA and do not require programming skills. Once a web scraping technique is selected, the next step is to apply the web scraper as shown in Figure 2. Subsequently, in accordance with Persson (2019), the steps of fetching, extracting, transforming and saving the data were executed prior to commencing the data analysis.

In our case study, the RPA web scraping solution offered by Microsoft Power Automate was identified as an attractive option that is very intuitive, making it easy to design a web scraping application. RPA tools provide users with pre-programmed process steps, commonly referred to as "actions", which can be easily incorporated into workflows. These actions offer a range of functionalities that users can select and utilize without requiring extensive programming knowledge. This capability enables users with low IT knowledge to automate complex tasks efficiently. The RPA solution "Microsoft Power Automate" also provides several benefits to web scrap data, including the use of the recorder-feature to facilitate the selection of HTML elements, without requiring knowledge of HTML.

Additionally, the RPA bot acts as a human user on the website, obviating the need for proxy rotation to conceal its activities. A further advantage of Microsoft Power Automate is its easy integration into a range of Microsoft products. It is evident that for accountants, knowledge on how to structure and replicate a process, as well as proficiency in working with process automation tools, is crucial for the successful implementation and utilization of web scraping with RPA.

Do Results from an RPA Solution Reach the Critical Quality Criteria for Data Inclusion in the Process of Decision-making and What are Limitations of the Method Compared to Other Tools in this Regard?

The reliance of the RPA solution on the GUI of the application resulted in reduced performance and increased error susceptibility. Furthermore, an inconsistency in the load times of websites caused significant delays and failures during the case study. This sometimes even resulyrf in the user's computer becoming unresponsive, which is not ideal for larger web scraping projects. Technically, although this issue can be partially addressed by employing a separate computer or virtual machine, the dependence of the RPA solution on the GUI of the application is a significant disadvantage when compared to other web scraping solutions. Therefore, the use of RPA is recommended only for smaller and non-repetitive or self-updating web scraping projects.

With respect to our case study, RPA would be beneficial only for an analysis at a single point in time, to determine housing prices. For the aim of a continuous and current dataset to evaluate historical price developments and trends, we would recommend switching to a popular programming language like Python or R using predefined libraries for web scraping. This switch, however, requires the accountant to work together with an IT specialist, and we also want to add that the use of libraries introduces additional difficulties and obstacles that need to be overcome. To be more precise, libraries can be problematic for web scraping when dealing with websites that use JavaScript elements or infinite loaders. In this context, workarounds such as specifying the number of loaded elements in the URL to limit that number may be required. While these restrictions could be lifted by using frameworks, in our experience, sometimes even experienced programming professionals are not familiar with specific frameworks. As a result, they may choose not to use them for web scraping, as it could disproportionately increase the complexity of the scraping project.

4.2 Discussion on Real Estate Data in Accounting

Data-driven analytics including real estate data is important not only for the real estate industry but also for the construction industry to make decisions regarding business models (Jain et al. 2022). Furthermore, real estate represents an important security for loans, which is why the real estate market is relevant for banks' risk management in determining the value of real estate transferred as collateral (Higgins et al. 2022).

To make purchase or sale decisions, timely and accurate data on the real estate market is useful and even essential for real estate companies (Ahmed et al. 2020). Thus, web scraped data cannot only be used for nowcasting real estate prices but also for modelling and identifying trends (Bricongne et al. 2021).

4.3 Limitations and Further Research

From an accountant's point of view, the information provided in the real estate market differs significantly from that in other markets such as the stock market. Shares are traded on regulated public markets, and there are clear guidelines for the disclosure of information, which means that all market participants (especially private investors, who are often dependent on free information) have complete and correct information available in a timely manner, even without using paid financial information services, such as Bloomberg Terminal (Healy and Palepu 2001). This not only makes real estate information more difficult to cluster, but our selected use case might not be replicable for other data sets.

Currently, we only use information presented as string (text) or integer. With respect to real estate information, special focus should also be placed on the uploaded pictures of the property. Scraping pictures or even small videos showcasing the place and using visual prompting in the analysis could potentially influence current modelling practice. In addition to ensuring high quality data, ensuring high quality models for accurate forecasting based on accurate causal relationships is a key task in accounting.

While accountants have traditionally been responsible for data collection and, manually extracting data from documents such as invoices, it has become increasingly evident that the era of big data requires the involvement of IT experts for data collection to effectively scrape large volumes of data. Upon request, IT specialists will be capable of designing and maintaining web scraping processes for the accountant, providing technical expertise for the development and upkeep of these processes. While IT specialists will design the web scraping tool, it is ultimately the accountant who determines the selection of data sources and the data used for decision-making, as well as the frequency of data collection. Given the limitations of data storage, decisions on data retention and deletion must be considered. In this regard, the accounting department, as a specialized department, is best placed to determine whether decisions are influenced by the decreasing or increasing frequency of data collection. Simultaneously, accountants must be aware of the legal and technical limitations of web scraping. The use of data obtained through web scraping is certainly a novelty that presents research opportunities for accountants to explore big data analytics. Nonetheless, there is a need to investigate opportunities for collaboration between IT specialists and accountants in developing effective web scraping processes.

We also see that Robotic Process Automation (RPA) is often promoted as a universal solution for automating processes with little or no IT knowledge. However, as exemplified by web scraping, we have shown in this study that although these tools are user-friendly, they have limitations. As a result, for future research we see a need to highlight the advantages and disadvantages of applying RPA solutions.

Acknowledgments

The authors gratefully acknowledge the federal state of Upper Austria for funding the research project FinCoM (Financial Condition Monitoring) and thus, the underlying research of this study. The authors are also inherently grateful for the ongoing support from additional members of the research project. Thus, we would like to mention Sebastian Dorl, and Christian Haider.

References

Ahmed, H., Jilani, T.A., Haider, W., Hasany, S.N., Abbasi, M.A. and Masroor, A. 2020. Producing standard rules for smart real estate property buying decisions based on web scraping technology and machine learning techniques. International Journal of Advanced Computer Science and Applications 11(3): 498–505.

Anand, V., Bochkay, K., Chychyla, R. and Leone, A. 2020. Using python for text analysis in accounting research. Foundations and Trends in Accounting 14(3-4): 128–359.

Apostolou, B., Dorminey, J.W., Hassell, J.M. and Hickey, A. 2019. Accounting education literature review (2018). Journal of Accounting Education 47: 1–27.

Appelbaum, D., Kogan, A., Vasarhelyi, M. and Yan, Z. 2017. Impact of business analytics and enterprise systems on managerial accounting. International Journal of Accounting Information Systems 25: 29–44.

Beręsewicz, M.E. 2015. On representativeness of Internet data sources for real estate market in Poland. Austrian Journal of Statistics 44(2): 45–57.

Boegershausen, J., Borah, A. and Stephen, A. 2021. Fields of Gold Web Scraping for Consumer Research. Marketing Science Institute Working Paper Series 21-101: 1–58.

Bradley, A. and James, R.J.E. 2019. Web scraping using R. Advances in Methods and Practices in Psychological Science 2(3): 264–270.

Bricongne, J.-C., Chatelais, N., Meunier, B., Pouget, S., Coffinet, J. and Kintzler, E. 2021. Covid-19 and house prices in the UK: what can be learned from web-scraping data? Economic Research 235: 5.

Bricongne, J.-C., Meunier, B. and Pouget, S. 2023. Web-scraping housing prices in real-time: The Covid-19 crisis in the UK. Journal of Housing Economics 59: 101906.

Bumblauskas, D., Nold, H., Bumblauskas, P. and Igou, A. 2017. Big data analytics: transforming data to action. Business Process Management Journal 23(3): 703–720.

Ciampi, F., Giannozzi, A., Marzi, G. and Altman, E.I. 2021. Rethinking SME default prediction: a systematic literature review and future perspectives. Scientometrics 126: 2141–2188.

Cooper, L.A., Holderness Jr, D.K., Sorensen, T.L. and Wood, D.A. 2019. Robotic process automation in public accounting. Accounting Horizons 33(4): 15–35.

Da Diniz Silva, A., Menezes Marques de Oliveira, B., Gonçalves Peixoto, Í. and Braga Sales de Souza, L. Overview of the use of big data for official statistics in Latin America and the Caribbean. Statistical Journal of the IAOS (Preprint) 1–7.

El Asikri, M., Krit, S. and Chaib, H. 2020. Using web scraping in a knowledge environment to build ontologies using python and scrapy. European Journal of Molecular & Clinical Medicine 7(03): 433–442.

Gabriel, J. 2021. RPARPAUse Case—"IFRS 9IFRS 9/SPPISPPI". pp. 295–310. *In*: Liermann, V. and Stegmann, C. (eds.). The Digital Journey of Banking and Insurance. Volume II: Digitalization and Machine Learning. Springer International Publishing, Cham, Switzerland.

Gartner Research. 2022. Magic Quadrants. https://www.gartner.com.

Glez-Peña, D., Lourenço, A., López-Fernández, H., Reboiro-Jato, M. and Fdez-Riverola, F. 2014. Web scraping technologies in an API world. Briefings in Bioinformatics 15(5): 788–797.

Green, S., McKinney Jr, E., Heppard, K. and Garcia, L. 2018. Big Data, digital demand and decision-making. International Journal of Accounting & Information Management 26(4): 541–555.

Grybauskas, A., Pilinkienė, V. and Stundžienė, A. 2021. Predictive analytics using Big Data for the real estate market during the COVID-19 pandemic. Journal of Big Data 8(1): 105.

Hajba, G.L. 2018. Website Scraping with Python. Apress, Sopron, Hungary.

Healy, P. and Palepu, K. 2001. Information asymmetry, corporate disclosure, and the capital markets: A review of the empirical disclosure literature. Journal of Accounting and Economics 31(1-3): 405–440.

Higgins, E., Yavas, A. and Zhu, S. 2022. Private mortgage securitization and loss given default. Real Estate Economics 50(5): 1334–1359.

Huang, F. and Vasarhelyi, M.A. [M.A.] 2019. Applying robotic process automation (RPA) in auditing: A framework. International Journal of Accounting Information Systems 35: 100433.

Jain, A., Soojin Yoon, F., Kang, K. and Hastak, M. 2022. Implementation of the data-driven analytics protocol through facility management and real estate industry cases. Journal of Management in Engineering 38(1): 4021077.

Kainz, M. 2017. Monitoring von Immobilienpreisen in Österreich. Doctoral Dissertation, Vienna University of Technology, Vienna.

Khalil, S. and Fakir, M. 2017. RCrawler: An R package for parallel web crawling and scraping. SoftwareX. 6: 98–106.

Khder, M. 2021. Web scraping or web crawling: state of art, techniques, approaches and application. International Journal of Advances in Soft Computing and Its Applications 13(3): 145–168.

Knoblock, C. 1997. Searching the World Wide Web. IEEE Intelligent Systems 12(01): 8–14.

Kościelniak, H. and Puto, A. 2015. BIG DATA in decision making processes of enterprises. Procedia Computer Science 65: 1052–1058.

Krotov, V. and Tennyson, M. 2018. Research note: Scraping financial data from the web using the R language. Journal of Emerging Technologies in Accounting 15(1): 169–181.

Krueger, C. 1992. Software reuse. ACM Computing Surveys (CSUR) 24(2): 131–183.

Kühnemann, H. 2021. Anwendungen des Web Scraping in der amtlichen Statistik. AStA Wirtschafts- und Sozialstatistisches Archiv 15(1): 5–25.

Langmann, C. and Turi, D. 2023. Robotic Process Automation (RPA)-Digitization and Automation of Processes: Prerequisites, Functionality and Implementation using Accounting as an Example. Springer Nature, Wiesbaden, Deutschland.

Leitner-Hanetseder, S., Lehner, O.M., Eisl, C. and Forstenlechner, C. 2021. A profession in transition: actors, tasks and roles in AI-based accounting. Journal of Applied Accounting Research 22(3): 539–556.

Lev, B. 2019. Ending the accounting-for-intangibles status quo. European Accounting Review 28(4): 713–736.

Li, H., Wei, D.K., Moffitt, K. and Vasarhelyi, M.A. 2023. Decoding PDF-Based Financial Reports: A Design and A Demonstration on Annual Comprehensive Financial Report (ACFR). Available at SSRN 4385883.

Lin, C.-F. and Yang, S.-C. 2022. Taiwan stock tape reading periodically using web scraping technology with GUI. Applied System Innovation 5(1): 28.

Macias, P., Stelmasiak, D. and Szafranek, K. 2023. Nowcasting food inflation with a massive amount of online prices. International Journal of Forecasting 39(2): 809–826.

Mahlendorf, M.D., Martin, M. and Smith, D. 2022. Innovative data–Use-cases in management accounting research and practice. European Accounting Review (Forthcoming).

Mauro, A. de, Greco, M., Grimaldi, M. and Ritala, P. 2018. Human resources for Big Data professions: A systematic classification of job roles and required skill sets. Information Processing and Management 54(5): 807–817.

Milev, P. 2017. Conceptual approach for development of web scraping. Economic Alternatives 3: 475–485.

Mirtaheri, S.M., Dinçktürk, M.E., Hooshmand, S., Bochmann, G.V., Jourdan, G.-V. and Onut, I.V. 2013. A Brief History of Web Crawlers.

Mishra, A., Mishra, S. and Kumar, N.S. (eds.). 2022. Data Analysis using Robot Process Automation Study on Web Scraping using UI Path Studio. IEEE, Greater Noida, India.

Mitchell, R. 2018. Web Scraping with Python: Collecting More Data from the Modern Web. O'Reilly Media, Inc, Sebastopol, CA, USA.

Mohapatra, B., Mohapatra, S. [Sanjana] and Mohapatra, S. [Sanjay]. 2023. Fundamentals of RPA. pp. 123–166. *In*: Process Automation Strategy in Services, Manufacturing and Construction. Emerald Publishing Limited, Bingley, UK.

Nigam, H. and Biswas, P. (eds.). 2021. Web Scraping: From Tools to Related Legislation and Implementation using Python. Springer, Singapore.

Patel, J.M. 2020. Getting Structured Data from the Internet. Apress, Berkeley, CA, USA.

Persson, E. 2019. Evaluating Tools and Techniques for Web Scraping. Master Thesis, School of Electrical Engineering and Computer Science, Stockholm, Sweden.

Polidoro, F., Giannini, R., Lo Conte, R., Mosca, S. and Rossetti, F. 2015. Web scraping techniques to collect data on consumer electronics and airfares for Italian HICP compilation. Statistical Journal of the IAOS 31(2): 165–176.

Raj, J.S., Iliyasu, A.M., Bestak, R. and Baig, Z.A. 2021. Innovative Data Communication Technologies and Application (Vol. 59). Springer Singapore.

Vargiu, E. and Urru, M. 2012. Exploiting web scraping in a collaborative filtering-based approach to web advertising. Artificial Intelligence Research 2(1): 44–54.

Vording, R. 2021. Harvesting Unstructured Data in Heterogenous Business Environments; Exploring Modern Web Scraping Technologies. Bachelor's thesis, University of Twente, Enschede, The Netherlands.

Wamba, S.F., Akter, S., Edwards, A., Chopin, G. and Gnanzou, D. 2015. How 'big data' can make big impact: Findings from a systematic review and a longitudinal case study. International Journal of Production Economics 165: 234–246.

Appendix

The Stored Procedure in MS SQL

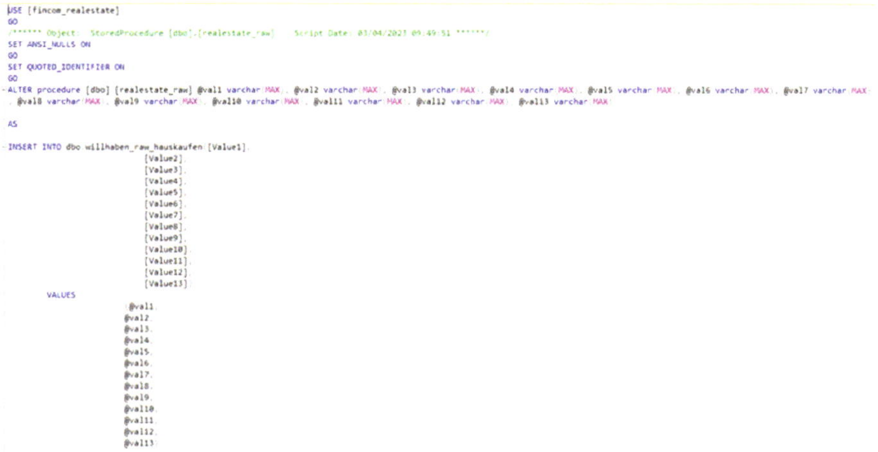

```sql
USE [fincom_realestate]
GO
/****** Object:  StoredProcedure [dbo].[realestate_raw]    Script Date: 03/04/2023 09:49:51 ******/
SET ANSI_NULLS ON
GO
SET QUOTED_IDENTIFIER ON
GO
ALTER procedure [dbo].[realestate_raw] @val1 varchar(MAX), @val2 varchar(MAX), @val3 varchar(MAX), @val4 varchar(MAX), @val5 varchar(MAX), @val6 varchar(MAX), @val7 varchar(MAX)
, @val8 varchar(MAX), @val9 varchar(MAX), @val10 varchar(MAX), @val11 varchar(MAX), @val12 varchar(MAX), @val13 varchar(MAX)

AS

INSERT INTO dbo.willhaben_raw_hauskaufen([Value1],
                        [Value2],
                        [Value3],
                        [Value4],
                        [Value5],
                        [Value6],
                        [Value7],
                        [Value8],
                        [Value9],
                        [Value10],
                        [Value11],
                        [Value12],
                        [Value13])
        VALUES
                      (@val1,
                      @val2,
                      @val3,
                      @val4,
                      @val5,
                      @val6,
                      @val7,
                      @val8,
                      @val9,
                      @val10,
                      @val11,
                      @val12,
                      @val13)
```

Figure 5. Screenshot of the stored procedure.

Chapter 4

Supervisory Approaches to AI Regulation in Insurance

The Case of the UK Prudential Framework

Stavros Pantos[*]

1. Introduction

There are different uses and applications of Artificial intelligence (AI) in financial services, and indeed the range of cases from banks, insurers and asset managers using AI is growing. There are growing AI capabilities and deployment at different sectors, with the financial services industry employing many of them (Allen and West 2020). Different innovative solutions powered by AI, developed internally and/or externally with support of start-ups, highlight the digitalisation of finance, driving innovation. More AI applications are observed, with certain associated opportunities for financial services, but also concerns and risks linked to that rising frequency, that has been well documented in the literature.[1] An interesting aspect beyond the technical examples of using AI for a range of operations and processes within financial services, is the evolving underlying legal and regulatory landscape (Maynard and Goodman 2020), with regulators striving to create sets of rules (Criddle et al. 2023), especially considering the risks of prudential nature and risk management practice. Building on those risks, this chapter focuses on the area of supervisory approaches in the prudential regulation of AI, using the UK insurance sector as a case study.

The chapter starts with a brief introduction of AI and its associated risks, before capturing an overview of existing regulatory practices from UK regulators and

Foxhill House, Whiteknights Road Reading, School of Law, University of Reading, RG6 7BA.
Email: s.pantos@pgr.reading.ac.uk

[1] For literature review studies on AI, please see Milana and Ashta (2021) and Ahmed et al. (2022).

supervisors, critically examining the gaps of the regulatory framework for prudential risks. The existing approach from UK's financial services regulators[2] shaping the policy framework is briefly discussed, before commenting on their limitations regarding prudential risks. The UK prudential regulatory framework underpinning AI applications within insurance is critically analysed after adopting a socio-legal methodology, to support the recommendations for enhancements. These preliminary findings with proposals for developments in the prudential regulatory framework are discussed in the final part of this chapter, after presenting an overview of AI applications and cases within the insurance industry in the UK, describing the different areas of use and examples.

The study of this chapter attempts to understand the prudential risks posed by AI, to support the development of appropriate regulatory responses to the AI applications within the insurance sector (Aitken et al. 2022). The underlying motivation is to increase regulatory effectiveness and efficiency, in the form of regulatory research and prudential supervision (Aitken et al. 2022). This chapter effectively captures the regulatory gap of existing supervisory practices in the UK for AI uses within insurance from a prudential lens (Aitken et al. 2022). AI applications have the potential to transform the nature of loss events and insurability, thus underlining the importance of prudent supervisory approaches for the use of AI within insurance (Eling et al. 2022).

2. Supervising AI in the UK

There are different definitions of AI[3] in practical and legal/regulatory terms. There is no single definition of AI (Madiega 2023); instead it is an umbrella term capturing a range of concepts and applications (Noordhoek 2023)—machine learning (ML), data and automation constitute the three key elements of AI innovation (Aitken et al. 2022). AI comprises of ML,[4] Deep Learning and Artificial Neural Networks, Natural Language Processing (NLP) and Knowledge Representation (ROFIEG 2019), with insurers using those techniques for useful insights (Curtis et al. 2019). Based on the Organisation for Economic Co-operation and Development (OECD) and the United Nations Commission on International Trade Law (UNCITRAL) AI refers to "systems about the use of algorithms and the processing of large quantities of data from multiple sources" (Kerrigan 2022). From a legal and regulatory perspective, a broad definition of AI is adopted in this study, based on the four types of AI explained in Fenwick et al. (2018), thus encompassing the characteristics of all those four types of AI technology.[5]

[2] For a map of all UK regulators, please see Table 3 on pp. 21 in Aitken et al. (2022).

[3] Please see different definition of AI in Box 1, pp. 12 from Lloyd's of London (Lloyd's 2019a).

[4] For a link between AI, Machine Learning, Representation Learning and Deep Learning please see Fig. 42, pp. 39 in Virdee (2022). The Machine Learning scheme from Fig. 4.3 in Virdee (2022) depicts the difference between supervised and unsupervised learning.

[5] Type 1: reactive machines specialised in one area or task, Type 2: machine possess just enough memory or experience to make decisions in specific situations or contexts, Type 3: AI has the capacity to understand human behaviour, Type 4: self-aware, super-intelligent, sentient and presumed to be conscious (Fenwick et al. 2018).

2.1 Risks of AI Uses

There are different risks associated with the use and application of AI within the insurance value chain and business model. There are various studies capturing the assessment of risks, robustness and vulnerability of AI systems (Royal Society 2019), with the studies of Kruse et al. (2019) and Fabri et al. (2022: Table 4) providing further insights about the general challenges of AI uses in financial services. AI technology is changing financial services while posing a number of risks, with regulatory pressures being highlighted (Hernández de Cos 2022). And because of the strict regulation, financial services, including insurers, might struggle to keep up with digitalisation (Hernández de Cos 2022). The use of AI leads to the emergence of potential risks, either linked to risks arising from traditional services and approaches, or new risks in their entirety (ROFIEG 2019). AI amplifies existing risks,[6] such as financial and operational risks, whilst introducing new risks that should be managed within financial services (AIPPF 2022). These new risks are associated with the AI-powered "black box" algorithms,[7] as well as the regulatory and legal responsibilities from the insurance processes (ROFIEG 2019). They are linked to the deployment of AI applications, exacerbating the risks inherent in the technology (Shabsign and Boukherouaa 2023). This explains the motivation of this study, commenting on how the regulatory approach towards prudential risks from the use of AI within in insurance could evolve. The primary drivers of AI risk in financial services are linked to the three key stages of the AI lifecycle, referring to (a) data, (b) model and (c) governance (PRA 2022a). The associated challenges and risks from the use of AI may amplify prudential risks with overall implications to financial soundness (PRA 2022a: par. 3.17). OECD and the AI principles[8] emphasise the systematic risk management approach to each part of the AI lifecycle (OECD 2022). The concern of AI is that it presents new and unknown risks with which current laws may not be able to cope with, thus requiring new rules to mitigate the risks of AI (Buiten 2019). Consequently, there is potential for severe legal issues and ramifications that could arise when a financial services company, an insurance one in this case, decides to implement AI into their business (Japonas 2020). AI could potentially bring new sources and transmission channels of (systemic) risks (Shabsign and Boukherouaa 2023). Considering the challenges associated with AI and ML, regulators and supervisors, as well as insurers are assessing existing risk management and governance practices to determine the identification and management of those risks (Hernández de Cos 2022). This highlights the need of regulation in the use of AI in financial services (Molton 2020), as this study suggests, focusing on prudential risks.

[6] Jellison and Erel (2023) present these standard risks, such as operational, performance, financial, IT, cybersecurity, privacy, processes and controls, legal and reputational risks and considerations among others.

[7] The systemic risk of AI and ML regarding the "black box" issue is highlighted in the literature (Black and Murray 2019).

[8] "AI actors should, based on their roles, the context, and their ability to act, apply a systematic risk management approach to each phase of the AI system lifecycle on a continuous basis to address risks related to AI systems, including privacy, digital security, safety and bias" (OECD 2022).

This is explained from the claim that traditional financial supervision focusing on external supervision is unlikely to be effective in addressing the risks created by AI (Zetzsche et al. 2020a, 2020b).

2.2 Regulatory Environment

Legal and regulatory requirements about the use of data and AI are ongoing policymaking initiatives that continue to evolve (Ostmann and Dorobantu 2021). The regulatory environmental and underlying legal framework to support the use of AI within financial services has been developing with various initiatives in the UK. At the UK's level, there are different existing regulatory and legal frameworks,[9] especially in the area of data governance that is the angle closest linked to prudential risk management (Noordhoek 2023). A major development and key milestone was the establishment of the AI Public-Private Forum (AIPPF) by the Bank of England and the FCA in 2019, focusing on sharing information and understanding the practical challenges and associated risks of using AI within financial services, as well as gathering views about principles, guidance and good practice examples (AIPPF 2022, Aitken et al. 2022). The AIPFF was initially set up to explore the challenges related to the use of AI and ML, as well as how to address and mitigate those risks (BoE 2022). The absence of a specific regime regulating the use of AI in financial services in the UK from prudential lens, is highlighted in this study, composing an area where this research attempts to explore and contribute with the findings presented (Hay and Le Vesconte 2022). AIPPF's work is focused on data, model risk management and governance (Hay and Le Vesconte 2022, AIPFF 2022). This is a promising step towards supervisory and regulatory approaches about AI applications, though the need for an enhanced prudential framework for the use of AI should be highlighted. AI poses challenges in relation to compliance with regulatory requirements, such as the FCA's and PRA's rules (as linked to this study) and in particular about specific regulation of prudential nature (Hay and Le Vesconte 2022). Specific examples are the Solvency II Own Risk and Solvency Assessment (ORSA), regulatory reporting as in the Solvency and Financial Conditions Report (SFCR) and stress and scenario testing for insurers. AI prudential regulation should be expanded, outside the narrow frame towards prominent, existing cross-cutting frameworks (HM Government 2021). Concerns about legal and regulatory compliance regarding AI systems are also expressed by Ostmann and Dorobantu (2021), further supporting the aim of this study to provide additional insight in that area. Therefore, what is needed in terms of developments in the underlying regulatory environment is (a) partnership building, (b) inter-organisational cooperation and (c) system-level leadership competence (Aitken et al. 2022).

In relation to regulatory development requirements, a collaborative approach to identify the regulatory gaps is underlined (Aitken et al. 2022), building on the regulatory weaknesses identified, with regulatory cooperation being very important

---

[9] Please see Table 2 in Noordhoek (2023) about the list of regulation and relevant article, along with their description.

(Gov UK 2022, Anderljung et al. 2023). The importance of cross-regulatory initiatives, and the need for collaboration with regulators across different fields is emphasised by certain regulators (CMA 2022, Aitken et al. 2022). An example of joint collaboration[10] is the AIPPF established by the BoE and the FCA as described in the previous sub-section (Aitken et al. 2022). Other examples of regulatory cooperation include the Digital Regulation Cooperation Forum (DRCF), comprising of the CMA, ICO, FCA and Ofcom, as well as the Regulators and AI Working Group, and the Digital Markets Taskforce, with those initiatives stressing the importance of and interest in collaboration among regulators to identify and address emerging challenges (Aitken et al. 2022, Gov UK 2022). The value of common capacity in the regulation of AI is linked to the mapping and understanding of the risks posed by AI, facilitating joint work/approach among regulators to identify more holistically common AI-related risks, informed by cross-sectoral and cross-remit perspectives, aiming towards the case for a unified approach across the regulation of AI (Aitken et al. 2022). A joined-up approach from regulators to increase AI readiness and enable coordination, knowledge generation and sharing, as well as resource pooling is highlighted by Aitken et al. (2022). Collaboration and exchange between regulators, such as the AI and Regulation Common Capacity Hub (ARCCH) are identified as areas for further improvements to make the UK regulatory landscape more robust (Aitken et al. 2022). The co-regulatory approach with the collaboration of the rest regulators and supervisors, could provide insights on the use of AI within the supervisory process (Wrigley 2018). The development of an AI regulatory sandbox with regulatory collaboration could support the advances in the prudent supervision of AI (Ringe 2023). This is validated by the FCA's approach to open their AI sandbox in the summer of 2023 (Rathi 2023). Regulatory testing of AI could be achieved with the use of a digital sandbox (Maple et al. 2023).

2.3 Regulatory Gap

Regulation of AI remains at preliminary stages, particularly regarding the regulatory compliance about law in AI, with questions remaining concerning the applicability of existing practices to AI legal issues (Lim 2022). Recognition of the form and stage of development of the disruptive technology is very important to shape the regulatory approach (Black and Murray 2019). The risks and concepts introduced by AI should be translated into regulatory standards and requirements (Hay and Le Vesconte 2022). Key examples include the transparency and explainability, and how this is reflected within the Second Line practices (Hay and Le Vesconte 2022). Firms and insurance in this case should consider all relevant risks against the controls and risk management frameworks already in place, with developments about changes to address diverging exposures (Hay and Le Vesconte 2022). Regulation is lagging in relation to the use of AI within prudential risk context, where a proactive ex-ante

[10] For a summary of existing collaboration within regulators focusing on regulation and AI at UK level, please see Table 7 pp. 73 in Aitken et al. (2022).

approach should have been followed, instead of the usual reactive ex-post approach (Margan 2020). AI-specific regulation is required, with proactive regulatory approaches to AI, as pointed out by Lloyd's of London (2019a). A standardisation of the AI codes of conduct with harmonised applications, shaped by the regulatory environment is required (Ulbrich 2020). Aitken et al. (2022) point to the significant gaps regarding regulation of AI at UK level vis-à-vis organisational, participant and system-level readiness—which is the focus of this chapter—with insights on the organisational readiness from the empirical analysis, looking at UK insurers.

There is a gap in the existing prudential framework regarding the use of AI about measuring risk accurately, associated with the reliance on big data, with this been highlighted by regulators in the study of Sadok et al. (2022). AI and ML are transforming the core components of the insurance business model and risk management in particular, observing a range of applications within credit, market and operational risk techniques (Aziz and Dowling 2019). AI and ML assist insurers at various stages of risk management process, such as the exposure, measurement, estimation and assessment of risks (Sanford and Moosa 2015), resulting in enhanced practices and improved risk management capabilities (Aziz and Dowling 2019). AI algorithms with big data process techniques enable more accurate and fast underwriting, with improved predictive models about the adequate premium estimation and loss reduction and overall risk management practices (Curtis et al. 2019). Risks arising from the use of AI in relation to data, model and governance should be addressed in the regulatory framework and supervision of insurance companies as highlighted by the AIPPF[11] as well (Croxson et al. 2019). In relation to model risk, the scale, speed and complexity of the underlying AI models leads to challenges and risks, either new or via the amplification of existing ones (Croxson et al. 2019, AIPPF 2022). Complexity with the interlinkage of different AI models, their parameters, variables, input, etc., exacerbates the risks arising from AI model applications (Croxson et al. 2019, AIPPF 2022). This complexity adds to the ability to explain the output and results, challenging the key concept of explainability in AI models (Croxson et al. 2019, AIPPF 2022). These make even more challenging the governance of AI models, especially the identification, management and application of changes (Croxson et al. 2019, AIPPF 2022). Model risks reinforce the need for a strengthened governance framework for AI models (Croxson et al. 2019, AIPPF 2022). Building on the interaction of AI models and systems with other risk and governance processes, data governance and model risk management frameworks within insurance should be further developed, reflecting the risk and materiality of the use-case and exact AI application (Croxson et al. 2019, AIPPF 2022). Model risk management regulation at UK level is currently very limited in scope, with explicit guidance required (PRA 2022a: par. 4.37). For instance, guidance is required vis-à-vis AI solutions in underwriting, pricing, capital modelling and reserving, with different internal governance frameworks, to capture the exact AI models deployed

[11] Data and Model are the two core components of the AI system. Data consists of ingestion, quality control, processing, validation, monitoring and reporting, whereas model's parts are the development, validation, deployment, change management and monitoring and reporting (AIPPF 2022).

(Croxson et al. 2019, AIPPF 2022). Therefore, a systematic framework is required to address the prudential risks associated with the use of AI models that are conditional on their exact application (Mueller and Ostmann 2020).

In relation to model governance and risk management, the Bank of England has conducted a study to establish an effective model risk management framework for banks (PRA 2022a, 2022e). This consists of model risk management principles underpinning the proposals for the embedding of supervisory expectations about model identification and risk classification, model development, implementation and use, model risk mitigation, independent model validation and its overarching governance (PRA 2022a, 2022e). However, these recommendations and proposals have not been extended to insurers, explaining the need to provide guidance specifically for insurance companies, capturing AI applications within the insurance business model (PRA 2022e: par. 1.3–1.4). In particular about AI/ML techniques and applications, adequate testing, monitoring and validation should be in place, based on the IOSCO guidance (IOSCO 2021: measure 2). PRA's risk element framework (PRA 2023: Figure 1) does not consider AI under the operational mitigation, financial or operational resilience component of the assessment.

AI prudential regulation for insurers should define exactly AI and its uses within underwriting, pricing, modelling and risk management, to allow the development of the framework shaping the AI applications (Buiten 2016). Further clarifications with respect to AI are central to developments in the regulatory framework (PRA 2022a). Therefore, specific guidance on the application of the PRA and the FCA rules should be provided (Kalifa 2021).[12] Effectively clarifying how the PRA Rulebook and the FCA Handbook guidance should be followed with respect to the use of AI within insurance, in relation to accountability, explainability and overall governance of AI models (Kalifa 2021). Currently neither the PRA Rulebook nor the FCA Handbook include any references to AI/ML and their applications or use cases in insurance. To support the establishment of the future regulatory framework to address these gaps about AI within prudential supervision, further guidance should be provided based on the exact AI uses, their associated risks and applications by type (e.g., pricing, underwriting, etc.) (Kalifa 2021).

3. AI in Insurance

This section presents a selection of AI cases and applications from the UK insurance sector.[13] Specifically, certain examples of using AI within the insurance business model and operations are discussed, presenting a review of how AI is used by insurance companies.[14]

---

[12] Looking at what the largest insurance companies in the UK state about using or consider using AI, as part of the reporting.

[13] For more detailed examples of applications of AI across sectors, please see Table 4, pp. 23 in Aitken et al. (2022). Additional examples about AI applications in the finance industry are summarised in ROFIEG (2019).

[14] For underwriting, pricing, reserving, capital modelling, handling claims, etc. looking at the disclosures of UK insurance companies and their press releases, about how AI is referenced.

3.1 Applications

The impact of artificial intelligence is observed along the insurance value chain (Eling et al. 2022) that is digitalised (Ocampo et al. 2023) and amplified via digital transformation (Hielkema 2022). In a recent Alan Turing report, Maple et al. (2023) comment on examples from the adoption of AI within the insurance sector. The insurance sector has seen and continues to see innovations in different areas, such as pricing, claims handling and fraud detection (Lloyd's 2019a), with different AI applications observed in the insurance sector (OECD 2020). AI enhances the insurance industry's value chain with the use of large data analytics and evolved algorithms, with insurance companies incorporating AI technologies into their business model to increase their overall performance, customer experience and market share (Kelley et al. 2018). Insurers experiment with AI in the business value chain to leverage its capabilities across three AI dimensions: insights, automation and (customer) engagement (Margan 2020). The use cases for AI in insurance consist of insights, automation and engagement for the proposition, distribution and operations components of the insurance value chain (Margan 2020). AI-based automation allows the streamline of operations creating better value for customers (Pirilä et al. 2022). Claims automation, fraud detection, pricing and underwriting comprise big categories of areas with AI applications (Insurance Europe 2021). Insurers use AI to improve insurance processes: customer service, underwriting, fraud detection, claims business development and (as the focus of this study) modelling, exposure management pricing (Lloyds 2019a).

There are a lot of benefits to insurers from the use of AI that are going to increase in the next years,[15] such as enhanced data and analytics, increased revenue, productivity and operational efficiency (BoE 2022). These are linked to better customer service, increased efficiency and lower costs, with improved claims handling and fraud detection, and overall enhanced value proposition and extended coverage of insurance risks (Noordhoek 2023). Sales, pricing, underwriting, claims management and customer experience are all areas in the insurance value chain where AI is going to transform, introducing several improvements (Deloitte 2019). Typical AI cases in the insurance value chain are observed in marketing, operations, claims management and risk planning and strategy (Gillhuber and Nagele 2022). AI in insurance is used in underwriting, claims processing, customer service and fraud detection (Noordhoek 2023). Price optimization, customer segmentation, fraud prevention and management risks are additional examples (Vandrangi 2022). Client risk profiling and insurance claims management are the most common instances from the insurance sector (Aitken et al. 2022). AI cases and application in insurance often refer to image recognition and AI art, anomaly detection, classification and prediction, as well as recommendation (Gillhuber and Nagele 2022). An area where AI and machine learning provide insights to insurers is fraud detection (Allen and West 2020, Aslam et al. 2022). Power-chatbots using natural-language processing

[15] For a detailed list of AI categories of benefits and their anticipated evolution over the next three years, please see Chart 12 from the BoE (2022).

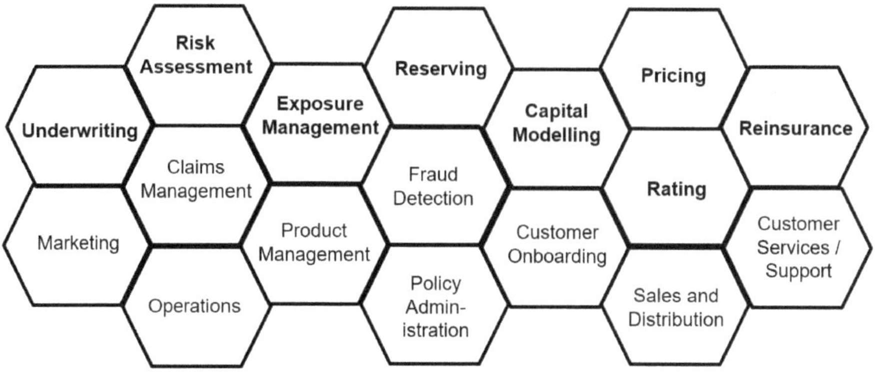

Figure 1. AI insurance applications.

(NLP) capabilities constitute another case of AI in insurance technology (Riikkinen et al. 2017). The above graph (Figure 1) depicts the range of areas and applications of AI within the insurance value chain (in bold the areas linked prudential risks), as adapted by Riikkinen et al. (2017: Figure 1), Sarkar (2020), and Gupta et al. (2022: Figure 3) and Ocampo et al. (2023: Graph 1).

AI uses in insurance processes of modelling and exposure management pricing which are linked to prudential risk management (Lloyds 2019a). In the area of pricing and underwriting, the use of AI can lead to enhanced risk assessments by enabling insurers to combine traditional and new data sources more efficiently and to price policies that more accurately reflect the risk (Insurance Europe 2021). Advances in pricing and underwriting with new risk monitoring approaches to improve existing processes, via automation and data analytics result in pricing efficiency and accuracy, while sophisticated, real-time risk monitoring improves capital efficiency in back-testing and model validation (Deloitte 2019). The results of a project carried out in the Lloyd's Lab provide further insights in relation to the use of AI in insurance pricing (Maynard et al. 2019). Specific examples include the use of ML applications life insurance underwriting and in motor risk pricing, where ML models predict the frequency and severity of expected claims for new business and renewals quotes (BoE 2022). However, as described above, there is a gap between AI and the regulatory landscape in those areas from a prudential angle, in relation to the surveillance capabilities of regulators and compliance of AI strategies in insurance industry (Deloitte 2019).

3.2 Cases

The insurance cases include examples from different parts of the insurance value chain (e.g., underwriting, claims) (Herrmann and Masawi 2022) and for different insurance lines of business capturing (e.g., product liability, professional indemnity

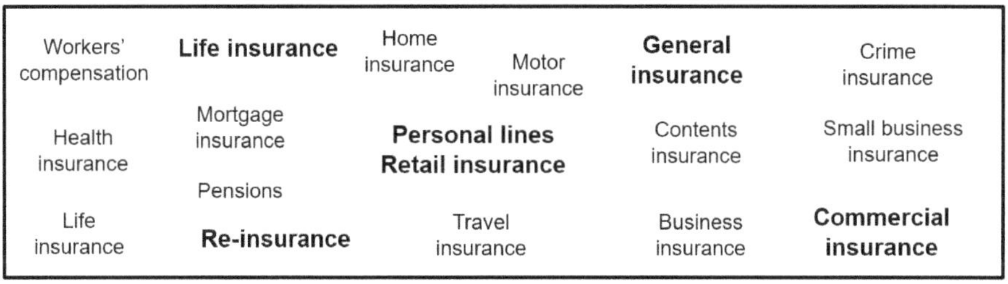

Figure 2. AI cases in insurance segments.

political risks, etc.) (Lloyd's 2019a). The different products and lines of business where AI is applied in the insurance industry[16] are captured in the graph above (Figure 2), based on Herrmann and Masawi (2022). Specific examples and cases drawn upon the UK insurance industry are described in this subsection below.

What is currently observed in the insurance industry, is the collaboration of AI start-ups with traditional insurers. These tech companies provide unique and tailored solutions to insurers, supporting them with improvements in existing processes within their operations. Insuretch companies have developed technological innovations using AI/ML models, leading to improvements in the insurance business model, with examples of claims settlement process and premium structuring (Gupta et al. 2022). AI allows the rapid processing and analysis of data, enabling accurate underwriting and efficient risk assessment (Noordhoek 2023). Traditional re-insurance companies, seek to improve their own AI capabilities-based external expertise from insurtech disruptors, with their partnership (or even acquisition) and integration within the traditional insurance business model often being observed. Another theme emerging is the partnership of these tech companies with multiple insurers competing in the same industry and sector. For instance, Tractable's[17] AI applications are employed by multiple UK-based general insurers, with another example being about Cytora and its risk engine capabilities. Both general and life insurers, operating in the personal/retail and commercial segments strive for innovative solutions using large datasets, seeking those partnerships. Sometimes they comment broadly about AI gains, without explicitly stating if and how they use AI. The exception is when they reference partnerships with AI tech companies and start-ups using AI supporting them. For example, Lloyds's of London presents specific cases (Zasti, Layr, Geollect)[18] of using AI, describing the operations and exact AI application (Lloyd's 2019a). It could be argued that there is a signalling effect of disclosing information about the use of AI.

[16] However, do note that the proportion and value in monetary terms with the commercial use of AI applications by insurance segment varies.

[17] For more information, please see Tractable's solutions and cases in supporting insurance companies globally (https://tractable.ai/en).

[18] Zasti (https://zasti.ai/), Layr (https://withlayr.com/), Geollect (https://www.geollect.com/). For a detailed list of insurtech start-ups operating in this space, please look at pp. 53–54 (Lloyd's 2019a).

Moreover, there are cases of AI applications developed at Group/parent level, being rolled out at subsidiary level for the UK-based entity. AXA and QBE, for instance, are two examples of large international insurance groups following this. Specifically, AXA is conducting research at Group level on AI, focusing on data security and privacy, the ethical and regulatory framework, whilst strengthening accountability through transparency (AXA 2018). However, the challenge about meeting different regulatory requirements and expectations about the use of AI within insurance should be noted for the Group vs. entity AI applications. For instance, cases from different jurisdictions, as well as the potential use of customer data to train the AI models deployed, originating from different countries and geographical areas, adding to the risks and complexities of using AI.

3.3 UK Insurance Uses Overview

For the empirical analysis, specific cases and application of AI within the insurance business model from the largest UK insurers are examined[19] as in the following table. Some insurers have provided information about how AI is used internally, denoted in the third column of the (Table 1). However, arguably there are probably additional insurers not disclosing the use of AI on the basis of commercially sensitive information, and/or because of the stage of their development. Therefore, the lack of information provided in that area, with insurers not disclosing the use of AI, adds to the transparency concerns in the AI models employed.

Insurance and reinsurance companies use AI targeting improvements and financial gains, as stated by QBE's aim to "help lower loss ratios, grow premiums and improve expense ratios" (Villanueva 2017). AI in insurance supports the analysis of data to design risk management and risk transfer solutions, via flexible data platforms with the effective use of large internal and external data, as an example of AI used by AXA's XL Catlin (Stanway 2018). Data and innovation via the use of ML and AI supports also re-insurers, in the underwriting decision making whilst transforming work practices, with TransRe constituting another example (2020a; 2020b). AI transforms the delivery of insurance solutions, with AI improving operational efficiency and the insurers' operations, evidently from AXA (Bamberger 2022). Hiscox uses AI aiming for efficiency improvements and productivity gains, in areas of processes and claims. In a specific example of a partnership, Hiscox has adopted the digital underwriting

[19] Specifically including the general and life insurers who participated at the most recent, 2022 version of the PRA's market-wide Insurance Stress Test (IST). These are the largest general and life insurers in the UK, thus being representative of the UK insurance sector. The exact general and life insurers who completed PRA's 2022 IST is presented below (PRA 2022c, 2022d). More information is available in Annex 2 of the Life Insurance Stress Test (LIST) and the General Insurance Stress Test (GIST) (PRA 2022c, 2022d).

Table 1. List of UK Insurers – AI applications cases.

Segment[20]	Insurer	AI application-case
GI	Admiral (Group)	Motor claims, Tractable
GI	Ageas Insurance Limited	Motor claims, Tractable
GI	Allianz Insurance plc	N/A
GI	American International Group UK Limited	N/A
GI	Aspen Insurance UK Limited	Crime insurance product, platform
GI	Aviva Insurance Limited	Tractable
GI	AXA Insurance UK plc	Cytora Risk Engine
GI	Convex Insurance UK Limited	Cytora Risk Engine
GI	UK Insurance Limited	N/A
GI	Flood Re Limited	N/A
GI	Hiscox Insurance Company Limited	Internal data processing, Convr, Eigen
GI	Lloyds Bank General Insurance Limited	N/A
GI	The National Farmers Union Mutual Insurance Society	Pricing
GI	QBE Limited	Internal data processing, HyperScience, TensorFlight, motor/home insurance claims
GI	Royal & Sun Alliance Insurance Limited	Motor claims
GI	XL Catlin Insurance Company UK Limited	Cytora Risk Engine
GI	TransRe London Limited	Underwriting decisions
GI	Lloyd's of London	Commercial property risk engineering
LI	Aviva International Insurance Limited	N/A
LI	Aviva Life & Pensions UK Limited	N/A
LI	Canada Life Limited	Conquest Planning
LI	Legal & General Assurance Society Limited	N/A
LI	Liverpool Victoria Financial Services Limited	Machine learning applications
LI	The National Farmers Union Mutual Insurance Society	N/A
LI	Partnership Life Assurance Company Limited	N/A
LI	Pension Insurance Corporation plc	N/A
LI	Phoenix Life Assurance Limited	N/A
LI	Phoenix Life Limited	N/A
LI	The Prudential Assurance Company Limited	N/A
LI	ReAssure Limited	N/A
LI	Rothesay Life plc	N/A
LI	The Royal London Mutual Insurance Society Limited	Machine learning applications
LI	Scottish Widows Limited	N/A
LI	Standard Life Assurance Limited	N/A

[20] Based on the insurance sector classification by the Bank of England, these are segmented into: (i) general insurers (GI), health insurers and life insurers (LI); (ii) and personal vs. commercial lines insurers (BoE 2022).

platform of Convr,[21] an AI tech company (Coverager 2021). The core use cases of AI within Convr's environment are (a) document processing, (b) risk insights for underwriting and pricing, (c) with business classification and underwriting questions responses and (d) risk selection (Coverager 2021). Hiscox has also partnered with Eigen,[22] another AI startup for internal data processing improvements (Ruel 2018). In that direction about data processing with automating processes, gaining speed and accuracy, QBE has partnered with HyperScience to realise this (Villanueva 2018). QBE has also partnered with TensorFlight[23] for property inspection, with the use of big data, targeting cost and time efficiency/savings for underwriting decisions using AI (Taylor 2021). XL Catlin, part of AXA, has partnered with Cytora, using AI to improve quantification, selection and pricing of risks, based on Cytora's Risk Engine (AXA XL 2017). QBE has also a commercial agreement with Cytora, using the Cytora Risk Engine for risk scoring, providing insight on anticipated claims at individual and aggregate/portfolio level (Villanueva 2017). Convex insurance has partnered with Cytora too, using its AI-powered platform for commercial insurance underwriting to improve risk selection (Cytora 2019), using advancements in data and analytics for decision making (Gallin 2019). Aspen Insurance uses the insurtech solution platform from Verisk, the "Mozart Form Composer" (Verisk 2019). That's similar to Lloyd's commercial property risk engineering AI applications (Lloyd's 2019a). Aspen has also partnered with Counterpart, using AI to support the crime insurance product for small business (Willard 2022). Glozman (2020) comments on commercial insurers using AI as a catalyst to accelerate their digital transformation, presenting use cases in commercial underwriting, adding to the validity of the above examples.

Beyond commercial insurance, there are certain AI applications within personal lines and retail insurance products. The use of AI in pricing is another example of the use of AI in key insurance areas and processes, with NFU confirming that, though caveating its evolving nature and the regulatory challenges underpinning it (NFU 2021). Another insurance segment in general and personal lines retail insurance is the application of machine learning on usage-based insurance, with the most common example coming from motor insurance, and the pay-as-you-drive model (Bamberger 2022). This has been highlighted by Kelley et al. (2018) commenting on the significant changes to the entire value chain of transportation, and as a consequence to the underlying insurance product in the motor insurance market. In the most popular case of AI use within insurance about claims management, Aviva partnered with Tractable to support its management of motor claims (Tractable 2022). Specifically, Tractable's AI helps Aviva to improve the efficiency and accuracy of repairs for auto claims, with a fast and remote repair assessment, realising gains across its UK repair network (Tractable 2022). Admiral Seguros, a subsidiary of

[21] Please see Convr's website for more information (https://www.convr.com/).

[22] More information about Eigen Technologies and its automated document processing with no-code intelligence document processing (IDP) platform please see its website (https://eigentech.com/).

[23] Please see TensorFlight's website (https://tensorflight.com/), about how AI and ML processing real-time data to support insurance decision making.

the UK based motor insurance Admiral Group uses AI, the solution from Tractable, for auto damages with immediate payments to customers (NS 2020, Ruel 2020). Actually, Ageas was the first insurer to use Tractable for car damage assessments and repairs, improving claims management in motor insurance (Ageas 2017, 2020). RSA also uses AI for the effective motor claims management, with customers being able to upload pictures of the damage incurred in their vehicles, with AI assessing this (RSA 2020). AI paired with the Internet of Things (IoT) capabilities enhances the customer experience of insurance products, easing the claims process and repairs for motor and home insurance (QBE 2020). A well-documented area of the insurance business model is claims, with image recognition and natural language processing (NLP) easing the claims experience for AXA's customers (Bamberger 2022). A machine learning tool, "RoRI" (Repair or Replace Intelligence) is used in claims handling by AXA, comparing the cost of total loss for vehicles in motor insurance, smoothing the claims lifecycle and experience (AXA 2020). Another machine learning tool used to support the streamlining and acceleration of complex property claims which has been built internally and deployed by AXA, the "BETSIE" (Buildings Enhanced Triage Steering Intelligence Engine) (AXA 2021a). Outside general insurance, AI supports the earlier and more accurate checks and detections in health insurance (Bamberger 2022), employed for predictive risk assessment (Abel and Kleipaβ 2020), with AXA's Doctor at Hand service, a private online GP service an example in that area (Genial 2021). Just employs AI and ML tools for fraud detection, providing early warning of suspicious activity on IT systems (Just 2021). Liverpool Victoria is another insurer using machine learning (LV = 2019). Royal London uses machine learning for mortgage protection innovation for underwriting purposes (McCaughey 2017). Canada Life has partnered with Conquest Planning,[24] creating a streamlined financial planning platform using AI (Canada Life 2021).

3.4 Risk Management and Prudential Oversight

Innovation in finance via the use of AI revolutionises non-customer facing functions (compliance, risk) resulting in significant changes to existing regulation and/or new regulatory approaches about how these functions operate (ROFIEG 2019). Application of AI by insurance companies allows for the development of more accurate prediction of loss probabilities, changing the risk landscape after transforming the frequency and severity of certain risks (Eling et al. 2022). AI in insurance has the potential to improve risk pooling, enhance risk reduction, mitigation and prevention (Keller 2020). It allows expanding the scope of risk pooling, supporting the prevention and mitigation of risks, whilst also reducing the cost of risk pooling (Noordhoek 2023).

AI reshapes the nature of risk management, compliance, compliance and prudential oversight (Shabsign and Boukherouaa 2023). AI solutions are emerging in risk management, but their application is conditional on the regulatory framework and the state of "explainable AI (XAI)" (Berns 2020). This underlines the importance of regulatory developments in relation to the prudential risks from the use of AI.

[24] For more information please Conquest Planning (https://www.conquestplanning.com/en-ca/home).

The application of AI in the context of Pillar I of Solvency II, regarding high level of data quality, with the case of technical provisions data quality from the actuarial function oversight, is another example of prudential nature (Deloitte 2019). Risk management functions have adopted AI, using ML techniques for the monitoring, detection and management of a range of risks (Hay and Le Vesconte 2022). For instance, capturing operational risks for fraud and cyber/information security, market risk about validation and stress testing, credit risk for counterparty exposure, among other examples (Hay and Le Vesconte 2022). Developments about the compliance and governance capabilities of AI applications are anticipated (Candelon et al. 2021), requiring the appropriate governance structures to address related risks (Keller 2020). The appropriate internal governance should be developed internally, consisting of policies, processes and operating procedures to manage the risks associated with the AI applications (NIST 2021b), with thorough risk assessments (Anderljung et al. 2023).

Risk management involves using data to price and manage exposure, including credit, market, operational and liquidity risk, with ML-based applications deployed to support risk management activities (IOSCO 2021). Changes in the risk profile of the insurer from the use of AI should be understood and documented, with developments in the underlying Enterprise Risk Management Framework (ERMF) reflected in the disclosures and reporting (Kelley 2018). AI considerations should be considered in the enterprise risk management programmes, deployed to understand the different risks associated with the use of AI, to ensure their identification, mitigation and adaptation (Jellison and Erel 2023). AI assurance is linked to the three-lines-of defence (3LoD) model, with an equivalent of the ICO's (2020) auditing framework for AI required for prudential risks (HM Government 2021). Documenting the AI governance hierarchy and the approach in the 3LoD model set up in relation to prudent risk management is recommended (AIPPF 2022), because of the complications across the three-lines-of-defence functions and operations observed from AI uses (Hay and Le Vseconte 2021). In the insurance context, looking at the Solvency II Directive for instance, Article 41 (1) of Solvency II Directive requires "insurance and reinsurance undertakings to have in place an effective system of governance which provides for sound and prudent management of the business" (Hielkema 2022). In relation to Solvency II, internal governance and risk management rules and requirements which are applicable to regulated financial institutions about the use of AI systems should document in detail AI system associated risks (EC 2021).

AI applications linked to prudential risks are observed within underwriting and capital management. In underwriting internal and external data is used to create a customer's financial and risk profile, whereas in capital management, a prediction of patterns for claims to create risk ratings is observed (Sarkar 2020). AI and ML models are employed in current risk assessment techniques (Malik 2020). The risks and challenges of AI and ML model "explainability" are the key concerns for insurers and prudential supervisors (Hernández de Cos 2022). Insurers and their supervisors need to understand the output of models, including potential biases, limitations and robustness, on the basis of being a key element of effective decision-making, risk management and supervisory oversight (Hernández de Cos 2022). In particular, they need to be aware of the model risk and complexity of input and variable relationship, explainability of model output and the overall model governance, involving the changes, monitoring and reporting of AI models (AIPPF 2022). Thus, the governance of AI systems reflecting risk and materiality of the use-case is vital, particularly in this context, with enhancements in the data governance and model risk management (MRM) frameworks (AIPPF 2022). It is even more important considering the gap in MRM regulatory guidance for insurance companies (PRA 2022e: par. 1.3–14). Therefore, it is of high importance to understand the interaction of AI models with other risk and governance processes, capturing those implications in existing governance frameworks and structures (AIPPF 2022). Risk management should be in line with the AI lifecycle, part of the pre-design, design/development, testing/evaluation, deployment as per the NIST Guidance (NIST 2021b: Fig. 1).

4. Towards an Effective AI Prudential Framework

This section discusses the recommendations based on the gaps identified from the existing supervisory practices of AI uses, as highlighted above, and also observed in the UK's Government's AI Regulation Policy Paper (Gov UK 2022). The aim of these recommendations is to build the regulatory framework to address existing limitations (Gov UK 2022). The proposals presented meet the AI governance criteria and unique characteristics that should be incorporated into existing governance frameworks as described by EIOPA's CEO (Hielkema 2022). Reviewing the existing legal framework with revisions aims to address the challenges and risks of AI, providing specific legal acts and/or other instruments to govern AI applications (Rodrigues et al. 2020). Aitken et al. (2022) highlight the need for regulators to understand the nature and implications of AI uses that fall within their regulatory remit, whilst also assessing the adequacy of regulatory arrangements in relation to them. The gaps in the prudential regulation and supervision of AI within insurance are linked to the Kalifa's policy and regulation recommendations (Kalifa 2021).[25] Regulatory collaboration and/or creation of a single cross-body, considering the current vertical-focus approach to fintech policy and regulation is required (Kalifa 2021). Kalifa highlighted the regulatory implication of AI, with further considerations required about AI under existing regulations (Kalifa 2021). The lack of alignment with other regulations and standards is perhaps the reason of the existing gaps, with the new regulatory environment for the prudential supervision of AI needed (BoE 2022). A cross-intra body Committee could be the solution for the prudent supervision of AI in insurance, building on the knowledge and expertise among the different regulators in the UK (Sherer 2016).

[25] In particular Kalifa's first recommendation about "delivering a digital finance package that creates a new regulatory framework for emerging technology" highlights the importance of the prudential supervision of the insurance industry in the UK (Kalifa 2021).

4.1 AI Model Governance

Inadequate controls and governance about the use of AI and ML are key limitations that should be addressed from prudential supervisors' oversight, to build an effective governance framework and model risk management practice (BoE 2022). AI model governance is of high importance considering the associated risks, such as inappropriate model choices, errors in the model design/construction, lack of explainability, model performance, inadequate validation and overall poor outcomes (PRA 2022a). Explainability of AI models should be considered by supervisory authorities, in a clear way, with a clear differentiation between technical AI (model) explainability requirements,[26] and the explainability requirements of the wider AI system in relation to applicable laws and regulations (Kuiper et al. 2021). In relation to explainability, insurers should be able to explain their decisions and actions linked to AI models to prudential supervisors (Shabsign and Boukherouaa 2023). In this sense, an additional layer of internal oversight should be created to ensure regulatory compliance regarding model risk governance. However, regulatory compliance is quite difficult to be achieved currently, since there is no clear guidance in the area of prudential risks. And beyond prudential risks, the non-financial risks linked to AI and how these could be transmitted/translated into prudential risks, such as creating issues of solvency and liquidity for instance from their inadequate risk management should also be accounted for and addressed in the supervisory guidance. Model risk management and governance of AI and ML applications with insurance should be the primary goals of effective prudential supervision in insurance (BoE 2022). From the PRA's recent consultation paper (CP6/22) and the five model risk management principles for banks,[27] those remain applicable for insurers subject to adjustments in line with the underlying regulatory framework of Solvency II (PRA 2022e). The model risk management principles for insurers should be developed by the UK prudential regulators and supervisors, replicating the approach for banks (PRA 2022e).[28] Developments in that area should be monitored and validated in the form of prudential reporting, such as in the Solvency II ORSA. Based on IOSCO's guidance and measures for AI, "regulators should consider what level of disclosure of the use of AI and ML is required by firms" (IOSCO 2021: Measure 5), with this linked to the ORSA and the SFCR, beyond the annual report and disclosures for insurers.

Financial regulation of AI applications within insurance should be embedded into the AI lifecycle, addressing model, technology and data risks (Azzutti et al. 2022). The regulatory framework to account for the application of AI with insurance consists of the regulation of specific portion and parts of AI defined applications, for instance, in pricing models and underwriting (Rodrigues et al. 2020). With

[26] An example of AI risk measurement framework linked to explainability is the KAIRI-SAFE risk measurement model, capturing the Sustainability, Accuracy, Fairness and Explainability (SAFE) of AI models developed by Guidici et al. (2024).

[27] Referring to Principle 1: Model identification and model risk classification, Principle 2: Governance, Principle 3: Model development, implementation and use, Principle 4: Independent model validation, Principle 5: Model risk mitigants (PRA 2022e: par 2.1).

[28] Please see Diagram 1 of CP6/22 provides the example from banking (PRA 2022e).

the monitoring of the results from using AI in pricing is recommended part of the regulatory oversight (OECD 2020). The model governance framework for the AI applications in insurance should be based on Buiten (2019) and Chaudhary (2020), as graphically depicted below (Figure 3). The different steps in the model governance framework, with supervisory and regulatory guidance observed at the AI and ML development and exact application with modelling for the specified insurance activity are shown the following graph (Figure 3). Although not graphically depicted below, a feedback loop between the customer and the insurer should exist. This feedback relationship using the obtained results for futuristic responses is associated with the Input-Data[29] component from the LHS of the graph (Figure 3).

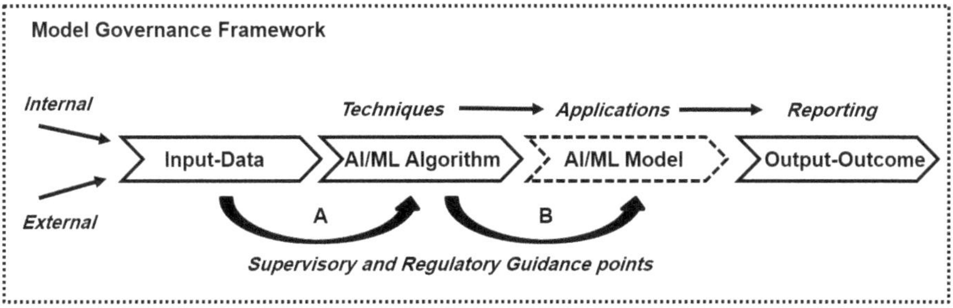

Figure 3. AI model governance framework in insurance.[30]

4.2 AI Regulation and Supervision

The use of AI in insurance continues to evolve, enhancing the accuracy and efficiency actuarial science techniques applications,[31] with improved rating and underwriting of risks, adding value to the society, explaining the importance of its effective supervision and regulation (Lior 2022, Kenny and Payne 2022). The prudential framework of supervising AI applications within insurance should be based on the specific characteristics of AI in insurance (Noordhoek 2023). To shape the prudential framework, AI should be clearly defined, applying existing regulations, as captured in the PRA's supervisory approach to insurance (Noordhoek 2023, PRA 2023). Building blocks of the effective AI regulatory regime, involve the development of safety standards, giving regulators visibility and ensure compliance with safety

[29] From a different angle on data sources part of the model development, the CMA published recently in September 2023 guidance in relation to found model development, training and deployment (CMA 2023: Fig. 1).

[30] It is important to comment on another layer of governance at internal level, linked to points A and B about the supervisory and regulatory guidance points. Therefore, beyond the AI model and as part of their governance, another layer of internal governance should be adopted, to ensure regulatory compliance of the AI models deployed. For instance, considering the three-lines-of-defence model (LoD), that another layer of governance providing assurance between the 2nd (2LoD) and the 3rd line (3LoD), will allow the effective application of AI solutions of prudential nature.

[31] Davies et al. (2023) in a report from the UK Government Actuary's Department present the findings from the use of AI/ML in actuarial work.

standards (Anderljung et al. 2023). The regulatory considerations arising from the use of AI capture consumer protection, competition concerns, market integrity and operational resilience (Maple et al. 2023). These are the principles that the prudential regulatory framework and supervisory approach for the insurance industry should adopt.

Regulatory options should provide a holistic framework for AI risks and challenges from applications within insurance processes (Rodrigues et al. 2020). Regulation should adapt and respond to the new and changed risks observed from the use of AI,[32] with developments in the underpinning regulatory framework and supervision (ROFIEG 2019). AI applications should be regulated, referring to the development and deployment of AI models in underwriting, pricing, risk management, etc., among other insurance processes of prudential nature (Rodrigues et al. 2020). However, the regulatory actions and overarching framework should be described by a balance between enabling beneficial AI and risk mitigation (Rodrigues et al. 2020). The enhanced regulatory framework for the applications of AI within insurance should be enabling and not stifling innovation or limiting the way AI is used (Michaels and Homer 2017, Rodrigues et al. 2020, Noordhoek 2023). Regulators and supervisors should focus on building the framework to address AI-related risks whilst maintaining an environment that encourages innovation, articulating clearly regulatory expectations (Aitken et al. 2022). They should adapt and be agile in their approach to understand the use and applications of AI within insurance (Aitken et al. 2022). In establishing the prudential regulation and supervisory framework for AI, a "responsive", "smart" and "dynamic" regulatory approach is recommended according to Fenwick et al. (2018). An agile and adaptable framework, responding to digital technologies and innovation disrupting existing practices should describe the approach about AI applications' prudential supervision (Fenwick et al. 2018).

Regulatory guidance is required to support the safe and responsible adoption of AI within the UK insurance sector (PRA 2022a). Specific guidelines on the use of AI within key insurance processes and operations should be developed by the Bank of England, the PRA and the FCA, in relation to prudential risks, based on the recommendations of the European Commission's Regulatory Obstacles to Financial Innovation Expert Group (ROFIEG) (ROFIEG 2019). ROFIEG's recommendation 13 regarding activity and risk-based regulation[33] is key to the prudential framework, with the same rules applicable to AI and existing practices in underwriting, pricing, risk management, etc., within the insurance business model (ROFIEG 2019). This is based on the insurance business model, with risk assessments constituting an integral part of the industry, for different insurance types and products (Pnevmatikakis et al. 2022). The regulatory framework for AI in the UK should be context-specific, pro-innovation and risk-based, but also coherent, proportionate and adaptable

[32] For the AI risks and concerns, with the approach of insurers to mitigate them, please see Fig. 3 in Noordhoek (2023).

[33] "Recommendation 13: The Commission and the ESAs should take the necessary steps to ensure that regulation of the financial sector follows the principle of same activity creating the same risks should be regulatory by the same rules" (ROFIEG 2019).

(UK Government 2022). Based on the NIST (2022a) guidelines, the AI Risk Management Framework should be risk-based, resource efficient, pro-innovation and voluntary. Therefore, the UK prudential supervisory approach should be in aligned to the principles underpinning UK's pro-innovation framework for regulating AI, being context specific, pro-innovation and risk-based, coherent, proportionate and adaptable (Gov UK 2022).

The development of the regulatory system is conditional on the context of the organisations subject to regulation, with the insurance market determining how prudential supervision of AI should be designed to address the differences by segment, line of business/product and application in the insurance value chain (Black and Murray 2019). A practical example of inspiration for the prudential supervision of AI, focusing on the governance dimensions is Generali's reference framework for operationalizing Trustworthy AI as in Bonaita (2022). Generali's "Responsible AI governance framework for the model lifecycle could be extended, but focusing on prudential areas, referring to the control function contributions that are Risk, Compliance and Audit (Bonaita 2022). Existing regulatory frameworks should be adapted to account for AI and certain types of AI in the area of prudential risk management and supervision for insurance (Japonas 2020). The following graph (Figure 4) presents developments towards the prudential framework for the applications of AI models in insurance, adapted from the guidance as in the AIPPF (2022), BoE (2022) and the PRA (2022a). Starting with the data and model components that are core elements of AI applications and techniques as in the underlying uses, with the exact cases are specified within the insurance context (AIPPF 2022, BoE 2022, PRA 2022a). The insurance cases and risks of prudential nature arising from the AI applications and techniques, should shape the regulatory approach in insurance supervision (AIPPF 2022, BoE 2022, PRA 2022a). The frontier AI regulation based on the AI lifecycle should capture the development and deployment of AI models (Anderljung et al. 2023: Fig. 1), as depicted in Figure 4 below for prudential risks.

The effective AI prudential framework should ensure regulatory consistency, whilst avoiding unnecessary regulatory overlaps and complexities (EIOPA 2022).

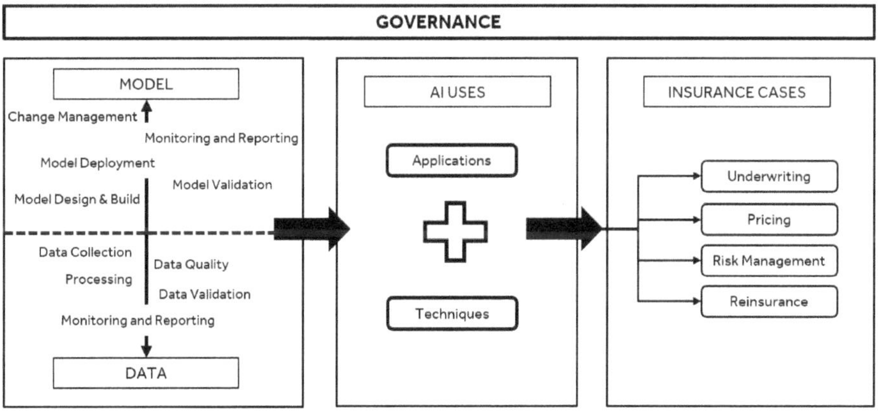

Figure 4. Regulatory and supervisory AI model governance in insurance.

Prudential supervision should evolve in line with the evolution of AI technology (Azzutti et al. 2022), and the corresponding policy adaptations to support the prudent AI applications within insurance (Shabsign and Boukherouaa 2023). In that direction, prudential oversight authorities (BoE, PRA, FCA) should strengthen their institutional capacity and intensify their monitoring and surveillance of AI applications (Shabsign and Boukherouaa 2023), explaining the importance of creating the prudential framework. Developments in the area of risk management and controls should be made in PRA's supervisory approach for insurers (PRA 2023: par. 64–71). Regulatory oversight of AI insurance applications should become part of the supervisory activity from the PRA, based on the overarching key principles of being (i) judgement-based, (ii) forward-looking and (iii) focused on key risks (PRA 2023). The principle of proportionality should be at the core of supervision and regulation of AI (EIOPA 2022), whilst distinguishing micro vs. macro levels of regulation (Daníelsson et al. 2022).

The proposed UK prudential framework should address adequately the AI risks observed in the insurance value chain, whilst also considering international approaches to AI supervision (e.g., EIOPA, IAIS, etc.) (Gov UK 2022). Regulators need to modify existing rules to take into account the specific risks raised by AI (FT 2023), with regulation supporting the mitigation of potential risks in AI (Maple et al. 2023). Existing regulation could be applied if remains fit for purpose, otherwise regulation that considers the specific characteristics of AI in insurance should be developed (Noordhoek 2023). This should be described by a proactive approach to regulate and supervise AI uses and associated implications in the insurance value chain (Maple et al. 2023). The above recommendations are linked to UK's strategy for Governance of AI (HM Government 2021). This entails the development of a clear, proportionate and effective regulatory framework, supporting AI innovation but addressing the actual risks (HM Government 2021). These proposals are in line with OECD's five recommendations and AI principles,[34] specifically about shaping an enabling policy environment for AI (IOSCO 2021, OECD 2022). Building on the work of Maple et al. (2023), Madiega (2023) and of Azzutti et al. (2022) about risk-based regulation, a risk-based approach with the pyramid of risks, where legal intervention tailored to the level of risk is recommended. This refers to segmenting the supervision of AI in (a) prohibited AI practices (unacceptable risks), (b) regulated high risk AI system (high risk), (c) transparency (limited risk) and (d) in no obligations (low or minimal risk) (Madiega 2023).

5. Further Directions and Discussion

This preliminary study adding to the area of AI governance from a prudential risk perspective could be extended at different directions, providing further insight about

[34] OECD's value-based principles: Inclusive growth, sustainable development and well-being; Human-centred values and fairness; Transparency and explainability; Robustness, security and safety; Accountability (OECD 2022). OECD's recommendations for policy makers: Investing in AI R&D; Fostering a digital ecosystem for AI; Providing an enabling policy environment for AI; Building human capacity and preparing for labour market transition; International co-operation for trustworthy AI (OECD 2022).

specific AI applications and cases in financial services, while also commenting on the underlying legal and regulatory environment. For instance, moving outside the UK framework, for a comparison with EU (Hay and Le Vesconte 2022), with gaps on the European AI Act & Liability Directive (Gillhuber and Nagele 2022), in line with OECD's AI principles,[35] and towards the future regulatory framework (EC 2020). Looking at the challenges of the use of AI for policymakers and regulators at EU level (Insurance Europe 2021), with the AI Act providing a framework for the regulatory developments for the use of AI in insurance (Hielkema 2023). Also attempting to capture the positioning and relationship of the UK with the EU following Brexit about regulatory and supervisory cooperation and collaboration (Criddle et al. 2023). At EU level, National Supervisory Authorities (NSAs) continue to be competent in the supervision and regulation of the use of AI in the insurance sector, whilst ensuring cooperation between the European Supervisory Authorities (ESAs) and the European Artificial Intelligence Board (EIOPA 2022). However, it would be interesting to understand the conditions under which UK regulators and supervisors could become part of that network, benefiting from sharing expertise and experience in the prudential supervision of AI within insurance.

Complexities linked to the underlying being insured and place of domicile could be examined further, to understand deviations in the prudential regulation (e.g., insurance policy underwritten in one country for cover in a different country, such as Lloyd's of London policies in the UK for US and EU cover). In relation to the AI insurance applications and cases presented, understanding examples from different jurisdictions and insurance segments might be interesting, such as commenting on dominant AI cases outside the UK for the EU and the US insurance markets. For instance, looking at the largest EU insurers[36] could be explored, allowing a comparison with the UK insurance sector. In terms of the insurance classification and segmentation, perhaps splitting commercial versus personal lines insurance could allow researchers to understand their idiosyncrasies and the exact AI applications (Glozman 2020). Additionally AI and robotics within insurance in further detail is worth examining, especially vis-à-vis cyber risks from an underwriting perspective (Lloyds 2019a, 2019b). Finally, another direction worth exploring originates from the entrance of big techs in the insurance market. This increases the level of complexity in the updating the prudential framework for the supervision of AI applications within insurance. However, it would be interesting.... It would be interesting to examine these implications from the developments in supervising big techs' activities in insurance. Building on the work of Ocampo et al. (2023) grouping the applicable regulatory requirements into (1) insurance underwriting, (2) digital distribution and (3) service provision. Monitoring of these insurance activities is of high importance, with the establishment of an overarching prudential framework (Ocampo et al. 2023).

[35] Referring to the five complementary values-based principles for the responsible stewardship of trustworthy AI (OECD 2022).

[36] For example, the ones in scope of EIOPA's Insurance Stress Test.

Acknowledgements

The author would like to acknowledge the feedback received from the attendees of the 2nd workshop on "Environmental Finance for the Common Good (EFCG)" at the University of Pavia, the 1st Interdisciplinary Conference on Management, Information Technology and Computer Sciences organized by the European Institute for Advanced Studies in Management (EIASM) and of the 2023 Economics of Financial Technology Conference (EFT) at the University of Edinburgh.

References

Abel, H. and Kleipaβ, U. 2020. Moving the AI needle: Strategies for health insurers to put AI into practice. *In*: Chishti, S., Bartoletti, I., Leslie, A. and Millie, S.M. (eds.). The AI Book: The Artificial Intelligence Handbook for Investors, Entrepreneurs and FinTech Visionaries (eds). John Wiley & Sons.

Ageas. 2017. Ageas pioneers UK-first artificial intelligence (AI) approach in claims handling. Press Release, 18 May 2017, Ageas. Retrieved from: https://www.ageas.co.uk/press-releases/2017-press-releases/ageas-pioneers-uk-first-ai/ (accessed 30 September 2023).

Ageas. 2020. Ageas is first UK insurer to use AI to create end-to-end car damage assessments and estimates. Press Release, 26 March 2020, Ageas. Retrieved from: https://www.ageas.co.uk/press-releases/2020-press-releases/ageas-is-first-uk-insurer-to-use-ai-to-create-end-to-end-car-damage-assessments-and-estimates/ (accessed 30 September 2023).

Ahmed, S., Alshater, M.M., El Ammari, A. and Hammami, H. 2022. Artificial intelligence and machine learning in finance: A bibliometric review. Research in International Business and Finance 61: 101646. https://doi.org/10.1016/j.ribaf.2022.101646.

AIPPF. 2022. Final report. Artificial Intelligence Public-Private Forum, February 2022, Bank of England. Retrieved from: https://www.bankofengland.co.uk/-/media/boe/files/fintech/ai-public-private-forum-final-report.pdf (accessed 30 September 2023).

Aitken, M., Leslie, D., Ostmann, F., Pratt, J., Margetts, H. and Dorobantu, C. 2022. Common regulatory capacity for AI. The Alan Turing Institute. https://doi.org/10.5281/zenodo.6838946.

Allen, J.R. and West, D.M. 2020. Turning Point: Policymaking in the Era of Artificial Intelligence. Project Muse, Brookings Institution Press. Project MUSE - Turning Point (jhu.edu).

Anderljung, M., Barnhart, J., Korinek, A., Leung, J., O'Keefe, C., Whittlestone, J. et al. 2023. Frontier AI Regulation: Managing Emerging Risks to Public Safety. Retrieved from: https://doi.org/10.48550/arXiv.2307.03718 (accessed 30 September 2023).

Arner, D.W., Barberis, J. and Buckley, R.P. 2017. RegTech: Building a better financial system. *In*: Chuen, K., Lee, D. and Deng, R.H. (eds.). Handbook of Blockchain, Digital Finance, and Inclusion: Volume 1: Cryptocurrency, FinTech, InsurTech, and Regulation. Elsevier Science & Technology.

Ashurst, S. 2022. Risk management. *In*: Kerrigan, C. (ed.). Artificial Intelligence: Law and Regulation, edited by Charles Kerrigan, Edward Elgar.

Aslam, F., Hunjra, A.I., Ftiti, Z., Louhichi, W. and Shams, T. 2022. Insurance fraud detection: Evidence from artificial intelligence and machine learning. Research in International Business and Finance 62: 101744. https://doi.org/10.1016/j.ribaf.2022.101744.

Aviva. 2022. Aviva partners with Tractable to bring the benefits of AI to motor claims. 27 April 2022, Newsroom, Aviva. Retrieved from: https://www.aviva.com/newsroom/news-releases/2022/04/aviva-partners-with-tractable-to-bring-the-benefits-of-ai-to-motor-claims/ (accessed 30 September 2023).

AXA. 2018. Artificial Intelligence: Fostering Trust. AXA Research Guide – Artificial Intelligence. AXA. Retrieved from: https://www.axa-research.org/en/news/AI-research-guide (accessed 30 September 2023).

AXA 2020. AXA UK deploys machine learning for motor claims. Product, 10 February 2020, AXA. Retrieved from: https://www.axa.co.uk/newsroom/media-releases/2020/axa-uk-deploys-machine-learning-for-motor-claims/ (accessed 30 September 2023).

AXA. 2021a. AXA UK rolls out machine learning tool to streamline complex property claims. Innovation, 20 July 2021, AXA. Retrieved from: https://www.axa.co.uk/newsroom/media-releases/2021/axa-uk-rolls-out-machine-learning-tool-to-streamline-complex-property-claims/ (accessed 30 September 2023).

AXA. 2021b. Towards the Right Kind of Fairness in AI. A guide on the different metrics. And the tool Fairness Compass to choose the best option for your project. AXA. Retrieved from: https://axa-rev-research.github.io/static/AXA_FairnessCompass-English.pdf (accessed 30 September 2023).

AXA XL. 2017a. XL Catlin partners with Artificial Intelligence start-up Cytora. Press Release, 2 October 2017, London, UK, AXA XL. Retrieved from: https://axaxl.com/press-releases/xl-catlin-partners-with-artificial-intelligence-startup-cytora (accessed 30 September 2023).

AXA XL. 2017b. Artificial intelligence & insurance: The unexpected love affair? Article, 27 November 2017, AXA XL. Retrieved from: https://axaxl.com/fast-fast-forward/articles/the-unexpected-love-affair (accessed 30 September 2023).

Aziz, S. and Dowling, M. 2019. Machine learning and AI for risk management. *In*: Lynn, T., Mooney, J.G., Rosati, P. and Cummins, M. (eds.). Disrupting Finance: FinTech and Strategy in the 21st Century. Palgrave Studies in Digital Business & Enabling Technologies, Palgrave MacMillan, Palgrave Pivot, Switzerland. https://doi.org/10.1007/978-3-030-02330-0.

Azzutti, A., Ringe, W.-G. and Stiehl, H.S. 2022. The Regulation of AI Trading from an AI Life Cycle Perspective. EBI Working Paper Series, 2022 – no. 130, European Banking Institute.

Balasubramanian, R., Ari Libarikian, A. and Doug McElhaney, D. 2021. Insurance 2030 – The impact of AI on the future of insurance. 12 March 2021, McKinsey. Retrieved from: https://www.mckinsey.com/industries/financial-services/our-insights/insurance-2030-the-impact-of-ai-on-the-future-of-insurance (accessed 30 September 2023).

Bamberger, M. 2022. AI – with greater power comes greater responsibility. Insight, 20 September 2022, AXA. Retrieved from: https://www.axa.com/en/insights/ai-greater-power-comes-responsibility (accessed 30 September 2023).

Berns, M. 2020. Robocop on wall street. *In*: Chishti, S., Bartoletti, I., Leslie, A. and Millie, S.M. (eds.). The AI Book: The Artificial Intelligence Handbook for Investors, Entrepreneurs and FinTech Visionaries. John Wiley & Sons.

Black, J. and Murray, A. 2019. Regulating AI and machine learning: setting the regulatory agenda. European Journal of Law and Technology 10(3).

BoE. 2019. New economy, new finance, new Bank. The Bank of England's response to the van Steenis review on the Future of Finance. Bank of England. Retrieved from: https://www.bankofengland.co.uk/-/media/boe/files/report/2019/response-to-the-future-of-finance-report.pdf (accessed 30 September 2023).

BoE. 2022. Machine learning in UK financial services. 11 October 2022, Bank of England. Retrieved from: https://www.bankofengland.co.uk/report/2022/machine-learning-in-uk-financial-services (accessed 30 September 2023).

Bonaita, A. 2022. AI Governance in Natural Catastrophes Risk Modelling. Generali, EIOPA Conference on AI Governance. Retrieved from: https://www.eiopa.europa.eu/sites/default/files/events/ai_governance_in_nat_cat_-_generali_group.pdf (accessed 30 September 2023).

Boukherouaa, E.B., Shabsign, G., Al Ajmi, K., Deodoro, J., Farias, A., Iskender, E. et al. 2021. Powering the Digital Economy: Opportunities and Risks of Artificial Intelligence in Finance. DP/2021/024, Departmental Papers, Money and Capital Markets and Information Technology Departments, International Monetary Fund, Washington, DC.

Buiten, M.C. 2019. Towards intelligent regulation of artificial intelligence. European Journal of Risk Regulation 10(1): 41–59. https://doi.org/10.1017/err.2019.8

Canada Life 2021. Canada Life partners with Conquest Planning, plans to roll out capability this summer. News and highlights, 15 April 2021, Canada Life. Retrieved from: https://www.canadalife.com/about-us/news-highlights/news/canada-life-partners-with-conquest-planning-plans-to-roll-out-capability-this-summer.html (accessed 30 September 2023).

Candelon, F., Charme di Carlo, R., De Bondt, M and Evgeniou, T. 2021. AI Regulation is Coming. AI and Machine Learning. Harvard Business Review. Retrieved from: https://hbr.org/2021/09/ai-regulation-is-coming (accessed 30 September 2023).

Chaudhary, H. 2020. Using artificial intelligence in commercial underwriting to drive productivity growth. *In*: Chishti, S., Bartoletti, I., Leslie, A. and Millie, S.M. (eds.). The AI Book: The Artificial Intelligence Handbook for Investors, Entrepreneurs and FinTech Visionaries. John Wiley & Sons.

Chishti, S., Bartoletti, I., Leslie, A. and Millie, S.M. 2020. The AI Book: The Artificial Intelligence Handbook for Investors, Entrepreneurs and FinTech Visionaries. John Wiley & Sons.

CMA. 2022. The Competition and Markets Authority's response to DCMS Policy Paper: Establishing a pro-innovation approach to regulating AI. 29 September 2022, Competition & Markets Authority, UK Government. Retrieved from: https://assets.publishing.service.gov.uk/government/uploads/system/uploads/attachment_data/file/1107669/CMA_response_to_DCMS_pro-innovation_approach_for_regulating_AI.pdf (accessed 30 September 2023).

CMA. 2023. AI Foundation Models. 18 September 2023, Competition & Markets Authority, UK Government. Retrieved from: https://www.gov.uk/government/publications/ai-foundation-models-initial-report (accessed 30 September 2023).

Conquest Planning. undated. Retrieved from: https://www.conquestplanning.com/en-ca/home (accessed 30 September 2023).

Convr. undated. Retrieved from: https://www.convr.com/ (accessed 30 September 2023).

Corrales, M., Fenwick, M. and Forgó, N. 2018. Robotics, AI and the Future of Law (eds). Perspectives in Law, Business and Innovation (PLBI). Springer.

Coverager. 2021. Hiscox to adopt Convr's digital underwriting platform. News, 28 September 2021. Retrieved from: https://coverager.com/hiscox-to-adopt-convrs-digital-underwriting-platform/ (accessed 30 September 2023).

Criddle, C., Espinoza, J. and Liu, Q. 2023. The global race to set the rules for AI. Financial Times. Retrieved from: https://www.ft.com/content/59b9ef36-771f-4f91-89d1-ef89f4a2ec4e (accessed 30 September 2023).

Croxson, K., Bracke, P. and Jung, C. 2019. Explaining why the computer says 'no'. Insight 31 May 2019, FCA. Retrieved from: https://www.fca.org.uk/insight/explaining-why-computer-says-no (accessed 30 September 2023).

Crown, S., Douglas, L, Ragha, M. and Sah, M. 2022. Fintech 2022. UK: Law & Practice. Clifford Chance LLP. Retrieved from: https://www.cliffordchance.com/insights/resources/blogs/talking-tech/en/articles/2022/04/Chambers-Global-Practice-Guide-2022-Fintech.html (accessed 30 September 2023).

Curtis, D., Debattista, J., Debono, J. and Farrell, M. 2019. InsurTech. *In*: Lynn, T., Mooney, J.G., Rosati, P. and Cummins, M. (eds.). Disrupting Finance: FinTech and Strategy in the 21st Century. Palgrave Studies in Digital Business & Enabling Technologies, Palgrave MacMillan, Palgrave Pivot, Switzerland. https://doi.org/10.1007/978-3-030-02330-0.

Cytora. undated. Retrieved from: https://cytora.com/ (accessed 30 September 2023).

Cytora. 2019. Cytora and Convex develop artificial intelligence powered solution for commercial insurance. News, 16 July 2019, Cytora. Retrieved from: https://cytora.com/news/cytora-and-convex-develop-artificial-intelligence-powered-solution-for-commercial-insurance/ (accessed 30 September 2023).

Daníelsson, J., Macrae, R. and Uthemann, A. 2022. Artificial intelligence and systemic risk. Journal of Banking and Finance 140: 106290.

Davies, S., Kinshuck, S. and Paterson, C. 2023. The use of Artificial Intelligence and Machine Learning in UK actuarial work. Government Actuary's Department, Financial Reporting Council.

Deloitte. 2019. Risk and compliance implications of AI in the Insurance Industry. Deloitte. Retrieved from: https://www2.deloitte.com/content/dam/Deloitte/de/Documents/risk/article-risk-and-compliance-implications-of-ai.pdf (accessed 30 September 2023).

Demajo, L.M., Vella, V. and Dingli, A. 2020. Explainable AI for interpretable credit scoring. pp. 185–203. David C. Wyld et al. (eds.). ACITY, DPPR, VLSI, WeST, DSA, CNDC, IoTE, AIAA, NLPTA – 2020. CS & IT - CSCP 2020. DOI: 10.5121/csit.2020.101516.

Detyniecki, M. undated. How to decide between explicability or transparency? Retrieved from: https://www-axa-com.cdn.axa-contento-118412.eu/www-axa-com/09a952fb-c7c7-4702-8006-406231045891_Article-RD-How-to-decide-between-explicability-or-transparency.pdf (accessed 30 September 2023).

Detyniecki, M. and Ruf, B. 2022. AI fairness. AXA. Retrieved from: https://www.eiopa.europa.eu/sites/default/files/events/ai_fairness_-_axa.pdf (accessed 30 September 2023).

DLG. The impact of AI on Insurance Risk. Direct Line Group (DLG). Retrieved from: https://www.directlinegroup.co.uk/en/insights/innovation/in-car-tech/the-impact-of-ai-on-risk-part-one.html (accessed 30 September 2023).

EC. 2020. On Artificial Intelligence – A European approach to excellence and trust. White paper COM(2020) 65 final, European Commission. Retrieved from: https://commission.europa.eu/system/files/2020-02/commission-white-paper-artificial-intelligence-feb2020_en.pdf (accessed 30 September 2023).

EC. 2021a. Proposal for a REGULATION OF THE EUROPEAN PARLIAMENT AND OF THE COUNCIL laying down harmonised rules on artificial intelligence (artificial intelligence act) and amending certain union legislative acts {SEC(2021) 167 final} - {SWD(2021) 84 final} - {SWD(2021) 85 final}. European Commission. Retrieved from: https://digital-strategy.ec.europa.eu/en/library/proposal-regulation-laying-down-harmonised-rules-artificial-intelligence (accessed 30 September 2023).

EC. 2021b. Proposal for a Regulation of the European Parliament and of the Council Laying Down Harmonised Rules on Artificial Intelligence (Artificial Intelligence Act) and Amending Certain Union Legislative Acts. Brussels, 21.4.2021 COM(2021) 206 final.

EC. 2022. Proposal for a DIRECTIVE OF THE EUROPEAN PARLIAMENT AND OF THE COUNCIL on adapting non-contractual civil liability rules to artificial intelligence (AI Liability Directive) COM/2022/496 final, European Commission. Retrieved from: https://eur-lex.europa.eu/legal-content/EN/TXT/PDF/?uri=CELEX:52022PC0496&from=EN (accessed 30 September 2023).

EigenTech. Eigen Technologies. Retrieved from: https://eigentech.com/ (accessed 30 September 2023).

EIOPA. 2022a. Artificial intelligence governance. AI Governance Event, 15 December 2022, European Insurance and Occupational Pensions Authority (EIOPA). Retrieved from: https://www.eiopa.europa.eu/media/event/artificial-intelligence-governance_en; https://www.eiopa.europa.eu/sites/default/files/events/ai-governance-agenda-december2022.pdf (accessed 30 September 2023).

EIOPA. 2022b. EIOPA letter to co-legislators on the Artificial Intelligence Act. 04 July 2022, Petra Hielkema, Chairperson, EIOPA-22-632, EIOPA.

Elicegui, I., Carrasco, J., Escribano, C.P., Gato, J., Becerra, A. and Politis, A. 2022. Usage-based automotive insurance. *In*: Soldatos, J. and Kyriazis, D. (eds.). Big Data and Artificial Intelligence in Digital Finance: Increasing Personalization and Trust in Digital Finance using Big Data and AI. Springer, Switzerland. https://doi.org/10.1007/978-3-030-94590-9.

Eling, M., Nuessle, D. and Staubil, J. 2022. The impact of artificial intelligence along the insurance value chain and on the insurability of risks. The Geneva Papers on Risk and Insurance - Issues and Practice 47: 205–241. https://doi.org/10.1057/s41288-020-00201-7.

Fabri, L., Wenninger, S., Kaymakci, C., Beck, S. and Klos, T. 2022. Potentials and challenges of artificial intelligence in financial technologies. Mediterranean Conference on Information Systems (MCIS), MCIS 2022 Proceedings, 14, Association for Information Systems. Retrieved from: https://aisel.aisnet.org/mcis2022/14 (accessed 30 September 2023).

Fenwick, M., Vermeulen, E.P.M. and Corrales, M. 2018. Business and regulatory responses to artificial intelligence: dynamic regulation, innovation ecosystems and the strategic management of disruptive technology. *In*: Corrales, M., Fenwick, M. and Forgó, N. (eds.). Robotics, AI and the Future of Law. Perspectives in Law, Business and Innovation (PLBI), Springer.

FRC. 2019. Artificial Intelligence and corporate reporting: How does it measure up? January 2019, Financial Reporting LAB, Financial Reporting Council.

FT. 2023. AI needs superintelligent regulation. 7 May 2023, The Editorial Board, Financial Times. Retrieved from: https://www.ft.com/content/7ba3e97b-d930-4f96-8365-f840eaabf523 (accessed 30 September 2023).

Fung, G., Polania, L.F., Choi, S.C.T., Wu, V. and Ma, L. 2021. Editorial: Artificial intelligence in insurance and finance. Frontiers in Applied Mathematics and Statistics 7: 795207. https://doi.org/10.3389/fams.2021.795207.

Gallin, L. 2019. Advanced tech, no legacy puts Convex in solid position. Press cutting, Reinsurance News, 6 November 2019. Retrieved from: https://convexin.com/2019/11/06/press-cutting-reinsurance-news/ (accessed 30 September 2023).

Gangcuangco, T. 2021. NFU Mutual announces partnership. News, 8 June 2021, Insurance Business Magazine. Retrieved from: https://www.insurancebusinessmag.com/uk/news/sme/nfu-mutual-announces-partnership-257248.aspx (accessed 30 September 2023).

Gienal, C. 2018. AI and health insurance: how will it change the industry? Innovation, 8 October 2021, AXA. Retrieved from: https://www.axa.co.uk/about/inside-axa/ai-and-health-insurance-how-will-it-change-the-industry/ (accessed 30 September 2023).

Gillhuber, A. and Nagele, J. 2022. Artificial Intelligence Explainability in Insurance. Alexander Thamm GmbH. EIOPA - AI Governance 2022. Retrieved from: https://www.eiopa.europa.eu/sites/default/files/events/ai_explainability_-_alexander_thamm_gmbh.pdf (accessed 30 September 2023).

Giudici, P., Centurelli, M. and Turchetta, S. 2024. Artificial Intelligence risk measurement. Expert Systems With Applications 235: 121220.

Glozman, R. 2020. The digitally-enabled underwriter: how AI is transforming commercial insurance underwriting. *In*: Chishti, S., Bartoletti, I., Leslie, A. and Millie, S.M. (eds.). The AI Book: The Artificial Intelligence Handbook for Investors, Entrepreneurs and FinTech Visionaries. John Wiley & Sons.

Gov UK. 2022. Establishing a pro-innovation approach to regulating AI. Policy Paper, Command Paper CP 728, Presented to Parliament by the Secretary of State for Digital, Culture, Media and Sport by Command of Her Majesty. Laid on Monday 18 July 2022.

Gramenga, A. and Guidici, P. 2020. Why to Buy Insurance? An explainable artificial intelligence approach. Risks 8: 137. https://doi.org/10.3390/risks8040137.

Gupta, S., Ghardallou, W., Pandey, D.K. and Sahu, G.P. 2022. Artificial intelligence adoption in the insurance industry: Evidence using the technology-organisation-environment framework. Research in International Business and Finance 63: 101757. https://doi.org/10.1016/j.ribaf.2022.101757.

Hernández de Cos, P. 2022. Trust, digitalisation and banking: from my word is my bond to my code is my bond? Keynote speech by Pablo Hernández de Cos, Chair of the Basel Committee on Banking Supervision and Governor of the Bank of Spain, at the Eurofi 2022 Financial Forum, Prague, Czech Republic, 9 September 2022. Retrieved from: https://www.bis.org/speeches/sp220909.htm (accessed 30 September 2023).

Hay, R. and Le Vesconte, S. 2022. Financial regulation. *In*: Kerrigan, C. (ed.). Artificial Intelligence: Law and Regulation, edited by Charles Kerrigan, Edward Elgar.

Herrmann, H. and Masawi, B. 2022. Three and a half decades of artificial intelligence in banking, financial services, and insurance: A systematic evolutionary review. Strategic Change 31: 549–569.

Hielkema, P. 2022. AI Governance Event Introductory Remarks. EIOPA European Insurance and Occupational Pensions Authority (EIOPA). Retrieved from: https://www.eiopa.europa.eu/sites/default/files/events/ai_governance_event_-_introductory_remarks.pdf (accessed 30 September 2023).

Hielkema, P. 2023. AI: Unleashing its potential in the finance. Digitalisation and Technology, 128 | VIEWS | The EUROFI Magazine | Santiago de Compostela 2023 | eurofi.net.

Hiscox. Four ways AI is already changing business. Retrieved from: https://www.hiscox.co.uk/broker/about-hiscox/news/Four-ways-AI-is-already-changing-business (accessed 30 September 2023).

HM Government. 2021. National AI Strategy. September 2021, Command Paper 525, HM Government.

HyperScience. undated. Retrieved from: https://hyperscience.com/ (accessed 30 September 2023).

ICO. 2020. Guidance on the AI auditing framework. Draft guidance for consultation, Information Commissioner's Office. Retrieved from ICO https://ico.org.uk/media/about-the-ico/consultations/2617219/guidance-on-the-ai-auditing-framework-draft-for-consultation.pdf (accessed 30 September 2023).

Insurance Europe. 2021. AI in the insurance sector. Insurance Europe. Retrieved online from: https://www.insuranceeurope.eu/publications/2608/artificial-intelligence-ai-in-the-insurance-sector/ (accessed 30 September 2023).

IOSCO. 2020. The use of artificial intelligence and machine learning by market intermediaries and asset managers. Consultation Report, CR02/2020, June 2020, The Board of the International Organization of Securities Commissions.

IOSCO. 2021. The use of artificial intelligence and machine learning by market intermediaries and asset managers. Final Report, FR06/2021, September 2021, The Board of the International Organization of Securities Commissions.

Japonas, E. 2020. AI and the law: challenges and risks for the financial services sector. *In*: Chishti, S., Bartoletti, I., Leslie, A. and Millie, S.M. (eds.). The AI Book: The Artificial Intelligence Handbook for Investors, Entrepreneurs and FinTech Visionaries. John Wiley & Sons.

Jellison, N. and Erel, I. 2023. Risk Institute: What is AI's evolving impact on risk and risk management? 21 April 2023, The Ohio State University, Fisher College of Business. Retrieved from: https://fisher.osu.edu/news/risk-institute-what-ais-evolving-impact-risk-and-risk-management (accessed 30 September 2023).

John, D. 2022. Telematics in Motor Insurance and AI Governance. HUK-COBURG Insurance Group, EIOPA AI Governance Event. Retrieved from: https://www.eiopa.europa.eu/sites/default/files/events/ai_governance_in_car_telematics_-_huk_coburg.pdf (accessed 30 September 2023).

Just Group plc. 2021. Just Group plc Annual Report and Accounts 2020. Retrieved from: https://www.justgroupplc.co.uk/~/media/Files/J/JRMS-IR/investor-docs/financial-reports-and-presentations/2021/Just%20Group%20plc%202020%20Annual%20Report%20and%20Accounts.pdf (accessed 30 September 2023).

Kalifa, R. 2021. Kalifa Review of UK Fintech. Independent report on the UK Fintech sector by Ron Kalifa OBE, Policy Paper. London: HM Treasury.

Keller, B. 2020. Promoting Responsible Artificial Intelligence in Insurance. The Geneva Association.

Kelley, K.H., Fontanetta, L.M., Heintzman, M. and Pereira, N. 2018. Artificial intelligence: Implications for social inflation and insurance. Risk Management and Insurance Review 21(3): 373–387.

Kenny, S. and Payne, C. 2022. Insurance. *In*: Kerrigan, C. (ed.). Artificial Intelligence: Law and Regulation, edited by Charles Kerrigan, Edward Elgar.

Kerrigan, C. 2022. Artificial Intelligence: Law and Regulation, edited by Charles Kerrigan, Edward Elgar.

Kerrigan, C. 2022a. Introduction to AI. *In*: Kerrigan, C. (ed.). Artificial Intelligence: Law and Regulation, edited by Charles Kerrigan, Edward Elgar.

Kourabas, S. and Tsang, C.-Y. 2023. Big Techs and Global Financial Regulation: Intersection, Challenges, and Solutions. 40.2 Banking & Finance Law Review (2024) (Forthcoming). Retrieved online from: https://papers.ssrn.com/sol3/papers.cfm?abstract_id=4556220 (accessed 30 September 2023).

Kruse, L., Wunderlich, N. and Beck, R. 2019. Artificial Intelligence for the Financial Services Industry: What Challenges Organizations to Succeed. Conference: Proceedings of the 52th Hawaii International Conference on System Sciences (HICSS 2019) At: Maui, Hawaii, USA. Retrieved online from: https://www.researchgate.net/publication/328215951_Artificial_Intelligence_for_the_Financial_Services_Industry_What_Challenges_Organizations_to_Succeed (accessed 30 September 2023).

Kuiper, O., van den Berg, M., van der Burgt, J. and Leijnen, S. 2021. Exploring Explainable AI in the Financial Sector: Perspectives of Banks and Supervisory Authorities. Retrieved online from: https://doi.org/10.48550/arXiv.2111.02244 (accessed 30 September 2023).

Lim, H.Y.F. (2022). Regulatory compliance. *In*: Kerrigan, C. (ed.). Artificial Intelligence: Law and Regulation, edited by Charles Kerrigan, Edward Elgar.

Lior, A. 2022. Insurance AI: the role of insurance in artificial intelligence regulation. Harvard Journal of Law & Technology 35(2): 467–530.

Lloyd's. 2018. Networked world Risks and opportunities in the Internet of Things. Emerging Risk Report 2018, Technology, Lloyd's of London. Retrieved from: https://assets.lloyds.com/assets/pdf-networked-world-2018/1/pdf-networked-world-2018.pdf (accessed 30 September 2023).

Lloyd's. 2019a. Taking control: Artificial intelligence and insurance. Emerging Risk Report 2019, Technology. Lloyd's of London. Retrieved from: https://assets.lloyds.com/assets/pdf-taking-control-aireport-2019-final/1/pdf-taking-control-aireport-2019-final.PDF (accessed 30 September 2023).

Lloyd's. 2019b. Taking control: Robots and risk. Emerging Risk Report 2019, Technology. Lloyd's of London. Retrieved from: https://assets.lloyds.com/assets/pdf-taking-control-robotics-2019-final/1/pdf-taking-control-robotics-2019-final.PDF (accessed 30 September 2023).

LV= 2019. What is machine learning and how can you get into it? - Q&A with Dapeng Wang, Data Scientist at LV= GI. Press Release, 8 November 2019, Liverpool Victoria (LV=). Retrieved from: https://www.lv.com/insurance/press/what-is-machine-learning-and-how-can-you-get-into-it (accessed 30 September 2023).

Lynn, T., Mooney, J.G., Rosati, P. and Cummins, M. 2019. Disrupting Finance: FinTech and Strategy in the 21st Century (eds). Palgrave Studies in Digital Business & Enabling Technologies, Palgrave MacMillan, Palgrave Pivot, Switzerland. https://doi.org/10.1007/978-3-030-02330-0.

Madiega, T. 2023. Artificial intelligence act. Briefing, EU Legislation in Progress, European Parliamentary Research Service. Retrieved from: https://www.europarl.europa.eu/RegData/etudes/BRIE/2021/698792/EPRS_BRI(2021)698792_EN.pdf (accessed 30 September 2023).

Malik, S. 2020. The changing face of regulatory, compliance and audit. *In*: Chishti, S., Bartoletti, I., Leslie, A. and Millie, S.M. (eds.). The AI Book: The Artificial Intelligence Handbook for Investors, Entrepreneurs and FinTech Visionaries. John Wiley & Sons.

Maple, C., Szpruch, L., Epiphaniou, G., Staykova, K., Singh, S., Penwarden, W. et al. 2023. The AI Revolution: Opportunities and Challenges for the Finance Sector. The Alan Turing Institute.

Margan, S.K. 2020. Drifting into algocratic insurance? *In*: Chishti, S., Bartoletti, I., Leslie, A. and Millie, S.M. (eds.). The AI Book: The Artificial Intelligence Handbook for Investors, Entrepreneurs and FinTech Visionaries. John Wiley & Sons.

Maslej, N., Fattorini, L., Brynjolfsson, E., Etchemendy, J., Ligett, K., Lyons, T. et al. 2023. The AI Index 2023 Annual Report. AI Index Steering Committee, Institute for Human-Centered AI, Stanford University, Stanford, CA, April 2023.

Maybe* undated. Maybe Tech. Retrieved from: https://www.maybetech.com/ (accessed 30 September 2023).

Maynard, T., Bordon, A., Rajagoapl, J., Shangkaranarayana, S.M., Wilkins, S., Berry, J. et al. 2019. What role for AI in insurance pricing? A preprint. Retrieved from: https://www.researchgate.net/publication/337110892_WHAT_ROLE_FOR_AI_IN_INSURANCE_PRICING_A_PREPRINT (accessed 30 September 2023).

Maynard, T. and Goodman, D. 2020. Risk, Science and Decision Making: How should risk leaders of the future work with AI? Report of a CRO Round-table Discussion. An IRM Occasional Paper, Institute of Risk Management.

McCaughey, R. 2017. Royal London launches machine learning mortgage protection innovation. News, 5 June 2017, Life Insurance International. Retrieved from: https://www.lifeinsuranceinternational.com/news/royal-london-launches-machine-learning-mortgage-protection-innovation/ (accessed 30 September 2023).

Michaels, L. and Homer, M. 2017. Regulation and supervision in a digital and inclusive World. *In*: Chuen, K., Lee, D. and Deng, R.H. (eds.). Handbook of Blockchain, Digital Finance, and Inclusion: Volume 1: Cryptocurrency, FinTech, InsurTech, and Regulation. Elsevier Science & Technology.

Milana, C. and Ashta, A. 2021. Artificial intelligence techniques in finance and financial markets: A survey of the literature. Strategic Change 30: 189–209. DOI: 10.1002/jsc.2403.

Millie, S.M. 2020. Insurance and AI: Choices in leadership, purpose and trust. *In*: Chishti, S., Bartoletti, I., Leslie, A. and Millie, S.M. (eds.). The AI Book: The Artificial Intelligence Handbook for Investors, Entrepreneurs and FinTech Visionaries. John Wiley & Sons.

Molton, T. 2020. Regulation of AI within the Financial Services Sector. *In*: Chishti, S., Bartoletti, I., Leslie, A. and Millie, S.M. (eds.). The AI Book: The Artificial Intelligence Handbook for Investors, Entrepreneurs and FinTech Visionaries. John Wiley & Sons.

Mueller, H. and Ostmann, F. 2020. AI transparency in financial services – why, what, who and when? Insight 19 February 2020, FCA. Retrieved from: https://www.fca.org.uk/insight/ai-transparency-financial-services-why-what-who-and-when (accessed 30 September 2023).

NFU Mutual. 2021. Our stories: 110 years old and still developing. National Farmers Union (NFU) Mutual. Retrieved from: https://careers.nfumutual.co.uk/our-stories/110-years-old-and-still-developing (accessed 30 September 2023).

NIST. 2021a. Taxonomy of AI Risk. October 15 2021, National Institute of Standards and Technology, U.S. Department of Commerce. Retrieved from: https://www.nist.gov/system/files/documents/2021/10/15/taxonomy_AI_risks.pdf (accessed 30 September 2023).

NIST. 2021b. AI Risk Management Framework Concept Paper. 13 December 2021, National Institute of Standards and Technology, U.S. Department of Commerce. Retrieved from: https://www.nist.gov/system/files/documents/2021/12/14/AI%20RMF%20Concept%20Paper_13Dec2021_posted.pdf (accessed 30 September 2023).

NIST. 2022a. AI Risk Management Framework: Second Draft. National Institute of Standards and Technology, U.S. Department of Commerce.

NIST. 2022b. AI Risk Management Framework: Initial Draft. March 17, 2022, National Institute of Standards and Technology, U.S. Department of Commerce. Retrieved from: https://www.nist.gov/system/files/documents/2022/03/17/AI-RMF-1stdraft.pdf (accessed 30 September 2023).

NIST. 2023a. Roadmap for the NIST Artificial Intelligence Risk Management Framework (AI RMF 1). National Institute of Standards and Technology, U.S. Department of Commerce. Retrieved from: https://www.nist.gov/itl/ai-risk-management-framework/roadmap-nist-artificial-intelligence-risk-management-framework-ai (accessed 30 September 2023).

NIST. 2023b. Artificial Intelligence Risk Management Framework (AI RMF 1.0). NIST AI 100-1, National Institute of Standards and Technology, U.S. Department of Commerce. Retrieved from. https://doi.org/10.6028/NIST.AI.100-1.

NIST. 2023c. Crosswalks to the NIST Artificial Intelligence Risk Management Framework (AI RMF 1.0). National Institute of Standards and Technology, U.S. Department of Commerce. Retrieved from: https://www.nist.gov/itl/ai-risk-management-framework/crosswalks-nist-artificial-intelligence-risk-management-framework (accessed 30 September 2023).

NIST. 2023d. NIST AI RMF Playbook. Retrieved from: https://airc.nist.gov/AI_RMF_Knowledge_Base/Playbook (accessed 30 September 2023).

Noordhoek, D. 2023. Regulation of Artificial Intelligence in Insurance: Balancing Consumer Protection and Innovation. The Geneva Association.

NS Insurance. 2020. Admiral Seguros to use artificial intelligence to assess vehicle damage. Article, 1 October 2020, NS Insurance. Retrieved from: https://www.nsinsurance.com/news/admiral-seguros-to-use-artificial-intelligence-to-assess-vehicle-damage/ (accessed 30 September 2023).

O'Sullivan, S. 2023. Britain badly needs a godfather of AI regulation, but we'll never be able to afford him (or her). Thursday 04 May 2023, City A.M.. Retrieved from: https://www.cityam.com/britain-badly-needs-a-godfather-of-ai-regulation-but-well-never-be-able-to-afford-him-or-her/ (accessed 30 September 2023).

Ocampo, D.G., Taneja, J., Yong, J. and Zhu, J. 2023. From clicks to claims: emerging trends and risks of big techs' foray into insurance. No. 51, FSI Insights on policy implementation, Financial Stability Institute, Bank for International Settlements.

OCED. undated. OECD AI Principles overview. Organisation for Economic Co-operation and Development. Retrieved online from: https://oecd.ai/en/ai-principles (accessed 30 September 2023).

OECD. 2020. The Impact of Big Data and Artificial Intelligence (AI) in the Insurance Sector. Organisation for Economic Co-operation and Development. Retrieved from: www.oecd.org/finance/Impact-Big-Data-AI-in-the-Insurance-Sector.htm (accessed 30 September 2023).

OECD. 2022. Recommendation of the Council on Artificial Intelligence, OECD/LEGAL/0449. OECD Legal Instrument, Organisation for Economic Co-operation and Development. Retrieved online from: https://legalinstruments.oecd.org/en/instruments/OECD-LEGAL-0449 (accessed 30 September 2023).

Ostmann, F. and Dorobantu C. 2021. AI in financial services. The Alan Turing Institute. https://doi.org/10.5281/zenodo.4916041.

Parliament. 2020. AI in the UK: No Room for Complacency. Liaison Committee. 7th Report of Session 2019–2021, published 18 December 2020, HL Paper 196, House of Lords. Retrieved from: https://publications.parliament.uk/pa/ld5801/ldselect/ldliaison/196/19602.htm (accessed 30 September 2023).

Petrin, M. 2022. Corporate Governance. *In*: Kerrigan, C. (ed.). Artificial Intelligence: Law and Regulation, edited by Charles Kerrigan, Edward Elgar.

Pirilä, T., Salminen, J., Osburg, V.-S., Yoganathan, V. and Jansen, B.J. 2022. Investigating the role of technical and process quality in chatbots: a case study from the insurance industry. Proceedings of the 55th Hawaii International Conference on System Sciences, 2022. Retrieved from: https://hdl.handle.net/10125/79484 (accessed 30 September 2023).

Pnevmatikakis, A., Kanavos, S., Perikleous, A. and Kyriazakos, S. 2022. Risk assessment for personalized health insurance products. *In*: Soldatos, J. and Kyriazis, D. (eds.). Big Data and Artificial Intelligence in Digital Finance: Increasing Personalization and Trust in Digital Finance using Big Data and AI. Springer, Switzerland. https://doi.org/10.1007/978-3-030-94590-9.

PRA. 2022a. Artificial intelligence and machine learning. Discussion Paper DP5/22, Prudential Regulation Authority, Bank of England. Retrieved from: https://www.bankofengland.co.uk/prudential-regulation/publication/2022/october/artificial-intelligence (accessed 30 September 2023).

PRA. 2022b. Appendices to Artificial intelligence and machine learning. DP5/22, October 2022, Prudential Regulation Authority, Bank of England. Retrieved from: https://www.bankofengland.co.uk/-/media/boe/files/prudential-regulation/consultation-paper/2022/october/dp522app1.pdf (accessed 30 September 2023).

PRA. 2022c. General Insurance Stress Test 2022. Scenario Specification, Guidelines and Instructions, 4 May 2022, Prudential Regulation Authority, Bank of England. Retrieved from: https://www.bankofengland.co.uk/-/media/boe/files/prudential-regulation/letter/2022/may/ist-2022-life-insurance-scenario-specification-guidelines-instructions.pdf (accessed 30 September 2023).

PRA. 2022d. Life Insurance Stress Test 2022. Scenario Specification, Guidelines and Instructions, 4 May 2022, Prudential Regulation Authority, Bank of England. Retrieved from: https://www.bankofengland.co.uk/-/media/boe/files/prudential-regulation/letter/2022/may/ist-2022-general-insurance-scenario-specification-guidelines-instruction.pdf (accessed 30 September 2023).

PRA. 2022e. Model risk management principles for banks. Consultation Paper CP6/22. 21 June 2022, Prudential Regulation Authority, Bank of England. Retrieved from: https://www.bankofengland.co.uk/prudential-regulation/publication/2022/june/model-risk-management-principles-for-banks (accessed 30 September 2023).

PRA. 2023. The Prudential Regulation Authority's approach to insurance supervision. July 2023, PRA, Bank of England.

QBE. 2020. How Artificial Intelligence will shape our future for insurance. News, 25 February 2020, QBE Insurance. Retrieved from: https://www.qbe.com/au/news/ai-the-intelligent-future-of-insurance (accessed 30 September 2023).

Rathi, N. 2023. Our emerging regulatory approach to Big tech and Artificial Intelligence. Speech by Nikhil Rathi, Chief Executive of the FCA, delivered at The Economist London on 12 July 2023, FCA. Retrieved from: https://www.fca.org.uk/news/speeches/our-emerging-regulatory-approach-big-tech-and-artificial-intelligence (accessed 30 September 2023).

Riikkinen, M., Saarijärvi, H., Sarlin, P. and Lähteenmäki, I. 2017. Using artificial intelligence to create value in insurance. International Journal of Bank Marketing 36(6): 1145–1168. DOI 10.1108/IJBM-01-2017-0015.

Ringe, W.-G. 2023. Why We Need A Regulatory Sandbox for AI. Faculty of Law Blogs, University of Oxford. Retrieved from: https://blogs.law.ox.ac.uk/oblb/blog-post/2023/05/why-we-need-regulatory-sandbox-ai (accessed 30 September 2023).

Rodrigues, R., Panagiotopoulos, A., Lundgren, B., Laulhé Shaelou, S. and Grant, A. 2020. Regulatory options for AI and big data. SHERPA Briefing. https://figshare.dmu.ac.uk/articles/online_resource/D3_3_Report_on_regulatory_options/11618211 (accessed 30 September 2023).

ROFIEG. 2019. Thirty Recommendations on Regulation, Innovation and Finance. Final Report to the European Commission – December 2019. Expert Group on Regulatory Obstacles to Financial Innovation (ROFIEG). Directorate-General for Financial Stability, Financial Services and Capital Markets Union, European Commission, European Union. Retrieved from: https://europa.eu/!yu87Xf (accessed 30 September 2023).

Royal Society. 2019. Explainable AI: the Basics. Policy Briefing, The Royal Society.

RSA. 2020. Insurance 2020: A look to the year ahead. News, 9 January 2020, Royal Sun Alliance (RSA) Insurance. Retrieved from: https://www.rsainsurance.co.uk/news/rsa-updates/insurance-2020-a-look-to-the-year-ahead/ (accessed 30 September 2023).

Ruel, C. 2018. Hiscox partners with AI startup Eigen to slash costs. Insurance Times, 9 August 2018. Retrieved from: https://www.insurancetimes.co.uk/news/hiscox-partners-with-ai-startup-eigen-to-slash-costs-/1427921.article (accessed 30 September 2023).

Ruel, C. 2020. Admiral subsidiary using Tractable's AI solution. News, 30 September 2020, Insurance Times. Retrieved from: https://www.insurancetimes.co.uk/news/admiral-subsidiary-using-tractables-ai-solution/1434760.article (accessed 30 September 2023).

Sadok, H., Sakka, F. and El Maknouzi, M.E.H. 2022. Artificial intelligence and bank credit analysis: A review. Cogent Economics & Finance 10(1): 2023262. DOI: https://doi.org/10.1080/23322039.2021.2023262.

Sanford, A. and Moosa, I. 2015. Operational risk modelling and organizational learning in structured finance operations: A Bayesian network approach. Journal of the Operational Research Society 66(1): 89–115. https://research.monash.edu/en/publications/operational-risk-modelling-and-organizational-learning-in-structu.

Sarkar, A. 2020. Disrupting the insurance value chain. *In*: Chishti, S., Bartoletti, I., Leslie, A. and Millie, S.M. (eds.). The AI Book: The Artificial Intelligence Handbook for Investors, Entrepreneurs and FinTech Visionaries. John Wiley & Sons.

Scherer, M.U. 2016. Regulating Artificial Intelligence Systems: Risks, Challenges, Competencies, and Strategies. Harvard Journal of Law & Technology 29(2): 354–400.

Shabsign, G. and Boukherouaa, E.B. 2023. Generative Artificial Intelligence in Finance: Risk Considerations. IMF Fintech Note 2023/006, August 2023, International Monetary Fund, Washington, DC.

Soldatos, J. and Kyriazis, D. 2022. Big Data and Artificial Intelligence in Digital Finance: Increasing Personalization and Trust in Digital Finance using Big Data and AI (eds.). Springer, Switzerland. https://doi.org/10.1007/978-3-030-94590-9.

Stanway, H. 2018. Artificial intelligence: more power to the risk manager? 31 January 2018, AXA XL. Retrieved from: https://axaxl.com/fast-fast-forward/articles/artificial-intelligence-more-power-to-the-risk-manager (accessed 30 September 2023).

Taylor, A. 2021. Why we invested in TensorFlight: leveraging AI to create a more sustainable industry for all. QBE Ventures. News, 31 October 2021, QBE Ventures. Retrieved from: https://www.qbe.com/ventures/news/why-we-invested-in-tensorflight--leveraging-ai-to-create-a-more-sustainable-industry-for-all (accessed 30 September 2023).

TensorFlight. Retrieved from: https://tensorflight.com/ (accessed 30 September 2023).

Tractable. undated. Retrieved from: https://tractable.ai/en (accessed 30 September 2023).

Tractable. 2022. Aviva partners with Tractable to bring the benefits of AI to auto claims. Tractable. Retrieved from: https://tractable.ai/en/resources/aviva-partners-with-tractable-to-bring-the-benefits-of-ai-to-auto-claims (accessed 30 September 2023).

TransRe. 2020a. The Insurer interview with Mike Sapnar, President and CEO of TransRe – Part 1. Podcast, 5 August 2020, TransRe. Retrieved from: https://www.transre.com/podcast/mike-sapnar-ceo-of-transre-part-one-of-the-insurers-the-best-policy-podcast/ (accessed 30 September 2023).

TransRe. 2020b. Data and Innovation in (Re)insurance. Podcast, 11 November 2020, TransRe. Retrieved from: https://www.transre.com/podcast/data-and-innovation-in-reinsurance/ (accessed 30 September 2023).

UK Government. 2022. Establishing a pro-innovation approach to regulating AI. Policy Paper, updated 20 July 2022, Command Paper: CP 728, Presented to Parliament by the Secretary of State for Digital, Culture, Media and Sport by Command of Her Majesty. Laid on Monday 18 July 2022. Retrieved from: https://www.gov.uk/government/publications/establishing-a-pro-innovation-approach-to-regulating-ai/establishing-a-pro-innovation-approach-to-regulating-ai-policy-statement (accessed 30 September 2023).

Ulbrich, E.K. 2020. Sure, AI can answer our questions – but who will answer our questions about AI? *In*: Chishti, S., Bartoletti, I., Leslie, A. and Millie, S.M. (eds.). The AI Book: The Artificial Intelligence Handbook for Investors, Entrepreneurs and FinTech Visionaries. John Wiley & Sons.

Van Steenis, H. 2019. Future of Finance. Review of the outlook for the UK financial system: what it means for the Bank of England. Bank of England. Retrieved from: https://www.bankofengland.co.uk/-/media/boe/files/report/2019/future-of-finance-report.pdf (accessed 30 September 2023).

Vandrangi, S.K. 2022. Predicting the insurance claim by each user using machine learning algorithms. Journal of Emerging Strategies in New Economics 1(1), The Netherlands Press.

Verisk. 2019. Aspen Insurance Selects Verisk's Mozart Form Composer to Research, Create, and Edit Policy Language. Newsroom 12 August 2019, Verisk. Retrieved from: https://www.verisk.com/newsroom/aspen-insurance-selects-verisks-mozart-form-composer-to-research-create-and-edit-policy-language/ (accessed 30 September 2023).

Villanueva, S. 2017. QBE partners with Cytora to leverage artificial intelligence and open source data. Press Release, 6 December 2017, QBE Europe. Retrieved from: https://qbeeurope.com/news-and-events/press-releases/qbe-partners-with-cytora-to-leverage-artificial-intelligence-and-open-source-data/ (accessed 30 September 2023).

Villanueva, S. 2018. QBE partners with HyperScience to drive immediate operational ROI with practical artificial intelligence. Press Release, QBE Europe. Retrieved from: https://qbeeurope.com/news-and-events/press-releases/qbe-partners-with-hyperscience-to-drive-immediate-operational-roi-with-practical-artificial-intelligence/ (accessed 30 September 2023).

Virdee, T. 2022. Understanding AI. *In*: Kerrigan, C. (ed.). Artificial Intelligence: Law and Regulation, edited by Charles Kerrigan, Edward Elgar.

Willard, J. 2022. Aspen backs Counterpart's AI-powered crime coverage for small businesses. 16 September 2022, Reinsurance News. Retrieved from: https://www.reinsurancene.ws/aspen-backs-counterparts-ai-powered-crime-coverage-for-small-businesses/ (accessed 30 September 2023).

Wrigley, S. 2018. Taming artificial intelligence: "Bots," the GDPR and regulatory approaches. *In*: Corrales, M., Fenwick, M. and Forgó, N. (eds.). Robotics, AI and the Future of Law. Perspectives in Law, Business and Innovation (PLBI), Springer.

Yan, T.C., Schulte, P. and Kuo Chuen, D.L. 2017. InsurTech and FinTech: Banking and insurance enablement. *In*: Chuen, K., Lee, D. and Deng, R.H. (eds.). Handbook of Blockchain, Digital Finance, and Inclusion: Volume 1: Cryptocurrency, FinTech, InsurTech, and Regulation. Elsevier Science & Technology.

Zetzsche, D.A., Arner, D.W., Buckley, R.P. and Tang, B. 2020a. Regulating AI in Finance: Putting the Human in the Loop. 2 March 2020, Oxford Business Law Blog. Retrieved online: https://blogs.law.ox.ac.uk/business-law-blog/blog/2020/03/regulating-ai-finance-putting-human-loop (accessed 30 September 2023).

Zetzsche, D.A., Arner, D.W., Buckley, R.P. and Tang, B. 2020b. Regulating AI in Finance: Putting the Human in the Loop. CFTE Academic Paper Serices: Centre for Finance, Technology and Entrepreneurship, no. 1, University of Hong Kong Faculty of Law Research Paper No. 2020/006. Retrieved from: https://papers.ssrn.com/sol3/papers.cfm?abstract_id=3531711 (accessed 30 September 2023).

CHAPTER 5

Digital Transformation in Cultural Organizations
New Emerging Technologies in the Italian Context

Eleonora Veglianti[1,]* and *Elisabetta Magnaghi*[2]

1. Introduction

The importance of cultural organizations has been demonstrated for a while. For instance, the Article 27 of the Universal Declaration of Human Rights (1948) describes how our society recognizes access to the life and cultural heritage of a territory as a fundamental right. From 1948 to the present, a number of national and international entities emerged to propose a concerted promotion and protection of the cultural heritage. Such interest of considering the relevant rule of cultural heritage for the overall society is still turned on. This is true especially in an era characterized by a higher number of tools which help the widespread of the importance of heritage among a largest portion of population.

In fact, in the current Industry 4.0 revolution, digital technologies have been influencing and impacting the whole society. In such scenario, to survive traditional organizations, processes and business models require to change introducing new technological elements. In this challenging digital context, cultural heritage organizations (i.e., museums) are not an exception. In fact, several governments and countries are involved in financing policies and programs which promote technologies in the cultural panorama.

New digital technologies become necessary to enhance the experience and the engagement of the visitors with the cultural heritage sector (Babu and Subramoniam

[1] Associate Professor, Management Department, KEDGE Business School, France.
[2] Deputy Director General and Dean, Kedge Business School, France.
* Corresponding author: eleonora.veglianti@kedgebs.com

2016). Moreover, social interactions become increasingly important to create and strength relationships with all the stakeholders involved both in the public and in the private sphere.

In other words, the digital innovation impacts the visitor experience due to the development of new processes and services highlighting a multi-stakeholder's approach with the goal of reaching a long-term value (Burton and Scott 2003).

In this outline, the cultural heritage can better face this social change with an efficient implementation of different kinds of technologies which help the stakeholders to deliver a more people-community centric service and experience that is aligned with a more sustainable approach. Hence, technological tools represent a crucial factor of our social life that are going to transform our culture in a steadily increasing manner (Sacco and Calveri 2021).

Technological innovation provides a new perspective on our cultural heritage, and consequently on the cultural organizations. Stated differently, today, we need to speak about digital culture as a phenomenon that is transforming our cultural organizations entities that need a deep rethinking of their business to better respond to the actual digital ecosystem (Giannini and Bowen 2019).

The influence of digital technologies on our cultural organizations is clear in terms of several aspects. For instance, organizations should look at the activities, the mission, the exposition of the heritage as well as at the management and stakeholder approach (Carpentieri 2020)

In tandem with this development of the Information and Communication Technologies (ICT), the cultural sector has to rethink its traditional way of "doing business" also taking into consideration the COVID-19 experience. The latter posed a crucial shock for these kind of organizations.

Given the above, the present paper wants to contribute to the literature about the digital transformation in the cultural sphere analysing the Italian context. Specifically, this article aims at understanding the technologies used to enhance the visibility and attractiveness of the cultural heritage. Consequently, the research question is the following: How are emergent technologies implemented in the cultural heritage organizations?

To answer to this question a qualitative research was conducted. The choice of Italy is the consequence of the authors' nationality, of their deep knowledge regarding the local context and the documentations in original language, without the filter of the translation. The last results a fundamental aspect in studying the materials as well as in enhancing the tacit knowledge of a specific country on a peculiar topic. In addition, Italy represents a unique ground in terms of numbers of cultural organizations. Following the above, the rest of the paper is structured in different sections. Section 2 presents the literature review; Section 3 describes the research methodology; Section 4 defines the emerging results and findings. Finally, Section 5 presents the discussion and conclusions, also suggesting further works.

2. Literature Review

During the digital era, new opportunities and challenges emerged to create value in various organization settings. Due to this digital wave, the cultural side has registered significant expansion in recent decades which was fostered by growth in the levels of citizens' income as well as of their education level.

Nowadays, the business behind the cultural side has become a valuable resource for Europe, especially for those countries with a large and widespread cultural heritage in their territories, such as Italy (Arostegui and Rius-Ulldemolins 2018). In such period, new technologies help the current paradigm shift (Navarrete 2014), providing a solution for cultural organizations to gain additional revenues and to stick to budgets.

Moreover, in this range of time identified as the 'new economy', the concept of the business model has become increasingly important for several academics and practitioners in different fields (Osterwalder et al. 2005, Zott et al. 2011). Hence, in this scenario, the cultural heritage sector has to rethink its services, processes because it cannot survive with the traditional way of doing business. Therefore, the development as well as the application of technologies promotes an innovative experience tailored on the needs of the today's users which attracts a growing audience (Ercolano et al. 2018). For these reasons, digital innovation has an increasing impact on the value proposition and, consequently, on the performance of cultural organizations.

As technologies are constantly evolving, an organization, in the cultural sector, has to change accordingly in terms of methods, services, strategies and information (Hooper-Greenhill 2013). In other words, the digital transformation changes the cultural entities both physically and virtually (Müller 2002). For instance, on one side, modern museums introduce various practices, starting from the creation of a website to the development of 3D experiences. On the other side, they shared information through social media, such as Facebook or Twitter. In addition, among the most relevant themes regarding the digital transformation of the cultural organization there is the idea of the virtual museum (Antinucci 2007, Bonacini 2011, Deloche 2011).

Today, we have to consider that the interactivity of digital devices and contents is going to impact the relationship with the clients that are profiled as digital "prosumers" (Esposti 2015) much more than in the past. This means that cultural organizations should not only care about the importance of their heritage but also, they have to have an increasing attention to the cultural contents and to the participations. The adoption of this new approaches is crucial in a digital transition as the design of experiences, through elements such as exhibition itineraries, it represents a powerful way to involve a larger number of people (Giannini and Bowen 2019).

Put it differently, the digital transformation creates a more direct relation with customers and final users due to the permanent information flow. Hence, the use of new technologies strengthens the participation of the audience not only during the exhibition. In fact, with the provision of innovative services (i.e., virtual tours, 3D, etc.), several cultural heritage organizations improve the so-called cultural dialogue (Rocchi et al. 2004, Spiliopoulou et al. 2014). This gives the opportunity to rediscover collection for new users by new users (Villaespesa and Navarrete 2019).

In addition, it is relevant to highlight that the digital setting of cultural organizations can be promoted in different ways developing strategies both to retain current visitors as well as to attract new ones. Thus, it can offer a new experiential activity which results a crucial approach to succeed (Deuschel et al. 2014).

Following this perspective, in several countries, as in the case of Italy, the cultural heritage has an influence not only at social and political level; instead, it represents also an important driver from a sustainable point of view. In this sense, the increasing relevance of adopting new technologies can help also these organizations in the implementation of a digital environment which emerged as a manner to reach and to involve a larger audience.

As a consequence, attracting more visitors is not only a matter of earnings and performance results; but, especially in the cultural heritage setting, it is linked to contents and experiences delivered (i.e., Domínguez-Quintero et al. 2018). In line with this, in the last years, tools such as apps, touch-screens panels, wearable technology, or Bluetooth enhance the request of digital guided tours in cultural organizations (Han et al. 2019). This happened because many visitors are more satisfied by the cultural experience (Antón et al. 2018).

Furthermore, the transition toward a digital environment in the cultural organization setting was also pushed by the recent event of the COVID-19 pandemic. This unexpected crisis opens new challenges for the cultural management field driving an important change which increases the access to the digital version of museums and other cultural institutions. Thus, the COVID-19 pandemic represents an occasional and unique acceleration of a path that had already started with the advent of the Information and Communication Technologies. Indeed, the digital transformation brings an evolution in the organization of the cultural heritage in both permanent and temporary exhibitions thanks to the introduction of a larger number of tools that creates a more inclusive experience not only in terms of contents.

Given the above, we can conclude that in a world that cannot be indifferent to the digital transformation, organizations, in general, and cultural heritage organizations, in particular, should rethink on how to provide an unforgettable outcome. Thus, it is crucial to understand how emergent technologies can be implemented in the cultural organizations.

3. Research Methodology

This article is based on a multiple case study approach which allows the exploration and understanding of a complex issue such the digitalization phenomenon in the cultural heritage organizations. This method of research gives an indepth analysis of the social and behavioral issues underlining the phenomenon under analysis. This research takes into consideration a broad level activity, both in terms of theoretical and empirical profiles (Bryman and Bell 2011).

The purpose of this work is to examine the data within a specific context. In line with this and, as discussed by different scholars (i.e., Yin 1984: p. 23), the case study method is: "an empirical inquiry that investigates a contemporary phenomenon within its real-life context; when the boundaries between phenomenon and context are not clearly evident; and in which multiple sources of evidence are used".

In addition, the authors can read the scientific literature and they can collect data from different sources (i.e., documents, conference, reports) in the Italian context due to their personal experience, knowledge as well as to their nationality. Therefore, this paper follows not only the relevant literature but, it considers also information coming from institutional and professional documents, websites, speeches and conferences. This research adopts a case design (Campbell 1975, Yin 1994a, Yin 1994b, Yin 2013).

Based on the relevant literature on this methodology and following the aim of this paper, it considers a descriptive approach to analyze the phenomenon under investigation. Specifically, a narrative form occurs within the analysis of the data in question (McDonough and McDonough 1997).

4. Emerging Results

As discussed previously, the digital transformation is modifying our lives and the way in which the cultural heritage is managed. In addition to this, the COVID-19 pandemic has pushed for an intense online migration of contents creating significant challenges and opportunities toward a new setting for these organizational entities. The improvements toward a digital access of the cultural heritage emerged from the results achieved in our investigation based on multiple cases of the technological cultural district of the Lazio Region, in Italy.

An important coalition of technology and art is the result of such unique transition that provides an advantage in term of sustainability. The exploration and implementation of different tools such as 3D screen, cyber-archaeology, and virtual tour play a driving role in the diversification of the proposals provided by the cultural organizations.

The virtual experience is well developed in the first case examined—the Franciscan sanctuary of the nativity in Greccio in Rieti. Here, the virtual tour is vital. It begins with an aerial image positioned over the Sanctuary as a union between architecture and nature that characterizes the path from Assisi to Rome. Moreover, a narrative voice comments on the visit: in each environment a friar appears as an interactive tutor who will explain to the visitor the characteristics of the environment being viewed or its history. In addition, a virtual book is presented which shows the Chorales, a particular category of liturgical codes of the 18th century. The latter, thanks to a conservative restoration and to technology, can be seen by visitors in high resolution while turning the pages virtually.

In this museum, there is also the possibility to download a mobile application named Toward Francis which retraces the stages of the path of St. Francis. It is a spiritual itinerary in an area of uncontaminated landscape beauty with historical and artistic aspects. Moreover, it is also possible to locate tourists via GPS, when the services are enabled and authorized. Therefore, this cultural heritage site was able, even before the COVID-19 pandemic, to develop and integrate virtual elements in its offer. The latter was also created in line with the traditional elements that are represented by the physical side due to the welcome centre that welcomes tourists with small cultural events as well as permanent exhibitions inherent to the life of St. Francis; but, at the same time, it works in conjunctions with the virtual sphere. In fact, it presents digital information regarding the territory.

In such case, we find a strong interaction between the physical and virtual aspects. This cultural organizations shows advanced technologies that are fully integrated with the "traditional" visit experience. As the analysis suggests, the aim of this well-organized integration is to make the culture usable particularly by the disabled and the elderly.

Therefore, from this first case, the main findings result the following. On one side, there is an impressive union between real and virtual. This is an important outcome that suggests the relevance of continuing with a hybrid experience driven by the traditional aspects as well as by virtual ones to deliver to the audience a unique experience. On the other side, the goal of this integration is to provide a service more adequate for a larger number of people. Thus, thanks to technologies, the cultural heritage organizations are going to create a more inclusive environment.

The second case is in Sperlonga where a virtual visit to the 'Marble Odyssey' that developed. The latter, thanks to 3D supports and an interactive interface, allows a visit through resources that could hardly be placed together in a physical space. For instance, this museum is able to create 3D representations that describes the long history of Sperlonga. In fact, the famous Tiberius Cave is represented with the play of 3D reconstructions, lights and sounds that offer to the public a scenario that bring them back to the time of Emperor Tiberius. In addition, the morphological and historical characteristics are presented. In this way, due to the technological and artistic contents provided by the digital narration and multimedia supports, the visitors are immerged in the culture and history of the place.

From our analysis, we can conclude that, in this case, the use of technologies finds multiple achievements. It creates an emotional effect from revisiting history that is very memorable. Therefore, from our findings, the digital transformation of cultural heritage can improve the learning educational process thanks to the usage of tools that help to impress visitors, especially younger ones. Put it differently, the experience in cultural organizations results more enjoyable having a stronger learning outcome.

The third case under investigation is Palazzo Braschi, in Rome, that develops an integrated system. In other terms, through the use of new technologies, it allows an innovative use of its collections together with its history and the urban evolution of the city. Specifically, the use of multimedia technologies provides a reconstruction of the historical urban situation in the past. The latter has been possible due to a careful scientific digitalization of different historical documents such as: fragments of the Forma Urbis, a recomposed map of Rome created in the era of Severo, cadastral maps, archived documents relating to building interventions, etc.

Using the digital tools, this museum offers visitors a journey back through the urban transformations of Rome. The digitalization of this case is based on augmented reality technologies and on virtual models and data (2D, 3D, 4D). For instance, in one of the main rooms, there is a digital table that provides an intuitive means of consultation to access the complex memories of the city. It represents a multitouch station that allows multiple users to interact simultaneously with the various installed applications. On one side, for example, there is the so-called MapVIEW that is a cartographic interface with several available information related to more than 1.200 point of interests enriched by photographs, videos and 3D models. On the other side, there is a MapSHOW that helps the understanding of Rome over the centuries and its urban evolution coming from an analytical and meticulous technical cartography approach. Finally, there is an application that helps people to connect and to share their favourite point of interests.

Therefore, from our analysis, it emerges that thanks to the digital reconstruction of archaeological and historical details, the visitors can have an immersive experience. This is suitable due to a huge effort: a strong scientific digitalization of the cultural heritage documentations that brings closer the virtual and the real side of the cultural organizations. Indeed, the application of advanced techniques and the digitalization of a great amount of documentation is an essential tool for the creation of a digital facsimile that allows a virtual experience that seems real.

5. Discussion and Conclusions

The digital transformation has been emerging all over the world as an essential transition for different organizations and sectors, reaching a high level of importance in cultural settings as well. The present paper contributes to shed a light on this relevant phenomenon analysing the Italian context, and, specifically, the cultural heritage in the Lazio region. The application and development of the digital sphere is beneficial for the today's organizational entities not only to improve the overall performance engaging the heritage resources but also to create an unforgettable experience.

The present work investigates multiple cases that implement the digital transformation in their organizations to answer to the research question. The research outcomes show that there is an integration between the digital and the physical aspects which provides important insights toward the development of hybrid approaches that are going to influence the organizational boundaries of this sector.

In other words, the aim is to contribute to the literature on digital transformation and its impact on organizations with a focus on its implementation in the cultural heritage context. The analysis of the Italian realities provides interesting inputs that can be generalized to other countries. In other words, the emerging results can be used as investigation canvas and applied to other countries. Hence, the results are not limited to the Italian scenario but are relevant also for other contexts.

This taxonomy permits to respond to the research question, emerging that the digital transformation could not be avoided. Therefore, today the concept of cultural heritage organizations is linked to the exhibition system, to its contents, but also it is linked to a new orientation that highlights the relevant role of the digital technologies.

Put it differently, there are still many traditional organizations in the cultural heritage setting with a weak approach toward digital tools as the ones that presents a basic website or a simple social profile, mainly with promotion purposes. However, many cultural organization entities are moving forward while presenting basic multimedia solutions (i.e., short videos or online catalogues of the exhibitions) or more advanced multimedia solutions (i.e., virtual tour, augmented reality, applications).

More and more, the adoption of digital technologies is definitely an interesting outcome that helps the risk of obsolescence. As this research suggests, the implementation of digital elements provides an important integration between the physical and the virtual which is going to ask further attention. In such way, cultural heritage organizations can propose a more inclusive environment. In fact, thanks to the implementation of such technologies disable and elder people can enjoy a more complete experience without obstacles and boundaries as well as without discriminating effects.

At the same time, the usage of digital tools is a valid choice to make available to the public a supplementary guidance that improves the contents. The latter creates the opportunity to have a more participate experience, producing a higher level of training and learning compared to "traditional" cultural institutions. Thus, the virtual side has an important teaching result. This learning possibility is of high value as it is strictly connected with the role of cultural heritage organizations in the whole society.

Furthermore, the digital transformation in such a context is going to be stronger and stronger following the need of our historical period. The development and implementation of advanced techniques is changing the organizations in comment as there is a higher possibility to bring visitors closer to the history and to culture, in general.

Despite its contribution to the relevant literature, this paper does not face some topics out of scope; but, it opens the debate for further scientific outcomes and reflections. This paper does not want to provide practical suggestions for best practices on how emergent technologies are implemented in the cultural organizations. However, it strives to deepen the knowledge of this important and relevant phenomenon which is increasingly useful also for the practitioners' discussion.

For example, the findings of the research suggest that the digital transformation is a fundamental element for the cultural context as, in this way, organizations are going to capture more general trends and attitudes. Besides, in many cultural heritage organization cases, this digital transition is still at the beginning stages and, thus, not completely implemented, or their outcomes are still not measured adequately to be assessed. Evenso, the purpose of this article is not to investigate their success or failure, but rather to present insights on the current situation of a peculiar context; we suggest considering our findings as a base to further contributions to the field of reference.

These results have implications for practitioners and future scholarly research alike. However, this paper shows some limitations. Indeed, further papers and researches could deepen the analysis, comparing more countries with a multinational approach to continue the investigation of this important transition so that it cannot be underestimated anymore.

References

Antinucci, F. 2007. Musei virtuali. Come non fare innovazione tecnologica. Roma/Bari: Laterza.

Antón, C., Camarero, C. and Garrido, M.J. 2018. A journey through the museum: Visit factors that prevent or further visitor satiation. Annals of Tourism Research 73(C): 48–61. doi: 10.1016/j.annals.2018.08.002.

Arostegui, J.A.R. and Rius-Ulldemolins, J. 2018. Cultural policies in the South of Europe after the global economic crisis: is there a Southern model within the framework of European convergence? International Journal of Cultural Policy. DOI: 10.1080/ 10286632.2018.1429421.

Babu, S. and Subramoniam, S. 2016. Tourism management in internet of things era. Journal of Information Technology & Economic Development 7(1).
Bryman, A. and Bell, E. 2011. Business Research Methods. Oxford University Press, Oxford.
Bonacini, E. 2011. Il museo contemporaneo: fra tradizione, marketing e nuove tecnologie. Roma: Aracne.
Burton, C. and Scott, C. 2003. Museums: challenges for the 21st century. International Journal of Arts Management 5(2): 56–68.
Campbell, D. 1975. Degrees of freedom and the case study. Comparative Political Studies 178–185.
Carpentieri, P. 2020. Digitalizzazione, banche dati digitali e valorizzazione dei beni culturali. Aedon 3.
Degli Esposti, P. 2015. Essere prosumer nella società digitale. Produzione e consumo tra atomi e bit. Milano: Franco Angeli.
Deloche, B. 2011. Le musée virtuel, Paris: Presses universitaires de France.
Deuschel, T., Heuss, T. and Humm, B. 2014. The digital online museum. A new approach to experience virtual heritage. pp. 38–48. In 4th International Workshop on Semantic Digital Archives (12-05-2014). London.
Domínguez-Quintero Ana, M., Rosario González-Rodríguez, M. and José Luis Roldán. 2019. The role of authenticity, experience quality, emotions, and satisfaction in a cultural heritage destination. Journal of Heritage Tourism 14(5-6): 491–505. DOI: 10.1080/1743873X.2018.1554666.
Ercolano, S., Gaeta, G.L. and Parenti, B. 2018 'Pompeii dilemma: a motivation-based analysis of tourists' preference for 'superstar' archaeological attractors or less renowned archaeological sites in the Vesuvius area'. Int. J. Tourism Res. 20: 345–354 [online] https://doi.org/10.1002/jtr.2186.
Giannini, T. and Bowen, J.P. 2019. Museums and Digital Culture: New Perspectives and Research.
Han, D.-I., Tom, C. and Jung, T. 2019. Augmented reality smart glasses (ARSG) visitor adoption in cultural tourism. Leisure Studies. doi: 10.1080/02614367.2019.1604790.
Hooper-Greenhill, E. 2013. Museums and their Visitors. Routledge.
McDonough, J. and McDonough, S. 1997. Research Methods for English Language Teachers. London: Arnold.
Müller, K. 2002. Museums and virtuality. Curator: The Museum Journal 45(1): 21–33.
Navarrete, T. 2014. Becoming digital: a Dutch heritage perspective. The Journal of Arts Management, Law, and Society 44(3): 153–168. DOI: 10.1080/10632921.2014.938385.
Osterwalder, A., Pigneur, Y. and Tucci, C.L. 2005. Clarifying business models: origins, present and future of the concept. Communications of the Association for Information Science (CAIS) 16: 1–25.
Rocchi, C., Stock, O., Zancanaro, M., Kruppa, M. and Kruger, A. 2004. The museum visit: Generating seamless personalized presentations on multiple devices. pp. 316–318. *In*: Vanderdonckt, J., Nunes, N.J. and Rich, C. (eds.). IUI '04 Proceedings of the 9th International Conference on Intelligent User Interfaces (Vol. 9). New York: ACM.
Sacco, P.L. and Calveri, C. 2021. La trasformazione digitale della cultura. Milano, Editrice Bibliografica.
Spiliopoulou, A., Mahony, S., Routsis, V. and Kamposiori, C. 2014. Cultural institutions in the digital age: British Museum's use of Facebook Insights. Journal of Audience & Reception Studies 11: 286–303.
Universal declaration of Human Rights. chrome-extension://efaidnbmnnnibpcajpcglclefindmkaj/https://www.un.org/sites/un2.un.org/files/2021/03/udhr.pdf.
Villaespesa, E. and Navarrete, T. 2019. Museum collections on Wikipedia: Opening up to open data initiatives. MW19: Museums and the Web 2019.
Yin, R.K. 1984. Case Study Research: Design and Methods. Beverly Hills, A: Sage Publications.
Yin, R.K. 1994a. Case Study Research Design and Methods: Applied Social Research and Methods Series (2nd ed.). Thousand Oaks, CA: Sage Publications Inc.
Yin, R.K. 1994b. Case Study Research: Design and Methods (2nd ed.). Beverly Hills, CA: Sage Publications Inc.
Yin, R.K. 2013. Case Study Research: Design and Methods. Sage Publication.
Zott, C., Amit, R. and Massa, L. 2011. The business model: recent developments and future research. Journal of Management 37(4): 1019–1042.

CHAPTER 6

Open Innovation and Industry 4.0 Digital Transformation

Literature Review and Preliminary Evidence[#]

Manuel Villasalero,[1] *Letizia Gasparri,*[2] *Agustín Zubillaga*[3] and *Martín Mora-Valbuena*[4,*]

1. Introduction

Firms are increasingly aware of the crucial challenges that innovation and digitalization represent in recent times to remain competitive in the marketplace. Along with other

[1] Associate professor at UCLM, Faculty of Law and Social Sciences, Campus Universitario, 13071 Ciudad Real (Spain).

[2] Torres Quevedo Postdoctoral Researcher at MEISA, Polígono Industrial El Cabezuelo, s/n, 13440 Argamasilla de Calatrava, Ciudad Real (Spain). Contract Professor at UCLM, Faculty of Law and Social Sciences, Campus Universitario, 13071 Ciudad Real (Spain).

[3] Bilbao office director at VICOMTECH, Zorrotzaurreko Erribera, 2, Deusto, 48014 Bilbao, Bizkaia (Spain).

[4] Managing director at MEISA, Polígono industrial El Cabezuelo, s/n, 13440 Argamasilla de Calatrava, Ciudad Real (Spain).

Emails: manuel.villasalero@uclm.es; letizia.gasparri@meisa-e.com; azubillaga@vicomtech.org

* Corresponding author: martin.mora@meisa-e.com

[#] This chapter has benefited from the comments and suggestions received from presentations of earlier versions at the international conferences held in Paris (DTS), Lille (MITCS) and Bilbao (WOIC) in 2023, and Dublin (IPDMC) and Valencia (ACEDE) in 2024. The authors acknowledge the funding the UCLM-MEISA university-business partnership for industrial digitalization provided to support the research leading to this chapter. This chapter publication is part of the aid PTQ2022-012725 financed by the MCIN/AEI/10.13039/501100011033 under the Torres Quevedo research project entitled "Open innovation-based international expansion through foreign subsidiaries" awarded to MEISA.

priorities, such as sustainability, governance, responsibility and globalization, the quest for innovative solutions and digital transformations are among the top concerns not only for managers but also investors, policymakers, consultants and scholars. In the last decades, openness has been the key recipe for innovation (Chesbrough 2003) and Industry 4.0 for digitalization (Kagermann et al. 2013). In the first case, the open innovation paradigm calls for firms to remain open to channel the inflow of external sources of knowledge for the firm's innovations (inbound innovation), facilitate internal knowledge outflow for other firms' innovations (outbound innovation) and internal and external knowledge bidirectional exchange for jointly innovating with selected partners (coupled innovation) (Gassmann and Enkel 2004). In the second case, the fourth industrial revolution perspective advocates for firms to adopt Industry 4.0 digital technologies (Cloud computing, Internet of Things, Big data, Artificial Intelligence) that go beyond task automation within the firm confines and control over some supply chain actors to pave the way to autonomous thinking with accompanying high levels of interconnectedness and interdependence with broader stakeholders, communities and ecosystems (BCG 2015).

Open innovation and Industry 4.0 digitalization have received tremendous attention as separate trends in scholarly, professional and political arenas. However, the interest on the openness-digitalization linkage remains much more modest. Policymaking is probably the exception to this rule, especially in the European Union (EU) and the United States of America (USA), where entrepreneurial innovations combined with smart manufacturing are seen as the way to reindustrialize western economies and regaining strategic autonomy confronting the labor-intensive model of eastern and developing economies in an increasingly context of deglobalization and geopolitical tensions. The EU's New Industrial Strategy and the USA's Chips and Science Act are recent good examples of the priority that policymakers attaches to innovation openness and Industry 4.0 digitalization dynamics (Villasalero et al. 2023b, Villasalero et al. 2024). In contrast, the existing research on this nexus is rather sparse, even after several calls made to understanding their linkages from both the open innovation (Bogers et al. 2018, Nambisan et al. 2019, Bercovitz and Chesbrough 2020, Enkel et al. 2020, Obradović et al. 2021, Colombo et al. 2023) and digitalization literatures (Ferrás-Hernández 2020, Okuwhere et al. 2022). Even in some cases in which open innovation and Industry 4.0 are simultaneously considered empirically, their relationship remains neglected and unexplored (for some recent examples, Ogiemwonyi et al. 2023, Dong and Xing 2024).

In this chapter, we review the studies dealing with the open innovation and Industry 4.0 digitalization relationship, propose a classifying framework based on the literature and provide some preliminary evidence based on a set of 733 manufacturing firms competing in Spain for illustrating the challenges ahead in the kind of research needed to uncover this connection. In doing so, we classify existing studies into three major categories according to the directionality addressed. Some studies view Industry 4.0 and openness as simultaneously co-occurring phenomena because their underlying forces are essentially the same or strongly overlap (Schlagwein et al. 2017, Wang and Islam 2017, Crupi et al. 2020, Lardo et al. 2020, Jiao et al. 2021, Anshari and Almunawar 2022). Other studies deal instead with how Industry 4.0

may enable open innovation practices, thus investigating from digitalization to openness (Dodgson et al. 2006, Cui et al. 2015, Dong and Netten 2017, Gómez et al. 2017, Trantopoulos et al. 2017, Cui et al. 2018, Trabucchi et al. 2018, Nellippallil et al. 2019, Cui et al. 2020, Mubarak and Petraite 2020, Urbinati et al. 2020, Wu and Ding 2020, Wu et al. 2021, Cui et al. 2022a, Cui et al. 2022b, Gao et al. 2022, Shehzad et al. 2022, Strazzullo et al. 2022, Wu et al. 2022, Wu and Gao 2022, Bettiol et al. 2023, Castillo et al. 2023, Eslami et al. 2023, Jiao et al. 2023, Rahmanzadeh et al. 2023, Yao and Li 2023, Wu et al. 2024). Others, in turn, focus on how open innovation practices may contribute to Industry 4.0 adoption, going consequently from openness to digitalization (Rocha et al. 2019, Ricci et al. 2021, Rocha et al. 2021, Benitez et al. 2022, Petruzzelli et al. 2022, Rocha et al. 2022, Capone et al. 2024, Pucci et al. 2024). From this, we propose a three-stage classifying framework for organizing the studies in the co-occurrence, enabling and driving perspectives across eight different models, thus revealing the research landscape on the Industry 4.0-openness relationship, including the opportunities to address unexplored issues, hybridize models and cross-fertilize perspectives. The illustrative evidence for Spanish manufacturing industry based on a recent large-sample assembly of secondary survey data shows a strong contemporary correlation between openness and Industry 4.0 and between them and innovation outcomes, consistent with the framework advanced in this chapter.

2. Open Innovation

The so-called open innovation paradigm has just turned its twentieth anniversary with the landmark Chesbrough (2003) book. Since then, it has positioned as a well-established perspective in the innovation studies literature, with an ever-increasing citation trend (for the latest accounts, Meireles et al. 2022, Laursen and Salter 2023, Sikandar et al. 2024), lots of literature reviews (Elmquist et al. 2009, Van de Vrande et al. 2010, Huizingh 2011, Lichtenthaler 2011, Chesbrough 2012, Remneland Wikhamn and Wikhamn 2013, Chesbrough and Bogers 2014, West and Bogers 2014, Randhawa et al. 2016, Bogers et al. 2017, Liu and Tang 2020, Sikandar and Abdul Kohar 2022, Laursen and Salter 2023, Sikandar et al. 2024), many special issues and sections (Gassmann 2006, Enkel et al. 2009, Gassmann et al. 2010, Galbraith and McAdam 2011, Holzmann et al. 2014, West et al. 2014, Tucci et al. 2016, Stanko et al. 2017, Bogers et al. 2019, Alexy et al. 2020, Bercovitz and Chesbrough 2020, Santos et al. 2021) and several books expanding its scope and strengthening its underpinnings (Chesbrough 2006, Chesbrough et al. 2006, Chesbrough 2011c, Chesbrough et al. 2014, Chesbrough 2020, Chesbrough et al. 2024).

In their initial version, Chesbrough (2003) documented extensively the practices of some well-known firms regarding how to innovate in a more open manner than it was the case in the past. In contrast with the traditional closed model based on an internal R&D department fueling all the firm innovations in a context of secrecy and vertical integration between the production of knowledge for innovation and its commercialization, some firms were starting to rely on externally-produced knowledge to innovate (inbound innovation) and let internally-generated knowledge be used for other firms to innovate (outbound innovation), being more permeable to external constituencies (von Hippel 2010) and vertically de-integrating the entire innovation process accordingly.

In the following years, a set of key academic studies contributed to consolidate this originally practical-oriented perspective within the literature (di Benedetto 2010) along three fundamental directions, such as recognizing additional open innovation modes with coupled solutions (Gassmann and Enkel 2004), distinguishing between breadth and depth of knowledge exchanges for innovation (Laursen and Salter 2006) and considering non-pecuniary knowledge flows in addition to pecuniary ones (Dahlander and Gann 2010). As a result of these advancements, the open innovation paradigm became more robust, articulated and consequential as a framework for studying innovation.

Another wave of studies served a different purpose. Instead of reinforcing the model with concepts, relations and approaches as the previous ones, other researchers decided to apply the open innovation scope to new contexts, such as mature industries (Chiaroni et al. 2010, Spithoven et al. 2010), service activities (Fasnacht 2009, Chesbrough 2011b, 2011a, 2011c, Mention 2011, Janeiro et al. 2013, Battisti et al. 2015), low-tech settings (Chesbrough and Crowther 2006), small and medium-sized enterprises (van de Vrande et al. 2009, Parida et al. 2012, Spithoven et al. 2013, Brunswicker and Vanhaverbeke 2015, Vanhaverbeke 2017, Torchia and Calabrò 2019, Son and Zo 2021), multinationals (Mortara and Minshall 2011, Asakawa et al. 2014, Ferraris et al. 2017a, Ferraris et al. 2017b, Ferraris et al. 2020), multidivisional firms (Villasalero 2018, Seran and Bez 2021) and start-ups (Audretsch et al. 2023). These studies expanded the phenomena explained and showed the vitality of a perspective capable of accounting for firm decisions beyond the restricted domain in which it originated; decisions adopted by large manufacturing firms in high-tech and fast-growing industries (Chesbrough and Brunswicker 2014).

A fourth set of studies trigger an even more profound shift in the open innovation research stream. In this case, openness does not only apply to different contexts but also spread throughout the firm's value chain and the value system (Groen and Linton 2010, von Krogh 2011) by redefining the business model (Chesbrough 2006, 2007b). The choice between openness and closedness does not longer revolve around the R&D department or merely technological decisions (Chesbrough 2007a), but become dependent on other departments and functions and how the firm relates with broader actors accordingly (Chesbrough 2010, Frankenberger et al. 2014, Saebi and Foss 2015, Moradi et al. 2021). Put another way, the innovation openness propagates to the entire firm and its relationship with stakeholders, including users (Vanhaverbeke and Du 2010, Laursen 2011, Bogers and West 2012, Piller and West 2014), communities (Hafkesbrink and Schroll 2011, Gould 2012, Shah and Nagle 2020, Urbinati et al. 2021) and ecosystems (Radziwon and Bogers 2019, Masucci et al. 2020, Vasudeva et al. 2020, Xie and Wang 2020). These studies provoked a double effect, first expanding the unit of analysis from firms to many other actors (universities, users, research institutes, etc.) (Villasalero 2014), the level of analysis from inter-organizational to intra-organizational (divisions, subsidiaries) (Villasalero 2018) and ecosystems (platforms, regional systems) (D'Ambrosio et al. 2017), and the exchange relation from dyadic to polyadic (communities, networks) (Battisti et al. 2019). Second, it pushes open innovation in related fields such as user, consumer, crowded, embedded and collaborative innovation (Ghasemzadeh et al. 2022, Villasalero et al. 2023a).

Finally, a fifth set of studies have tried to provide some theoretical underpinnings to the open innovation paradigm in an attempt to correct for major criticisms against it; lack of theory and insufficient cross-fertilization with related fields (van de Vrande and de Man 2011). This perspective has usually been seem as a workable framework for innovation studies still waiting for theoretical grounds (Vanhaverbeke and Cloodt 2014, Alexy et al. 2020), even adding some redundancies to established ones in strategic management or organization studies (Linstone 2010, Bercovitz and Chesbrough 2020). To counter this widespread view, open innovation has been linked to resource-based (Huang et al. 2015, Liu et al. 2022), knowledge-based (Barrena-Martínez et al. 2020) and dynamic capabilities perspectives (Bogers et al. 2019, Teece 2020, Engelsberger et al. 2022, Al Nuaimi et al. 2024, Song et al. 2024) in strategic management, and organizational learning (Naqshbandi et al. 2023), resource dependence (Biscotti et al. 2018, Wang et al. 2021), transaction costs (Remneland-Wikhamn and Knights 2012, Hsieh et al. 2016), institutional (Tran et al. 2022) and social exchange (Roldán Bravo et al. 2017) perspectives in organizational studies, to cite only the most frequent examples.

The foundational, reinforcing, expanding, spreading and grounding stages described above have positioned the open innovation paradigm in a progressive path (Kuhn 1970) to become a serious framework to advance the understanding of firms' decisions in many issues, going beyond innovation and encompassing many other instances.

3. Industrial Digitalization

The massive application of advances in computing and electronics to manufacturing settings began in the 70s, resulting in breakthrough automations of industrial firms. The change was so substantial that the term Industry 3.0 was coined to refer to it as the third industrial revolution (Klingenberg et al. 2022), after the introduction of machines in the seventeenth century (Industry 2.0) and the adoption of electricity in the eighteenth century (Industry 1.0).

Some key technologies in an Industry 3.0 context are computer numerical control (CNC) machines and automated robot arms to sensor and intervene in the physical world, computer-aided manufacturing (CAM) and flexible manufacturing systems (FMS) to implement decisions and integrate the manufacturing process, computer-aided design (CAD) to support simulation and decision making in the digital world and local area networks (LAN) and electronic data interchange (EDI) to communicate and keep everything connected to one another (Laffi and Boschma 2022). Adopting these technologies provided managers autonomy and control in manufacturing, with limited impact beyond the manufacturing function and industrial facilities' confines in a still highly human-controlled environment and relatively simple human-machine interfaces. Although CAD paves the way to coordinate product development with manufacturing processes and EDI does so to communicate with some key suppliers and distributors, the consequences for other functions and supply chain actors remained significantly restricted to a handful of scenarios.

The computerization of manufacturing characterizing Industry 3.0 settings evolved to a point in which new technologies pointing to new directions became available (Klingenberg et al. 2021). In the 2010s, some advances related to smart, connected sensors (Internet of Things, IoT) were starting to provide the opportunity to monitor and remotely manage any machine or device or track even persons, receiving large amounts of information in real-time (Big Data, BD). The resulting vast amounts of information could be easily stored for the first time and made available securely anytime, anywhere (Cloud Computing, CC) to support decision-making using analytic tools increasingly based on machines rather than humans (Artificial Intelligence, AI). These four technological pillars exhibiting strong complementarities and mutually reinforcing loops were noticed in industrial settings and acknowledged at the Hannover fair in 2011, later documented in a formal report (Kagermann et al. 2013), giving place to a so-called fourth industrial revolution coined as Industry 4.0 since then.

The previously mentioned technologies (IoT, BD, CC, AI) were the barebone of this fundamental change in the digitalization path with varied applications beyond the industry (Caruso 2018). In the specific industrial setting, such technologies were combined and adapted to the manufacturing context in the form of computer vision, autonomous robots, self-driven vehicles, smart storage and retrieval systems, additive manufacturing, augmented/virtual reality, cyber-physical systems, digital twins, natural language processing or touch kiosks, to cite a few of the most common examples (Agostini and Filippini 2019, Büchi et al. 2020, Cugno et al. 2021, Petruzzelli et al. 2022).

Although some argue that Industry 4.0 technologies are simply an evolutionary step from the Industry 3.0 ones (Qin et al. 2016, Yin et al. 2018, Nakayama et al. 2020, Laffi and Boschma 2022, Sari 2022), even suggesting talking about a fourth revolution may be premature or somewhat excessive (Xu et al. 2018, Soluk and Kammerlander 2021), they unleash notably different managerial implications. First, the applications go beyond the manufacturing function to reach almost all the firm's value chain activities, both primary and even support ones, thus allowing an increase in horizontal integration within the value chain across different tasks and vertical integration across the supply chain from suppliers to the final customer (Heppelmann 2014). As a result, it also goes beyond the manufacturing facilities' confines, promoting a high level of interconnectedness with external constituencies, including collaborators, users, communities, crowds and ecosystems. Second, machines not only continue to support the physical world tasks in a more autonomous (opposed to automatic) fashion, but they also make significant inroads, complementing or substituting human thinking in many non-recurring, unstructured decisions reserved for experts in the past. Even when humans retain the control of decisions, they become strongly technologically mediated with advanced simulation tools, such as those based on augmented/virtual reality, cyber-physical systems and digital twins (Brettel et al. 2017).

From the control and automation within the manufacturing facilities' boundaries in human-dominated settings with relatively simple specialized interfaces (Industry 3.0), the new digital technologies emphasize interconnectedness and autonomy across the supply chain in machine-driven settings with sophisticated technical interfaces (Industry 4.0). As such, an evolutionary technological evolution from one set of digital technologies to another, as many suggest, becomes a disruptive managerial revolution because of its profound impact on how firms behave, unleashing completely new ways of getting things done (Zonnenshain and Kenett 2020, Jiao et al. 2021, da Silva et al. 2022a).

The far-reaching and all-encompassing implications of the Industry 4.0 revolution have been extensively explored in many scholarly studies (Cannavacciuolo et al. 2023, Marino-Romero et al. 2024), consulting reports and policy plans (Horváth and Szabó 2019), with an overarching interest in contributing to accelerating industrial digitalization in different firms and countries (da Silva et al. 2022b, Cordero et al. 2023, Karuppiah et al. 2023, Santos et al. 2023, Virmani et al. 2023).

4. Openness and Industry 4.0

Considering that innovation and digitalization are top priorities for firms (Ayming 2023) and openness and Industry 4.0 are the dominant perspectives for addressing them, what do they have in common? How do they relate to each other? Which one impacts the other? The existing studies may be classified into three broad categories, depending on whether they address some commonalities between open innovation and Industry 4.0 digitalization (Schlagwein et al. 2017, Wang and Islam 2017, Crupi et al. 2020, Lardo et al. 2020, Jiao et al. 2021, Anshari and Almunawar 2022, Rahmanzadeh et al. 2023), deal with the causality from Industry 4.0 adoption to open innovation practices (Dodgson et al. 2006, Cui et al. 2015, Dong and Netten 2017, Gómez et al. 2017, Trantopoulos et al. 2017, Cui et al. 2018, Trabucchi et al. 2018, Nellippallil et al. 2019, Cui et al. 2020, Mubarak and Petraite 2020, Urbinati et al. 2020, Wu and Ding 2020, Mubarak et al. 2021, Wu et al. 2021, Cui et al. 2022a, Cui et al. 2022b, Gao et al. 2022, Shehzad et al. 2022, Strazzullo et al. 2022, Wu et al. 2022, Wu and Gao 2022, Bettiol et al. 2023, Castillo et al. 2023, Eslami et al. 2023, Jiao et al. 2023, Yao and Li 2023, Wu et al. 2024) or treat the reversed link between openness and Industry 4.0 (Rocha et al. 2019, Ricci et al. 2021, Rocha et al. 2021, Benitez et al. 2022, Petruzzelli et al. 2022, Rocha et al. 2022, Capone et al. 2024, Pucci et al. 2024).

4.1 Openness Co-occurrence with Industry 4.0

A first wave of studies view innovation and digitalization as knowledge-related challenges that force firms to recur to external knowledge pieces and embrace knowledge-sharing practices (Anshari and Almunawar 2022). In the case of digitalization, firms are prompted to rely on specialized digital providers and consultancy advice to successfully incorporate sophisticated digital technologies into business processes (Lardo et al. 2020). As for innovation, firms are also overloaded to keep the pace of delivering new products into the marketplace and implementing enhanced processes into practice using solely internally generated knowledge, thus looking for external ones to complement and accelerate the rhythm of innovation (Wang and Islam 2017). Whether the reason is responding to complex technological sophistication or an accelerated innovation race, knowledge sharing and sourcing are the common answers to both digitalization and innovation (Crupi et al. 2020).

The above discussion highlights the reliance on external knowledge sourcing as an imperative to confront some challenges in innovation and digitalization. While keeping the same argument about parallel directions and same underlying logic, some studies emphasize tapping into opportunities at the intersection between openness and Industry 4.0. In particular, a widely acknowledged intersection is one related to co-creating new products or processes by allowing the firm to be in touch with customers, users, engineers or suppliers and embracing an open innovation mindset to make it that possible. The synchronization of the human (stakeholder) through open innovation and the realization (process) through Industry 4.0 with the artifact (product) unleashes a whole array of opportunities for co-designing and co-creating (Jiao et al. 2021). In this case, open innovation and Industry 4.0 digitalization need each other as one provides the human-related input and another the technology-related platform, respectively (Rahmanzadeh et al. 2023).

On the empirical front, these studies view open innovation and Industry 4.0 adoption as co-occurring events. As both run in parallel directions because of sharing a common logic, one would expect that more openness is accompanied by more Industry 4.0 digitalization and vice versa (Crupi et al. 2020). Besides, this joint occurrence is expected to be favorable for achieving results since openness consequences will be stronger in the presence of Industry 4.0 (Rahmanzadeh et al. 2023).

This co-occurrence perspective on the relationship between open innovation and Industry 4.0 has evolved to the point of considering that both issues are part of the same in which openness, supply chain management and digitalization are viewed as indistinguishable (Groen and Linton 2010, Linstone 2010) or overlapping (von Hippel 2010, von Krogh 2011), including some proposals that coin expressions to refer to it, such as digital supply chain management (Scuotto et al. 2017), supply chain management 4.0 (Zekhnini et al. 2021) and open supply chain management (Rahmanzadeh et al. 2023).

A brilliant editorial essay summarizes this first position on the relationship between openness and digitalization by stating that "Open phenomena and IT [Information Technology] are often inseparable. That is, openness is often so deeply embedded in IT that it cannot be meaningfully analyzed and discussed separately from the IT platforms on which and through which open phenomena take place" (Schlagwein et al. 2017: 297).

4.2 Industry 4.0 Enables Openness

A second wave of studies conceives new digital technologies as enabling open innovation, regardless of whether they have to do with information technology in general (Cui et al. 2015, Dong and Netten 2017, Gómez et al. 2017, Trantopoulos et al. 2017, Cui et al. 2018, Wu and Ding 2020, Wu et al. 2021, Cui et al. 2022a,

Cui et al. 2022b, Gao et al. 2022, Shehzad et al. 2022, Wu and Gao 2022, Castillo et al. 2023, Eslami et al. 2023, Jiao et al. 2023, Rahmanzadeh et al. 2023, Yao and Li 2023, Wu et al. 2024) or specific digital technologies applied to industrial settings in particular (Trabucchi et al. 2018, Nellippallil et al. 2019, Mubarak and Petraite 2020, Strazzullo et al. 2022, Wu et al. 2022, Bettiol et al. 2023). In both instances, the technologies allow for performing open innovation better than without adopting them, thereby assuming that digital adoption drives openness.

From this common logic, some studies investigate directly how Industry 4.0 technologies facilitate different open innovation practices (Nellippallil et al. 2019, Strazzullo et al. 2022, Bettiol et al. 2023), modes (Trabucchi et al. 2018), mechanisms (Strazzullo et al. 2022) and phases (Dodgson et al. 2006, Urbinati et al. 2020), proposing in some cases even matching tables between those technologies and the corresponding innovation counterparts based on platform examples (Nellippallil et al. 2019), literature reviews (Strazzullo et al. 2022) or case studies (Dodgson et al. 2006, Trabucchi et al. 2018, Urbinati et al. 2020). This set of studies is meaningful in managerial terms because they link well-known Industry 4.0 technologies with the practice of open innovation in real-world situations. However, they do not go so deeply into the underlying connections between industrial digitalization and open innovation, that is to say, the enabling lever that each Industry 4.0 technology unleashes on openness for innovation. Only Bettiol et al. (2023) considers both the open innovation practices enabled by Industry 4.0 technologies and the subsequent impact that those practices have on a firm's outcomes, but it does so using cross-sectional data.

Instead of using individual Industry 4.0 technologies as the starting point, other studies take the capabilities they enabled as the determining factors impacting open innovation performance. Those capabilities range from integration (Wu and Gao 2022), flexibility or integration (Cui et al. 2015, Yao and Li 2023), connectivity or data (Trantopoulos et al. 2017), trust, assimilation or exploitation (Mubarak and Petraite 2020), exploration, exploitation and integration (Cui et al. 2020), external (Wu and Ding 2020), internal or external (Wu et al. 2021, Cui et al. 2022a, Gao et al. 2022), acquisition or utilization (Wu et al. 2022) and acquisition or operation (Cui et al. 2022b). In this way, these studies overcome the abovementioned limitations about the need for detailed explanations of the enabled capabilities that the enabling technologies provide. As apparent from the conceptualizations, some digital technologies help connect externally to valuable knowledge pieces (e.g., connectivity, flexibility, acquisition, trust, assimilation). In contrast, others support integrating those knowledge pieces internally with existing ones to take action (e.g., data, integration, utilization, operation, exploitation). In some studies, these digitalization-enabled organizational capabilities are presumed rather than measured directly using proxied variables such as self-reported information technology resources (Shehzad et al. 2022), expenditures on information technology hardware and software (Wu et al. 2024), expenditures on information technology hardware, software, services and labor (Dong and Netten 2017), investment in information technology infrastructure and professionals (Gómez et al. 2017, Castillo et al. 2023), information technology adoption (Jiao et al. 2023) or information technology use intensity (Eslami et al. 2023). In other studies, those digitalization-enabled organizational capabilities are neither explicitly considered, treating instead their more impactful consequences, such as the novelty or speed of open product innovations (Cui et al. 2018). Only one study considers simultaneously the impact of information technology-enabled capabilities on open innovation practices, on the one hand, and how those open innovation practices enhance, in turn, firm outcomes, on the other hand. It does so, however, using a research design based on cross-sectional data (Yao and Li 2023).

This literature on enabling technology and enabled capability (Braojos et al. 2020) as it has to do with the relationship between Industry 4.0 digitalization and open innovation looks promising, especially if it achieves a better articulation of the more intuitive and managerial stream with the more deductive and conceptual one. It is also noteworthy that the general studies dealing with information technology outnumber those more centered on Industry 4.0 in particular. Therefore, opportunities arise for importing some concepts and relations from the general to the particular. In either case, it implies that Industry 4.0 precedes openness. Therefore, firms may expect to become more open regarding innovation in the future as a result of investing in industrial digitalization in the present.

4.3 Openness Drives Industry 4.0

Finally, a third wave of studies examines how open innovation may contribute to accelerating Industry 4.0 adoption (Rocha et al. 2019, Ricci et al. 2021, Rocha et al. 2021, Petruzzelli et al. 2022, Rocha et al. 2022, Capone et al. 2024, Pucci et al. 2024) or making it more effective (Benitez et al. 2022, Pucci et al. 2024). The arguments used are similar to the ones employed by those defending the natural co-occurrence of openness and digitalization, that is, Industry 4.0 is too complex to be accomplished only internally without recurring to open innovation; Industry 4.0 is a systemic innovation that requires practicing openness as any other innovation project if not more; -openness is crucial to recognizing digital opportunities as a step in driving Industry 4.0 adoption. What is different is that open innovation and Industry 4.0 adoption are viewed as different domains (as opposed to indistinguishable or overlapping) in which openness drives digitalization.

Whether the open innovation practices are generic (Ricci et al. 2021, Petruzzelli et al. 2022, Capone et al. 2024) or targeted specifically to Industry 4.0 technologies (Rocha et al. 2019, Rocha et al. 2021, Benitez et al. 2022, Rocha et al. 2022, Pucci et al. 2024), they prove helpful in the race for industrial digitalization. This is an important distinction since the generic category of openness captures the overall posture of the firm regarding external knowledge sources for innovative purposes, whereas the specific category of openness refers only to the use of external knowledge sources for Industry 4.0 adoption. The fact that both measurement approaches to openness in the context of Industry 4.0 technologies reaches similar findings suggests a robust relationship from open innovation to industrial digitalization. Relatedly, the findings are also consistent for the entire range of manufacturing industries (Petruzzelli et al. 2022), medium- and high-tech industries (Ricci et al. 2021), an array of representative industries (Pucci et al. 2024), subsets more specialized in Industry 4.0 technologies

(Rocha et al. 2019, Benitez et al. 2022, Capone et al. 2024) or those that make more intensive use of them (Rocha et al. 2021, Rocha et al. 2022).

There are only eight studies in this research stream, five of them quantitative (dealing with all Industry 4.0 technologies) (Ricci et al. 2021, Benitez et al. 2022, Petruzzelli et al. 2022, Capone et al. 2024, Pucci et al. 2024) and three qualitative (addressing some of them) (Rocha et al. 2019, Rocha et al. 2021, Rocha et al. 2022). Only Benitez et al. (2022) and Pucci et al. (2024) consider the performance consequences of adopting industrial digitalization with open innovation practices; the former obtaining generally favorable effects with few exceptions while the latter detecting more complex interactions including curvilinear U-shaped effects with some thresholds for digitalization and asymmetrical moderated relations from openness. Both studies employed cross-sectional data.

Overall, this linkage from open innovation to industrial digitalization is the least investigated thereby offering ample research opportunities.

4.4 A Classifying Framework

From the co-occurrence of openness and Industry 4.0 to the view of open innovation driving industrial digitalization, passing through the enabling approach in which digital technologies support open innovation practices, the literature review on the openness-digitalization relationship offers three different responses (Figure 1).

In each perspective, there are at least two variations depending on whether the aim is to describe the determinants of the linkage or to prescribe the best form that it may take for performance, thus reflecting the traditional distinction between descriptive and prescriptive studies.

A crucial remark based on this classifying framework is how to deal with time in the studies trying to shed light on the openness-digitalization relationship for descriptive purposes. In the co-occurrence perspective, open innovation and

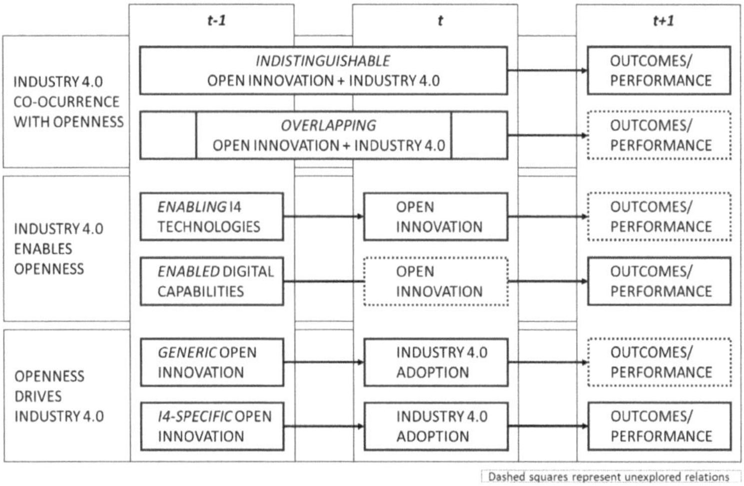

Figure 1. Perspectives on the openness-Industry 4.0 linkage.

Industry 4.0 adoption are contemporary phenomena that appear strongly intertwined over time at any observation point. In contrast, the enabling and driving perspectives need an appropriate lagged time structure to deal with the preceding order of the phenomena considering openness and Industry 4.0. Industrial digitalization must be time-lagged compared to open innovation for testing the enabling linkage. On the contrary, open innovation must be time-lagged against industrial digitalization to test the driving linkage. For prescriptive studies, it is always preferable to have a time-lagged temporal structure to isolate better the performance implications of the co-occurrence, enabling or driving relationships between openness and Industry 4.0.

The classifying framework also allows uncovering some research opportunities on the relationship between Industry 4.0 digitalization and open innovation (Figure 1, dashed lines). In particular, there are plenty of unexplored issues on the prescriptive side, because most of the limited number of studies reviewed are predominantly focused on the descriptive side.

5. Some Evidence for Manufacturing Industries

In what follows, we provide some preliminary evidence on the relationship between open innovation and Industry 4.0 adoption based on Spain's experience.

5.1 Setting and Data

The Survey on Business Strategies is a database compiled by the Minister of Finance's Spanish State Industrial Holding Company Foundation (Fundación SEPI, in Spanish) with detailed information about 1,200 manufacturing firms since 1990. Although the data collection is done every year, the information about some variables is surveyed every four years to keep the workload for respondents manageable. Generally, this database is similar to the well-known Profit Impact of Market Strategies (PIMS) (Moore and Farris 2004).

The latest full-fledged database release was made available to researchers in late 2022, reporting information for the 2018 fiscal year. A notable update for this newest version includes an all-new scale capturing the Industry 4.0 adoption phenomenon. Therefore, this database collects detailed information about last-generation industrial digitalization for the first time. We take advantage of this critical addition to explore the relationship between open innovation and Industry adoption.

In particular, we have information from 733 firms across 21 manufacturing industries without missing data in any of the variables of interest. The sample covers small and medium-sized enterprises (646) and large ones (87).

5.2 Measures

Similar to the vast majority of previous studies and consistent with the range of Industry 4.0 technologies considered as such (Agostini and Filippini 2019, Büchi et al. 2020, Cugno et al. 2021, Petruzzelli et al. 2022), the new scale asks firms whether they have adopted as many as 12 technologies: touch screens/kiosks for customer interface (orders via screen); (augmented/virtual reality and cyber-physical systems; automatically guided vehicles or systems self-driving vehicles, drones…);

automated storage and retrieval systems; 3D printing/additive manufacturing; machine learning data-driven management/big data; cloud computing; natural language processing; radio frequency identification and inventory systems and sensors; industrial internet or service internet of things; industrial robotics. We counted the number of technologies used for measuring Industry 4.0 adoption, thus ranging from 0 to 12, and applied a ln(x+1) to correct for skewness and truncation.

The proportion of external over total expenditures in R&D is one of the most widely employed measures to gauge openness, as closed innovators allocate almost all their R&D expenditures to internally developed projects, whereas open innovators follow an opposite pattern (Bönte 2003, Berchicci 2013, Gómez et al. 2017, 2020). We took this objective value then to capture open innovation.

Finally, we also explore a performance measure directly related to the issues of innovation and digitalization: innovation outcomes. We consider whether the firm has successfully introduced product, process and organizational innovations resulting from its research, development and innovation projects. As suggested in previous studies, innovation implies complementarities among different forms (Ballot et al. 2015, Hullova et al. 2016, Carboni and Russu 2018, Torres and Augusto 2020, Zhang 2022), especially in the case of digital innovations related to Industry 4.0 (Laubengaier et al. 2022). We take a count measure for measuring innovation outcomes ranging from 0 to 3 depending on whether the firm has achieved innovations in the product, process and organizational domains.

5.3 Preliminary Results

The first question is whether a strong relationship exists between Industry 4.0 adoption and open innovation. A simple correlational analysis shows this is the case, as Pearson's $r = .249$ is strongly statistically significant ($p = .000$, two-tailed). This a contemporary correlation between our measures for Industry 4.0 adoption and open innovation since both indicators are computed for the same year with no lagging effects between each other. Although the correlation is highly significant, the value indicates that open innovation and Industry 4.0 digitalization are different phenomena.

The second question concerns the impact of Industry 4.0 adoption and open innovation on innovation outcomes. Again, the contemporary correlations are strong and highly significant, with Industry 4.0 adoption reaching a remarkable $r = .444$ ($p = .000$, two-tailed) and a more modest openness $r = .197$ ($p = .000$, two-tailed). Therefore, there is a notable association of both open innovation and industrial digitalization with innovation outcomes, with the latter more than two times higher than the former.

6. Discussion

These preliminary findings based on an extensive sample database show that open innovation and Industry 4.0 digitalization are intertwined phenomena with good prospects in terms of innovation outcomes (Figure 2).

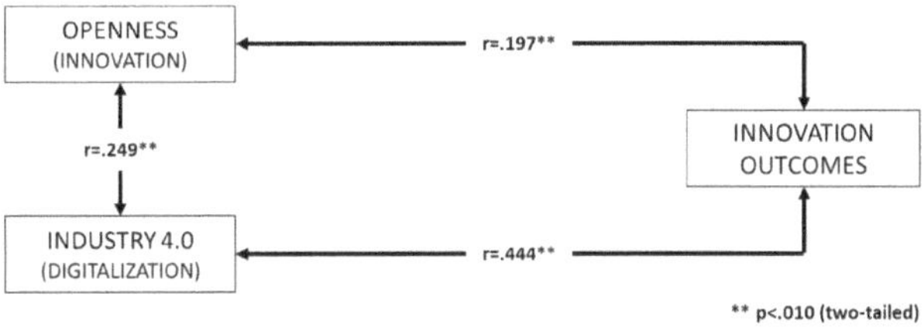

Figure 2. Summary of preliminary findings.

Beyond this point, more research is needed to understand whether this relationship better accommodates the co-occurrence, enabling or driving perspectives articulated in the literature review and organized around the classifying framework proposed in this study. Although our results are preliminary for illustrative purposes, they offer at least some tentative answers about crucial controversies.

6.1 Discussion of Findings

Some studies classified in the co-occurrence perspective argue that open innovation and Industry 4.0 are essentially the same under a supply chain management view, in what is called supply chain management 4.0 (Frazzon et al. 2019, Hofmann et al. 2019, Chauhan and Singh 2020, Frederico et al. 2020, Zekhnini et al. 2021) and open supply chain management (Rahmanzadeh et al. 2023). Although our measures may be somewhat imperfect, the correlation between open innovation and Industry 4.0 adoption is substantial at about r = .250 but remains low vis-à-vis indistinguishable phenomena. Instead, our results, based on widely accepted measures for both issues, point to an overlapping view; they overlap significantly (25%) but are distinct realities (75%). Accordingly, managers should be aware of matching openness and digitalization to get the best possible alignment; they do not appear to be naturally occurring joint events, even though some forces push towards their convergence over time.

The strong correlation between Industry 4.0 adoption and innovation outcomes is consistent with the idea that digitalization is simply a particular form of innovation, a complex one called systemic innovation that simultaneously involves product, process and organizational innovations in an interrelated manner (Ballot et al. 2015, Hullova et al. 2016, Carboni and Russu 2018, García-Piqueres et al. 2020, Torres and Augusto 2020, Laubengaier et al. 2022, Zhang 2022). This may likely explain why there is almost a 45% overlap between Industry 4.0 adoption and innovation outcomes. This is one of the prominent arguments lending support to the perspective of open innovation driving Industry 4.0. As digitalization is simply an additional manner of innovation, the firm will be better off applying an open innovation approach to industrial digitalization.

The correlation between open innovation and innovation outcomes is positive and significant, with Pearson's r = .197. Although a more sophisticated analysis is needed regarding these preliminary results, this finding is quite relevant because we employed a relative measure of open innovation that controls for firms' variations in R&D expenditures. It means that openness is beneficial for innovation outcomes as a general rule. There will undoubtedly be some contingencies and situations in which open innovation turns out to be neutral or even detrimental to innovation outcomes. Still, the general finding of a favorable effect with this sizeable firm sample is noteworthy in light of the recent studies that call for identifying unfavorable consequences resulting from practicing open innovation (Ebersberger et al. 2021, Schäper et al. 2023).

6.2 Research Implications

The classifying framework proposed in this study has three implications for research purposes. First, the research design issues concerning the temporal structure of data are crucial in a puzzling relationship between Industry 4.0 digitalization and open innovation that has just started to be explored. Mainly, a lagged-time design is a benchmark against which to elucidate whether co-occurrence, enabling or driving causalities prevail. Our study based on preliminary contemporaneous data intentionally exemplifies the challenges ahead for shedding light on such a controversial relationship. In this sense, this study mounts to the recent calls for more fine-grained research designs to position these fields better in mainstream management and organizational research (Laursen and Salter 2023).

Second, several opportunities await to be addressed in any of the three perspectives as our classifying framework identifies many unexplored issues. For example, the studies positing that Industry 4.0 adoption enables open innovation (Dodgson et al. 2006, Trabucchi et al. 2018, Nellippallil et al. 2019, Urbinati et al. 2020, Strazzullo et al. 2022) have not been complemented regarding the consequences of openness-enabled practices for outcomes or performance yet, with the sole exception of Bettiol et al. (2023). Similarly, the studies by Ricci et al. (2021), Petruzzelli et al. (2022) and Capone et al. (2024) showed that open innovation breadth and depth fosters Industry 4.0 adoption according to the driving perspective. Still, it remains to be investigated what the consequences of adopting those technologies supported by such open innovation practices look like, with the few exceptions of Benitez et al. (2022) and Pucci et al. (2024).

An interesting third implication is related to hybridizing the variants in each perspective or even different perspectives. For example, the enabling Industry 4.0 technologies and the resulting enabled digital capabilities are two sides of the same coin. However, the studies within this perspective run parallel without reaching intersections, such as which Industry 4.0 technologies favor one digital capability over another for open innovation. Another case is represented by generic open innovation to adopt Industry 4.0 compared to practices specifically targeted at sourcing Industry 4.0 technologies. A potential fruitful research may analyze whether Industry 4.0-specific open innovation practices are more effective when the firm enjoyed openness in other domains previously different from the digital ones.

As for cross-perspective fertilization, an evolutionary integration of the co-occurrence, enabling and driving responses to the Industry 4.0-openness relationship may be helpful to understand potential changing dynamics over time. The possibility of some circle in which driving and enabling mechanisms alternate virtuously reinforcing one another in enhancing dynamics seems likely. As indicated by Schlagwein et al. (2017), “Openness can be a driver for, or a consequence of, new

IT" (p. 297). Or, as put forth by Whelan et al. (2014), "IS [Information Systems] has played a prominent role in creating the necessity for, and the implementation of, open innovation models" (p. xxi).

6.3 Managerial Implications

One of the latest published consulting barometers reports that top managers rank innovation as their second-biggest priority (only surpassed by operational efficiency) and digital transformation ranked eleventh (Ayming 2023). If the priorities related to the bottom line are taken from the list, innovation becomes the top priority, while digital transformation elevates to sixth place, after internationalization, sustainability, reputation and talent. Almost 90% of over 1,000 firms surveyed support open innovation as the way to conduct their R&D and innovative projects. More than one-third use AI and automation to accelerate the innovation process (Ayming 2023).

These trends reveal a lot about the relevance of the topics addressed in this study as separate priorities among managers. More importantly, they show how innovation, openness and digitalization are increasingly closely intertwined in their mindsets, practices and real-world business problems. What has chief implications for our study is that their worries are compatible with the three identified perspectives on the relationship between Industry 4.0 digitalization and open innovation; they see both issues as something with many two-way commonalities, and consequently, recognizing, enabling and driving one-way relations between them.

In practical terms, regarding the one-way linkages, managers want to know whether they should invest in digitalization in the present to have openness as a result in the future. If this is the case, they also want to know how long it will take between digitalization being unleashed and the resulting open mindset making an impact in terms of product, process or organizational innovations, their novelty or radicalness or exploitative or transformative consequences. Moreover, they are likely interested in having some clues about the elasticity of the relationship from digitalization to openness; for example, an investment of one unit in Industry 4.0 will render two units in sales from open-derived product innovations or instead half of it. What is more, if they can do something about accelerating the time lapse or strengthening the impact, some hints are needed about whether to invest in information systems to fuel access to external knowledge or prioritize the integration of internal one, prioritize skilled digital employees over technological infrastructures or adopt an investment or spending approach to digitalization. Unfortunately, the review presented in this chapter indicated that existing research adds little to answering these managerial questions on the Industry 4.0-openness relationship regarding real-world worries such as payback period, payoff slope and accompanying discretionary decisions. The situation is quite the same or even worse about the other one-way relationship from openness to digitalization since fewer studies have addressed it.

Concerning potential two-way linkages, managers would willingly like to know more about the virtuous loops between open innovation and Industry 4.0 digitalization, what the reinforcing spirals look like, how to couple them over time and which actions prioritize to accelerate the advancement pace. Again, this chapter shows that we are far from providing even simple models about how openness and

Industry 4.0 intertwine along specific coevolutionary paths that managers may influence. If anything, a recommendation would be that innovation, operations, marketing and information technology managers must be in permanent touch now more than ever before with these trends. A proper supply chain management approach is also needed to integrate the firm better for these challenges (Rahmanzadeh et al. 2023). Echoing the design literature, an orchestration of the human (stakeholders), realization (processes) and artifact (products) is necessary to provide answers to and take opportunities from these vast changes (Jiao et al. 2021).

We hope this study's classifying framework and preliminary evidence contribute to managerial thinking about these critical issues and foster further research to illuminate how to deal with them in practice.

References

Agostini, L. and Filippini, R. 2019. Organizational and managerial challenges in the path toward Industry 4.0. Eur. J. Innov. Manag. 22: 406–421.

Al Nuaimi, F.M.S., Singh, S.K. and Ahmad, S.Z. 2024. Open innovation in SMEs: a dynamic capabilities perspective. J. Knowl. Manag. (in press).

Alexy, O., Frederiksen, L. and Hutter, K. 2020. Quo Vadis, open and user innovation theory? Innovation 22: 97–104.

Anshari, M. and Almunawar, M.N. 2022. Adopting open innovation for SMEs and industrial revolution 4.0. J. Sci. Technol. Policy Manag. 13: 405–427.

Asakawa, K., Song, J. and Kim, S.-J. 2014. Open innovation in multinational corporations: new insights from the global R&D research stream. pp. 157–168. *In*: Chesbrough, H., Vanhaverbeke, W. and West, J. (eds.). New Frontiers in Open Innovation. Oxford: Oxford University Press.

Audretsch, D.B., Belitski, M., Caiazza, R. and Siegel, D. 2023. Effects of open innovation in startups: Theory and evidence. Technol. Forecast Soc. Change 194: 122694.

Ayming. 2023. International innovation barometer 2024. Levallois-Perret, Île-de-France (France): Ayming Institute.

Ballot, G., Fakhfakh, F., Galia, F. and Salter, A. 2015. The fateful triangle: Complementarities in performance between product, process and organizational innovation in France and the UK. Res. Pol. 44: 217–232.

Barrena-Martínez, J., Cricelli, L., Ferrándiz, E., Greco, M. and Grimaldi, M. 2020. Joint forces: Towards an integration of intellectual capital theory and the open innovation paradigm. J. Bus. Res. 112: 261–270.

Battisti, E., Miglietta, N., Nirino, N. and Villasalero, M. 2019. Value creation, innovation practice, and competitive advantage: Evidence from the FTSE MIB index. Eur. J. Innov. Manag. 23: 273–290.

Battisti, G., Gallego, J., Rubalcaba, L. and Windrum, P. 2015. Open innovation in services: knowledge sources, intellectual property rights and internationalization. Econ. Innovation New Tech. 24: 223–247.

BCG. 2015. Industry 4.0: The Future of Productivity and Growth in Manufacturing Industries. Boston, M.A., United States.

Benitez, G.B., Ferreira-Lima, M., Ayala, N.F. and Frank, A.G. 2022. Industry 4.0 technology provision: the moderating role of supply chain partners to support technology providers. Supply Chain Manag. 27: 89–112.

Berchicci, L. 2013. Towards an open R&D system: Internal R&D investment, external knowledge acquisition and innovative performance. Res. Pol. 42: 117–127.

Bercovitz, J. and Chesbrough, H. 2020. Hopping tables—An introduction to the SMR special issue on open innovation. Strateg. Manag. Rev. 1: 207–222.

Bettiol, M., Capestro, M., Di Maria, E. and Grandinetti, R. 2023. Leveraging on intra- and inter-organizational collaboration in Industry 4.0 adoption for knowledge creation and innovation. Eur. J. Innov. Manag. 26: 328–352.

Biscotti, A.M., Mafrolla, E., Giudice, M.D. and D'Amico, E. 2018. CEO turnover and the new leader propensity to open innovation. Manag. Decis. 56: 1348–1364.
Bogers, M. and West, J. 2012. Managing distributed innovation: strategic utilization of open and user innovation. Creativity Innov. Manag. 21: 61–75.
Bogers, M., Zobel, A.-K., Afuah, A., Almirall, E., Brunswicker, S., Dahlander, L. et al. 2017. The open innovation research landscape: established perspectives and emerging themes across different levels of analysis. Ind. Innov. 24: 8–40.
Bogers, M., Chesbrough, H. and Moedas, C. 2018. Open innovation: research, practices, and policies. Calif. Manage. Rev. 60: 5–16.
Bogers, M., Chesbrough, H., Heaton, S. and Teece, D.J. 2019. Strategic management of open innovation: a dynamic capabilities perspective. Calif. Manage. Rev. 62: 77–94.
Bönte, W. 2003. R&D and productivity: Internal vs. external R&D - evidence from west german manufacturing industries. Econ. Innovation New Tech. 12: 343–360.
Braojos, J., Benitez, J., Llorens, J. and Ruiz, L. 2020. Impact of IT integration on the firm's knowledge absorption and desorption. Inf. Manag. 57: 103290.
Brettel, M., Friederichsen, N., Keller, M. and Rosenberg, M. 2017. How virtualization, decentralization and network building change the manufacturing landscape: An Industry 4.0 perspective. FormaMente 12: 47–62.
Brunswicker, S. and Vanhaverbeke, W. 2015. Open innovation in small and medium-sized enterprises (SMEs): External knowledge sourcing strategies and internal organizational facilitators. J. Small Bus. Manag. 53: 1241–1263.
Büchi, G., Cugno, M. and Castagnoli, R. 2020. Smart factory performance and Industry 4.0. Technol. Forecast Soc. Change 150: 119790.
Cannavacciuolo, L., Ferraro, G., Ponsiglione, C., Primario, S. and Quinto, I. 2023. Technological innovation-enabling Industry 4.0 paradigm: A systematic literature review. Technovation 124: 102733.
Capone, F., Innocenti, N., Baldetti, F. and Zampi, V. 2024. Firm's openness and innovation in Industry 4.0. Competitiveness Rev. (in press).
Carboni, O.A. and Russu, P. 2018. Complementarity in product, process, and organizational innovation decisions: evidence from European firms. R D Manag. 48: 210–222.
Caruso, L. 2018. Digital innovation and the fourth industrial revolution: epochal social changes? AI Soc 33: 379–392.
Castillo, A., Ruiz, L., Benitez, J., Schuberth, F. and Reina, R. 2023. IT impact on open innovation performance: Insights from a large-scale empirical investigation. Decis Support Syst. 175: 114025.
Chauhan, C. and Singh, A. 2020. A review of Industry 4.0 in supply chain management studies. J. Manuf. Technol. Manag. 31: 863–886.
Chesbrough, H.W. 2003. Open Innovation: The New Imperative for Creating and Profiting from Technology. Boston, MA. Harvard Business School Press.
Chesbrough, H.W. 2006. Open Business Models: How to Thrive in the New Innovation Landscape. Harvard Business Press.
Chesbrough, H.W. and Crowther, A.K. 2006. Beyond high tech: early adopters of open innovation in other industries. R D Manag. 36: 229–236.
Chesbrough, H.W., Vanhaverbeke, W. and West, J. (eds.). 2006. Open Innovation: Researching a New Paradigm. Oxford: Oxford University Press.
Chesbrough, H.W. 2007a. Business model innovation: it's not just about technology anymore. Strategy Leadersh. 35: 12–17.
Chesbrough, H.W. 2007b. Why companies should have open business models. Sloan Manage. Rev. 48: 22–28.
Chesbrough, H.W. 2010. Business Model Innovation: Opportunities and Barriers. Long Range Plann 43: 354–363.
Chesbrough, H.W. 2011a. Bringing open innovation to services. MIT Sloan Manag. Rev. 52: 85–90.
Chesbrough, H.W. 2011b. The case for open services innovation: The commodity trap. Calif. Manage. Rev. 53: 5–20.
Chesbrough, H.W. 2011c. Open Services Innovation: Rethinking your Business to Grow and Compete in a New Era. San Francisco: Jossey-Bass.

Chesbrough, H.W. 2012. Open innovation: where we've been and where we're going. Res. Technol. Manag. 55: 20–27.
Chesbrough, H.W. and Bogers, M. 2014. Explicating open innovation: clarifying an emerging paradigm for understanding innovation. pp. 3–28. *In*: Chesbrough, H., Vanhaverbeke, W. and West, J. (eds.). New Frontiers in Open Innovation. Oxford: Oxford University Press.
Chesbrough, H.W. and Brunswicker, S. 2014. A fad or a phenomenon?: the adoption of open innovation practices in large firms. Res. Technol. Manag. 57: 16–25.
Chesbrough, H.W., Vanhaverbeke, W. and West, J. 2014. New Frontiers in Open Innovation. New York: Oxford University Press.
Chesbrough, H.W. 2020. Open Innovation Results: Going beyond the Hype and Getting Down to Business. Oxford: Oxford University Press.
Chesbrough, H.W., West, J., Vanhaverbeke, W. and Radziwon, A. 2024. The Oxford Handbook of Open Innovation. New York: Oxford University Press.
Chiaroni, D., Chiesa, V. and Frattini, F. 2010. Unravelling the process from closed to open innovation: Evidence from mature, asset-intensive industries. R D Manag. 40: 222–245.
Colombo, M.G., Hoisl, K., Reichstein, T. and Torrisi, S. 2023. Open innovation, value creation and value capture: an introduction. J. Ind. Bus. Econ. 50: 731–742.
Cordero, D., Altamirano, K.L., Parra, J.O. and Espinoza, W.S. 2023. Intention to Adopt Industry 4.0 by Organizations in Colombia, Ecuador, Mexico, Panama, and Peru. IEEE Access 11: 8362–8386.
Crupi, A., Del Sarto, N., Di Minin, A., Gregori, G.L., Lepore, D., Marinelli, L. et al. 2020. The digital transformation of SMEs—a new knowledge broker called the digital innovation hub. J. Knowl. Manag. 24: 1263–1288.
Cugno, M., Castagnoli, R. and Büchi, G. 2021. Openness to Industry 4.0 and performance: The impact of barriers and incentives. Technol Forecast Soc. Change 168: 120756.
Cui, T., Ye, H., Teo, H.H. and Li, J. 2015. Information technology and open innovation: A strategic alignment perspective. Inf. Manag. 52: 348–358.
Cui, T., Wu, Y. and Tong, Y. 2018. Exploring ideation and implementation openness in open innovation projects: IT-enabled absorptive capacity perspective. Inf. Manag. 55: 576–587.
Cui, T., Tong, Y., Teo, H.-H. and Li, J. 2020. Managing knowledge distance: IT-enabled inter-firm knowledge capabilities in collaborative innovation. J. Manag. Inf. Syst. 37: 217–250.
Cui, T., Tong, Y. and Tan, C.-H. 2022a. Open innovation and information technology use: Towards an operational alignment view. Inf. Syst. J. 32: 932–972.
Cui, T., Ye, J.H. and Tan, C.H. 2022b. Information technology in open innovation: A resource orchestration perspective. Inf. Manag. 59: 103699.
D'Ambrosio, A., Gabriele, R., Schiavone, F. and Villasalero, M. 2017. The role of openness in explaining innovation performance in a regional context. J. Technol. Transf. 42: 389–408.
da Silva, L.B.P., Soltovski, R., Pontes, J., Treinta, F.T., Leitão, P., Mosconi, E. et al. 2022a. Human resources management 4.0: Literature review and trends. Comput. Ind. Eng. 168: 108111.
da Silva, N.A., Abreu, J.L., Orsolin Klingenberg, C., Antunes Junior, J.A.V. and Lacerda, D.P. 2022b. Industry 4.0 and micro and small enterprises: systematic literature review and analysis. Prod. Manuf. Res. 10: 696–726.
Dahlander, L. and Gann, D.M. 2010. How open is innovation? Res. Pol. 39: 699–709.
di Benedetto, A. 2010. Comment on 'Is open innovation a field of study or a communication barrier to theory development?'. Technovation 30: 557.
Dodgson, M., Gann, D. and Salter, A. 2006. The role of technology in the shift towards open innovation: the case of Procter & Gamble. R D Manag. 36: 333–346.
Dong, H. and Xing, G. 2024. Enhancing organisational resilience of 'Gazelle enterprises' through network embeddedness and knowledge search: the moderating effect of digital transformation. Technol. Anal. Strateg. Manag. (in press).
Dong, J.Q. and Netten, J. 2017. Information technology and external search in the open innovation age: New findings from Germany. Technol. Forecast Soc. Change 120: 223–231.
Ebersberger, B., Galia, F., Laursen, K. and Salter, A. 2021. Inbound open innovation and innovation performance: a robustness study. Res. Pol. 50: 104271.
Elmquist, M., Fredberg, T. and Ollila, S. 2009. Exploring the field of open innovation. Eur. J. Innov. Manag. 12: 326–345.

Engelsberger, A., Halvorsen, B., Cavanagh, J. and Bartram, T. 2022. Human resources management and open innovation: the role of open innovation mindset. Asia Pacific J. Hum. Resour. 60: 194–215.
Enkel, E., Gassmann, O. and Chesbrough, H. 2009. Open R&D and open innovation: exploring the phenomenon. R D Manag. 39: 311–316.
Enkel, E., Bogers, M. and Chesbrough, H. 2020. Exploring open innovation in the digital age: A maturity model and future research directions. R D Manag. 50: 161–168.
Eslami, M.H., Pellegrini, L., Lazzarotti, V., Puliga, G., Manzini, R. and Boer, H. 2023. The effect of knowledge collaboration on innovation performance: the moderating role of digital technologies. Int. J. Technol. Manag. 91: 162–189.
Fasnacht, D. 2009. Open Innovation in the Financial Services: Growing Through Openness, Flexibility and Customer Integration. Berlin: Springer.
Ferraris, A., Santoro, G. and Bresciani, S. 2017a. Open innovation in multinational companies' subsidiaries: the role of internal and external knowledge. Eur. J. Int. Manag. 11: 452–468.
Ferraris, A., Santoro, G. and Dezi, L. 2017b. How MNC's subsidiaries may improve their innovative performance? The role of external sources and knowledge management capabilities. J. Knowl. Manag. 21: 540–552.
Ferraris, A., Bogers, M.L.A.M. and Bresciani, S. 2020. Subsidiary innovation performance: Balancing external knowledge sources and internal embeddedness. J. Int. Manag. 26: 100794.
Ferrás-Hernández, X. 2020. Rethinking Industry 4.0: is there life beyond manufacturing? Int. J. Bus. Environ. 11: 404–416.
Frankenberger, K., Weiblen, T. and Gassmann, O. 2014. The antecedents of open business models: an exploratory study of incumbent firms. R D Manag. 44: 173–188.
Frazzon, E.M., Rodriguez, C.M.T., Pereira, M.M., Pires, M.C. and Uhlmann, I. 2019. Towards supply chain management 4.0. Braz. J. Oper. Prod. Manag. 16: 180–191.
Frederico, G.F., Garza-Reyes, J.A., Anosike, A. and Kumar, V. 2020. Supply Chain 4.0: concepts, maturity and research agenda. Supply Chain Manag. 25: 262–282.
Galbraith, B. and McAdam, R. 2011. The promise and problem with open innovation. Technol. Anal. Strateg. Manag. 23: 1–6.
Gao, H., Ding, X.-H. and Wu, S. 2022. Impact of knowledge search on product and process innovation: mediating role of absorptive capacity and moderating role of IT capability. Eur. J. Innov. Manag. 25: 325–346.
García-Piqueres, G., Serrano-Bedia, A.M., López-Fernández, M.C. and Pérez-Pérez, M. 2020. Relatedness in the adoption of different innovation types: product, process, organisational and commercial innovations. Technol. Anal. Strateg. Manag. 32: 44–57.
Gassmann, O. and Enkel, E. 2004. Towards a Theory of Open Innovation: Three Core Process Archetypes. Paper read at Proceedings of the R&D Management Conference, at Lisbon, Portugal, July 6–9.
Gassmann, O. 2006. Opening up the innovation process: towards an agenda. R D Manag. 36: 223–228.
Gassmann, O., Enkel, E. and Chesbrough, H.W. 2010. The future of open innovation. R D Manag. 40: 213–221.
Ghasemzadeh, K., Escobar, O., Yordanova, Z. and Villasalero, M. 2022. User innovation rings the bell for new horizons in e-health: a bibliometric analysis. Eur. J. Innov. Manag. 25: 656–686.
Gómez, J., Salazar, I. and Vargas, P. 2017. Does information technology improve open innovation performance? An examination of manufacturers in Spain. Inf. Syst. Res. 28: 661–675.
Gómez, J., Salazar, I. and Vargas, P. 2020. The role of extramural R&D and scientific knowledge in creating high novelty innovations: an examination of manufacturing and service firms in Spain. Res. Pol. 49: 104030.
Gould, R.W. 2012. Open innovation and stakeholder engagement. J. Technol. Manag. Innov. 7: 1–11.
Groen, A.J. and Linton, J.D. 2010. Is open innovation a field of study or a communication barrier to theory development? Technovation 30: 554.
Hafkesbrink, J. and Schroll, M. 2011. Innovation 3.0: embedding into community knowledge - collaborative organizational learning beyond open innovation. J. Innov. Econ. Manag. 7: 55–92.
Heppelmann, J. 2014. How the Internet of Things could Transform the Value Chain. New York: McKinsey & Company.
Hofmann, E., Sternberg, H., Chen, H., Pflaum, A. and Prockl, G. 2019. Supply chain management and Industry 4.0: conducting research in the digital age. Int. J. Phys. Distrib. Logist. Manag. 49: 945–955.

Holzmann, T., Sailer, K., Galbraith, B. and Katzy, B.R. 2014. Matchmaking for open innovation – theoretical perspectives based on interaction, rather than transaction. Technol. Anal. Strateg. Manag. 26: 595–599.

Horváth, D. and Szabó, R.Z. 2019. Driving forces and barriers of Industry 4.0: Do multinational and small and medium-sized companies have equal opportunities? Technol. Forecast Soc. Change 146: 119–132.

Hsieh, C.-T., Huang, H.-C. and Lee, W.-L. 2016. Using transaction cost economics to explain open innovation in start-ups. Manag. Decis. 54: 2133–2156.

Huang, H.-C., Lai, M.-C. and Huang, W.-W. 2015. Resource complementarity, transformative capacity, and inbound open innovation. J. Bus. Ind. Mark. 30: 842–854.

Huizingh, E.K. 2011. Open innovation: State of the art and future perspectives. Technovation 31: 2–9.

Hullova, D., Trott, P. and Simms, C.D. 2016. Uncovering the reciprocal complementarity between product and process innovation. Res. Pol. 45: 929–940.

Janeiro, P., Proenca, I. and Goncalves, V.D. 2013. Open innovation: Factors explaining universities as service firm innovation sources. J. Bus. Res. 66: 2017–2023.

Jiao, H., Yang, J., Jiang, C. and Yu, J. 2023. Openness and technological innovation: the moderating effect of information technology adoption and political ties. Int. J. Emerg. Mark. 18: 4037–4063.

Jiao, R., Commuri, S., Panchal, J., Milisavljevic-Syed, J., Allen, J.K., Mistree, F. et al. 2021. Design Engineering in the Age of Industry 4.0. J. Mech. Des. 143: 070801.

Kagermann, H., Wahlster, W. and Helbig, J. 2013. Recommendations for Implementing the Strategic Initiative INDUSTRIE 4.0. Frankfurt, Germany.

Karuppiah, K., Sankaranarayanan, B., D'Adamo, I. and Ali, S.M. 2023. Evaluation of key factors for industry 4.0 technologies adoption in small and medium enterprises (SMEs): an emerging economy context. J. Asia Bus. Stud. 17: 347–370.

Klingenberg, C.O., Borges, M.A.V. and Antunes, J.A.V. Jr. 2021. Industry 4.0 as a data-driven paradigm: a systematic literature review on technologies. J. Manuf. Technol. Manag. 32: 570–592.

Klingenberg, C.O., Borges, M.A.V. and Antunes, J.A.d.V. 2022. Industry 4.0: What makes it a revolution? A historical framework to understand the phenomenon. Technol. Soc. 70: 102009.

Kuhn, T.S. 1970. The Structure of Scientific Revolutions. 2nd ed. Chicago: Chicago University Press.

Laffi, M. and Boschma, R. 2022. Does a local knowledge base in Industry 3.0 foster diversification in Industry 4.0 technologies? Evidence from European regions. Pap. Reg. Sci. 101: 5–35.

Lardo, A., Mancini, D., Paoloni, N. and Russo, G. 2020. The perspective of capability providers in creating a sustainable I4.0 environment. Manag. Decis. 58: 1759–1777.

Laubengaier, D.A., Cagliano, R. and Canterino, F. 2022. It Takes Two to Tango: Analyzing the relationship between technological and administrative process innovations in Industry 4.0. Technol. Forecast Soc. Change 180: 121675.

Laursen, K. and Salter, A. 2006. Open for innovation: the role of openness in explaining innovation performance among U.K. manufacturing firms. Strateg. Manag. J. 27: 131–150.

Laursen, K. 2011. User-producer interaction as a driver of innovation: costs and advantages in an open innovation model. Sci. Public Policy 38: 713–723.

Laursen, K. and Salter, A. 2023. What we know about open innovation, unresolved issues, and a checklist for future research. J. Ind. Bus. Econ. 50: 743–764.

Lichtenthaler, U. 2011. Open innovation: Past research, current debates, and future directions. Acad. Manag. Perspect. 25: 75–93.

Linstone, H.A. 2010. Comment on 'Is open innovation a field of study or a communication barrier to theory development?'. Technovation 30: 556.

Liu, F., Lai, K.h. and He, C. 2022. Open innovation and market value: an extended resource-based view. IEEE Trans Eng. Manag: 1–14.

Liu, T. and Tang, L. 2020. Open innovation from the perspective of network embedding: knowledge evolution and development trend. Scientometrics 124: 1053–1080.

Marino-Romero, J.A., Palos-Sánchez, P.R. and Velicia-Martín, F. 2024. Evolution of digital transformation in SMEs management through a bibliometric analysis. Technol. Forecast Soc. Change 199: 123014.

Masucci, M., Brusoni, S. and Cennamo, C. 2020. Removing bottlenecks in business ecosystems: The strategic role of outbound open innovation. Res. Pol. 49: 103823.

Meireles, F.R.d.S., Azevedo, A.C. and Boaventura, J.M.G. 2022. Open innovation and collaboration: A systematic literature review. J. Eng. Technol. Manag. 65: 101702.

Mention, A.-L. 2011. Co-operation and co-opetition as open innovation practices in the service sector: Which influence on innovation novelty? Technovation 31: 44–53.

Moore, M.J. and Farris, P.W. 2004. The Profit Impact of Marketing Strategy Project: Retrospect and Prospects. Cambridge: Cambridge University Press.

Moradi, E., Jafari, S.M., Doorbash, Z.M. and Mirzaei, A. 2021. Impact of organizational inertia on business model innovation, open innovation and corporate performance. Asia Pac. Manag. Rev. 26: 171–179.

Mortara, L. and Minshall, T. 2011. How do large multinational companies implement open innovation? Technovation 31: 586–597.

Mubarak, M.F. and Petraite, M. 2020. Industry 4.0 technologies, digital trust and technological orientation: What matters in open innovation? Technol. Forecast Soc. Change 161: 120332.

Mubarak, M.F., Tiwari, S., Petraite, M., Mubarik, M. and Raja Mohd Rasi, R.Z. 2021. How Industry 4.0 technologies and open innovation can improve green innovation performance? Manag. Environ. Qual. 32: 1007–1022.

Nakayama, R.S., de Mesquita Spínola, M. and Silva, J.R. 2020. Towards I4.0: A comprehensive analysis of evolution from I3.0. Comput. Ind. Eng. 144: 106453.

Nambisan, S., Wright, M. and Feldman, M. 2019. The digital transformation of innovation and entrepreneurship: Progress, challenges and key themes. Res. Pol. 48: 103773.

Naqshbandi, M.M., Meeran, S. and Wilkinson, A. 2023. On the soft side of open innovation: the role of human resource practices, organizational learning culture and knowledge sharing. R D Manag. 53: 279–297.

Nellippallil, A.B., Ming, Z., Allen, J.K. and Mistree, F. 2019. Cloud-based materials and product realization—fostering ICME via Industry 4.0. Integr. Mater. Manuf. Innov. 8: 107–121.

Obradović, T., Vlačić, B. and Dabić, M. 2021. Open innovation in the manufacturing industry: A review and research agenda. Technovation 102: 102221.

Ogiemwonyi, O., Alam, M.N., Hago, I.E., Azizan, N.A., Hashim, F. and Hossain, M.S. 2023. Green innovation behaviour: Impact of industry 4.0 and open innovation. Heliyon 9: e16524.

Okuwhere, M.P., Huynh, T., Hoyte, C. and Johnston, A. 2022. SMEs digitalisation through clustering, the role of open innovation: a research agenda. Proc. Eur. Conf. Innov. Entrep. 17: 386–393.

Parida, V., Westerberg, M. and Frishammar, J. 2012. Inbound open innovation activities in high-tech SMEs: The impact on innovation performance. J. Small Bus. Manag. 50: 283–309.

Petruzzelli, A.M., Murgia, G. and Parmentola, A. 2022. How can open innovation support SMEs in the adoption of I4.0 technologies? An empirical analysis. R D Manag. 52: 615–632.

Piller, F.T. and West, J. 2014. Firms, users, and innovation: An interactive model of coupled open innovation. pp. 29–49. *In*: Chesbrough, H., Vanhaverbeke, W. and West, J. (eds.). New Frontiers in Open Innovation. Oxford: Oxford University Press.

Pucci, T., Casprini, E., Zanni, L. and Bonaccorsi, A. 2024. Profiting from the digital integration of the value chain and digital competencies: does open innovation matter for manufacturing SMEs? Technol. Anal. Strateg. Manag. (in press).

Qin, J., Liu, Y. and Grosvenor, R. 2016. A categorical framework of manufacturing for Industry 4.0 and beyond. Procedia CIRP 52: 173–178.

Radziwon, A. and Bogers, M. 2019. Open innovation in SMEs: Exploring inter-organizational relationships in an ecosystem. Technol. Forecast Soc. Change 146: 573–587.

Rahmanzadeh, S., Pishvaee, M.S. and Govindan, K. 2023. Emergence of open supply chain management: the role of open innovation in the future smart industry using digital twin network. Ann. Oper. Res. 329: 979–1007.

Randhawa, K., Wilden, R. and Hohberger, J. 2016. A bibliometric review of open innovation: setting a research agenda. J. Prod. Innov. Manage 33: 750–772.

Remneland-Wikhamn, B. and Knights, D. 2012. Transaction cost economics and open innovation: implications for theory and practice. Creativity Innov. Manag. 21: 277–289.

Remneland Wikhamn, B. and Wikhamn, W. 2013. Structuring of the open innovation field. J. Technol. Manag. Innov. 8: 173–185.

Ricci, R., Battaglia, D. and Neirotti, P. 2021. External knowledge search, opportunity recognition and industry 4.0 adoption in SMEs. Int. J. Product. Econ. 240: 108234.
Rocha, C.F., Mamédio, D.F. and Quandt, C.O. 2019. Startups and the innovation ecosystem in Industry 4.0. Technol. Anal. Strateg. Manag. 31: 1474–1487.
Rocha, C.F., Quandt, C.O., Deschamps, F. and Philbin, S. 2022. R&D collaboration strategies for industry 4.0 implementation: A case study in Brazil. J. Eng. Technol. Manag. 63: 101675.
Rocha, C.F., Quandt, C.O., Deschamps, F., Philbin, S. and Cruzara, G. 2021. Collaborations for digital transformation: case studies of Industry 4.0 in Brazil. IEEE Trans Eng. Manag: 1–15.
Roldán Bravo, M.I., Lloréns Montes, F.J. and Ruiz Moreno, A. 2017. Open innovation in supply networks: an expectation disconfirmation theory perspective. J. Bus. Ind. Mark. 32: 432–444.
Saebi, T. and Foss, N.J. 2015. Business models for open innovation: Matching heterogeneous open innovation strategies with business model dimensions. Eur. Manag. J. 33: 201–213.
Santos, A.B., Bogers, M.L.A.M., Norn, M.T. and Mendonça, S. 2021. Public policy for open innovation: Opening up to a new domain for research and practice. Technol. Forecast Soc. Change 169: 120821.
Santos, B., Dieste, M., Orzes, G. and Charrua-Santos, F. 2023. Resources and capabilities for Industry 4.0 implementation: evidence from proactive Portuguese SMEs. J. Manuf. Technol. Manag. 34: 25–43.
Sari, T. 2022. The relationship between the implementation levels of Industry 4.0 technologies and advanced manufacturing technologies. Manag. Prod. Eng. Rev. 13: 52–60.
Schäper, T., Jung, C., Foege, J.N., Bogers, M.L.A.M., Fainshmidt, S. and Nüesch, S. 2023. The S-shaped relationship between open innovation and financial performance: A longitudinal perspective using a novel text-based measure. Res. Pol. 52: 104764.
Schlagwein, D., Conboy, K., Feller, J., Leimeister, J.M. and Morgan, L. 2017. “Openness” with and without Information Technology: A framework and a brief history. J. Inf. Technol. 32: 297–305.
Scuotto, V., Caputo, F., Villasalero, M. and Del Giudice, M. 2017. A multiple buyer – supplier relationship in the context of SMEs’ digital supply chain management. Prod. Plan. Control. 28: 1378–1388.
Seran, T. and Bez, S.M. 2021. Open Innovation’s “Multiunit Back-End Problem”: How corporations can overcome business unit rivalry. Calif. Manage. Rev. 63: 135–157.
Shah, S.K. and Nagle, F. 2020. Why do user communities matter for strategy? Strateg. Manag. Rev. 1: 305–353.
Shehzad, M.U., Zhang, J., Alam, S. and Cao, Z. 2022. Determining the role of sources of knowledge and IT resources for stimulating firm innovation capability: a PLS-SEM approach. Bus. Process Manag. J. 28: 905–935.
Sikandar, H. and Abdul Kohar, U.H. 2022. A systematic literature review of open innovation in small and medium enterprises in the past decade. Foresight 24: 742–756.
Sikandar, H., Kohar, U.H.A., Corzo-Palomo, E.E., Gamero-Huarcaya, V.K., Ramos-Meza, C.S., Shabbir, M.S. et al. 2024. Mapping the development of open innovation research in business and management field: a bibliometric analysis. J. Knowl. Econ. (in press).
Soluk, J. and Kammerlander, N. 2021. Digital transformation in family-owned Mittelstand firms: A dynamic capabilities perspective. Eur. J. Inf. Syst. 30: 676–711.
Son, S.C. and Zo, H. 2021. Do R&D resources affect open innovation strategies in SMEs: the mediating effect of R&D openness on the relationship between R&D resources and firm performance in South Korea’s innovation clusters. Technol. Anal. Strateg. Manag.: 1–13.
Song, D., Zhang, P., Shi, R. and Yin, Y. 2024. Impact of strategic human resource management on open innovation: a chain mediation analysis of intellectual capital and supply chain integration. Chinese Manag. Stud. (in press).
Spithoven, A., Clarysse, B. and Knockaert, M. 2010. Building absorptive capacity to organise inbound open innovation in traditional industries. Technovation 30: 130–141.
Spithoven, A., Vanhaverbeke, W. and Roijakkers, N. 2013. Open innovation practices in SMEs and large enterprises. Small Bus. Econ. 41: 537–562.
Stanko, M.A., Fisher, G.J. and Bogers, M. 2017. Under the wide umbrella of open innovation. J. Prod. Innov. Manage 34: 543–558.
Strazzullo, S., Cricelli, L., Grimaldi, M. and Ferruzzi, G. 2022. Connecting the path between open innovation and Industry 4.0: A review of the literature. IEEE Trans Eng. Manag.: 1–13.
Teece, D.J. 2020. Hand in glove: open innovation and the dynamic capabilities framework. Strateg. Manag. Rev. 1: 233–253.

Torchia, M. and Calabrò, A. 2019. Open innovation in SMEs: A systematic literature review. J. Enterprising Cult. 27: 201–228.
Torres, P. and Augusto, M. 2020. Understanding complementarities among different forms of innovation. Eur. J. Innov. Manag. 23: 813–834.
Trabucchi, D., Buganza, T., Dell'Era, C. and Pellizzoni, E. 2018. Exploring the inbound and outbound strategies enabled by user generated big data: Evidence from leading smartphone applications. Creativity Innov. Manag. 27: 42–55.
Tran, H.T., Santarelli, E. and Wei, W.X. 2022. Open innovation knowledge management in transition to market economy: integrating dynamic capability and institutional theory. Econ. Innovation New Tech. 31: 575–603.
Trantopoulos, K., von Krogh, G., Wallin, M.W. and Woerter, M. 2017. External knowledge and information technology: implications for process innovation performance. MIS Q. 41: 287–300.
Tucci, C.L., Chesbrough, H., Piller, F. and West, J. 2016. When do firms undertake open, collaborative activities? Introduction to the special section on open innovation and open business models. Ind. Corp. Change 25: 283–288.
Urbinati, A., Chiaroni, D., Chiesa, V. and Frattini, F. 2020. The role of digital technologies in open innovation processes: an exploratory multiple case study analysis. R D Manag. 50: 136–160.
Urbinati, A., Landoni, P., Cococcioni, F. and De Giudici, L. 2021. Stakeholder management in open innovation projects: a multiple case study analysis. Eur. J. Innov. Manag. 24: 1595–1624.
van de Vrande, V., de Jong, J.P.J., Vanhaverbeke, W. and de Rochemont, M. 2009. Open innovation in SMEs: Trends, motives and management challenges. Technovation 29: 423–437.
Van de Vrande, V., Vanhaverbeke, W. and Gassmann, O. 2010. Broadening the scope of open innovation: past research, current state and future directions. Int. J. Technol. Manag. 52: 221–235.
van de Vrande, V. and de Man, A.-P. 2011. A response to "Is open innovation a field of study or a communication barrier to theory development?". Technovation 31: 185–186.
Vanhaverbeke, W. and Du, J.S. 2010. Reframing the role of lead users in radical innovations: an open innovation perspective. Int. J. Bus. Environ. 3: 202–220.
Vanhaverbeke, W. and Cloodt, M. 2014. Theories of the firm and open innovation. pp. 256–278. *In*: Chesbrough, H., Vanhaverbeke, W. and West, J. (eds.). New Frontiers in Open Innovation: Oxford University Press.
Vanhaverbeke, W. 2017. Managing Open Innovation in SMEs. Cambridge: Cambridge University Press.
Vasudeva, G., Leiponen, A. and Jones, S. 2020. Dear enemy: the dynamics of conflict and cooperation in open innovation ecosystems. Strateg. Manag. Rev. 1: 355–379.
Villasalero, M. 2014. University knowledge, open innovation and technological capital in Spanish science parks: Research revealing or technology selling? J. Intellect. Cap. 15: 1469–1930.
Villasalero, M. 2018. Multi-business firms, knowledge flows and intra-network open innovations. J. Knowl. Econ. 9: 162–179.
Villasalero, M., Gasparri, L., Yordanova, Z., Ghasemzadeh, K. and Escobar, O. 2023a. Open innovation in the neighborhood: open, collaborative, user, consumer, embedded and crowd innovation, June 7–9. Paper read at 30th Innovation and Product Development Management Conference, at Lecco, Como Lake, Milan (Italy).
Villasalero, M., Guadamillas, F. and Donate, M.J. 2023b. La estrategia industrial europea [The European industrial strategy]. pp. 163–186. *In*: Benedicto Solsona, M.Á. (ed.). La Unión Europea como poder global. Autonomía estratégica y despertar geopolítico [The European Union as a Global Power. Strategic Autonomy and Geopolitical Awakening]. Valencia (Spain): Tirant lo Blanch.
Villasalero, M., Guadamillas, F. and Gasparri, L. 2024. La autonomía estratégica abierta de la industria europea [The open strategic autonomy of European industry]. pp. (in press). *In*: Benedicto Solsona, M.Á. (ed.). Europa durante la guerra en Ucrania. Geopolítica y autonomía estratégica abierta [Europe during the War in Ukraine. Geopolitics and Open Strategic Autonomy]. A Coruña (Spain): Colex.
Virmani, N., Sharma, S., Kumar, A. and Luthra, S. 2023. Adoption of industry 4.0 evidence in emerging economy: Behavioral reasoning theory perspective. Technol. Forecast Soc. Change 188: 122317.
von Hippel, E. 2010. Comment on 'Is open innovation a field of study or a communication barrier to theory development?'. Technovation 30: 555.
von Krogh, G. 2011. Is open innovation a field of study or a communication barrier to theory development? A commentary. Technovation 31: 286.

Wang, H. and Islam, S.M.N. 2017. Construction of an open innovation network and its mechanism design for manufacturing enterprises: a resource-based perspective. Front. Bus. Res. China 11: 1–21.

Wang, T., Wu, J., Gu, J. and Hu, L. 2021. Impact of open innovation on organizational performance in different conflict management styles: based on resource dependence theory. Int. J. Confl. Manag. 32: 199–222.

West, J. and Bogers, M. 2014. Leveraging external sources of innovation: A review of research on open innovation. J. Prod. Innov. Manage 31: 814–831.

West, J., Salter, A., Vanhaverbeke, W. and Chesbrough, H. 2014. Open innovation: The next decade. Res. Pol. 43: 805–811.

Whelan, E., Conboy, K., Crowston, K., Morgan, L. and Rossi, M. 2014. Editorial: The role of information systems in enabling open innovation. J. Assoc. Inf. Syst. 15: xx–xxx.

Wu, L., Sun, L., Chang, Q., Zhang, D. and Qi, P. 2022. How do digitalization capabilities enable open innovation in manufacturing enterprises? A multiple case study based on resource integration perspective. Technol. Forecast Soc. Change 184: 122019.

Wu, S.-M. and Ding, X.-H. 2020. Unpacking the relationship between external IT capability and open innovation performance: evidence from China. Bus. Process Manag. J. 26: 1789–1805.

Wu, S., Ding, X., Liu, R. and Gao, H. 2021. How does IT capability affect open innovation performance? The mediating effect of absorptive capacity. Eur. J. Innov. Manag. 24: 43–65.

Wu, S. and Gao, H. 2022. How internal IT capability affects open innovation performance: from dynamic capability perspective. SAGE Open 12: 21582440211069389.

Wu, W., Zhang, P. and Tsai, S.-B. 2024. IT investment and corporate collaborative innovation: the moderating role of the top management team's educational background and absorptive capacity. Internet Res. (in press).

Xie, X. and Wang, H. 2020. How can open innovation ecosystem modes push product innovation forward? An fsQCA analysis. J. Bus. Res. 108: 29–41.

Xu, L.D., Xu, E.L. and Li, L. 2018. Industry 4.0: state of the art and future trends. Int. J. Prod. Res. 56: 2941–2962.

Yao, W. and Li, L. 2023. Information technology capability, open technological innovation and firm growth. PLoS One 18: e0291227.

Yin, Y., Stecke, K.E. and Li, D. 2018. The evolution of production systems from Industry 2.0 through Industry 4.0. Int. J. Prod. Res. 56: 848–861.

Zekhnini, K., Cherrafi, A., Bouhaddou, I., Benghabrit, Y. and Garza-Reyes, J.A. 2021. Supply chain management 4.0: a literature review and research framework. Benchmarking 28: 465–501.

Zhang, H. 2022. Does combining different types of innovation always improve SME performance? An analysis of innovation complementarity. J. Innov. Knowl. 7: 100192.

Zonnenshain, A. and Kenett, R.S. 2020. Quality 4.0—the challenging future of quality engineering. Qual. Eng. 32: 614–626.

Chapter 7

Developing Digital Marketing Strategy to Promote Summer Schools to Generation Z

Mariia Simchuk[1] and *Monica C. Scarano*[2,*]

1. Introduction

In response to the constant changes in our external environment and human life, consumer behavior is evolving significantly. Due to this, different profiles of customers are presenting new types of demands for educational programs and the related customer experience. More than ever, this concerns the younger generation, so-called Generation Z, who represent a relatively new customer profile for higher education institutions. Influenced by the consequential development of technologies, which make access to information more affordable and easier to obtain, Generation Z are laying down new requirements for how educational programs should be shaped, promoted, and delivered in order to meet their expectations.

To drive and meet demand, universities should focus on understanding the holistic experience of their students and improving interactions where possible. In this sense, digital marketing is becoming an essential component of promotional activities. Thus, it is crucial for universities nowadays to stay up to date with the most recent trends in the sphere of digital marketing for educational programs and adapt their marketing strategy to these changes for more effective promotion.

[1] Master's graduate – Université Catholique de Lille.
[2] Associate Professor – Université Catholique de Lille.
Email: Mariia.simchuk@univ-catholille.fr
* Corresponding author: Monica.scarano@univ-catholille.fr

There have been numerous attempts to study the characteristics of Generation Z and how digital marketing tools are influencing the promotion of educational programs. This includes the application of the new Marketing 4.0 concept, which is human-centered and empowered by technologies to provide a better customer experience (Kotler et al. 2020). From a managerial standpoint, there have been few attempts to study how a digital marketing strategy can be built to promote a summer school by outlining its unique characteristics, building a brand identity, and increasing engagement with alumni, as well as current and prospective students, by identifying the full range of student experiences. This is possible by understanding the personal qualitative experience of students at international summer programs.

The goals of our research are twofold. Theoretically, we integrate knowledge of how Generation Z experiences an international university summer school, focusing on the motivations to choose it. From a managerial point of view, we aim to help university marketing managers and international relations managers develop a successful digital marketing strategy to promote their international summer programs to digital natives, attract more international students, gain a wider and stronger international presence, and build communication and loyalty with their alumni and future students.

This chapter is structured as follows. First, we present a literature review on the role of international summer schools for universities and students and the recent marketing trends in the promotion of educational programs, allowing us to identify the research question. Second, we justify our qualitative methodology based on interviews. Third, our results are presented and discussed. Finally, we make recommendations on how to adapt a digital strategy to our research findings.

2. International University Summer Programs: from Theoretical Knowledge to our Evidence about the Experience of Generation Z

2.1 Growth of University Summer Schools Due to Technology

The first summer schools in universities are believed to have been established in the late 19th and early 20th centuries, primarily in the United States, where the self-financed education system was more common than in Europe. The so-called ‘third semester’ was created to help students graduate more quickly at a relatively lower cost by attending additional courses during the summer and earning the required number of credits. In recent years, summer schools have experienced phenomenal growth, and more and more universities are opening such programs around the world. According to a report prepared by the co-founders of research platforms dedicated to the promotion of summer schools (Torenbeek and Van Rest 2014), the number of courses on offer rose from 378 in 2009 to 1544 in 2014, with the largest number of courses offered by institutions in the Netherlands (346), United Kingdom (286), Germany (154), Russia (83), and Italy (79). Nowadays, depending on the particular program, summer schools can welcome participants both online and on campus. International summer schools typically span multiple weeks and facilitate social, cultural, and professional exchanges between students from diverse countries (Koster et al. 2022). These short-term programs usually include academic courses, as well as leisure activities such as excursions, field trips, and international socializing events. Some focus on the local language and culture, while others provide courses based on the university's profile and area of expertise.

The main target groups of summer schools differ and may include students already enrolled in the university, international students from partner and non-partner universities, university professors, and international guest lecturers.

According to a study conducted by Helsky-Lehtola (2015), students are interested in participating in summer school because it allows them to earn the credits needed for the validation of their diploma while having a unique experience of studying and living abroad for several weeks, meeting other students from around the world, and discovering other cultures through travel.

Overall, summer schools play an important role in universities' international strategies and serve several goals at the institutional level (Helsky-Lehtola 2015):

1) *Strengthening the international presence and academic reputation of the university*: summer schools present an opportunity to increase the international reach of the university and invite international educational institutions to establish or build on partnerships and new ways of collaborating. By bringing together students from various countries, diverse backgrounds, and cultures, summer schools facilitate social, cultural, and professional exchanges, fostering cross-cultural understanding. The variety of courses offered in specific fields promotes the academic reputation of the university by showcasing its expertise and unique and innovative teaching methods, as well as the quality and content of its education. Strengthening partnerships can be achieved by inviting lecturers from various universities to teach certain courses. Universities can also cooperate by signing interuniversity partnership agreements, allowing their students to participate in the summer school through customized short-term exchange programs tailored to their academic needs (Torenbeek and Van Rest 2014).
2) *Generating revenue*: summer schools can serve as a significant source of revenue for universities and their international relations departments. These programs are offered in return for tuition fees and administrative and hospitality fees for additional personalized services such as organizing visits and field trips, providing accommodation facilities, and more.
3) *Promoting educational programs and attracting talented students*: with specialized courses and programs during summer school, students have the opportunity to experience international student life at the university while earning the credits needed for their diploma. For some students, this is an alternative to a longer exchange period. For others, it may be their first experience of studying abroad, which could encourage them to return to the same university in the future for a longer exchange program or to pursue a degree.

The existing academic articles related to summer schools mainly focus on analyzing how specific schools are organized (Helsky-Lehtola 2015, Romanovska 2021), the motivations of different student groups to participate in summer schools (Cooper et al. 2000) and the components of a successful summer school from the participants' perspective (Borman 2000, Denton 2002). Most of these studies were conducted and published in the early 2000s, when most students belonged to Generation Y. Thus, the current body of knowledge lacks information on the interests and preferences of today's Generation Z students when it comes to summer schools, as well as their decision-making process. Torenbeek and Van Rest (2014) emphasize the need for further research on the motivation of students to enroll in summer schools and the outcomes of their participation to gain a broader understanding of the role of summer schools in the educational sphere. This would be useful for universities keen to adapt their summer schools and marketing activities to the prevailing trends resulting from global changes in education, the needs of the current generation of students and the development of technologies.

2.2 *Technological Prowess in the Digital Marketing Strategies of Universities*

The development of digital technologies is significantly transforming customers' lifestyles, purchasing preferences, and decision-making processes. Statistics indicate that in 2023, there are approximately 5.16 billion internet users, accounting for 64.4% of the world's population. Among them, 4.76 billion are active social media users, and the average daily internet usage is 6 hours and 37 minutes (DataReportal 2023). Institutions, including universities, need to adapt their communication strategies to effectively engage with their target audience. Understanding the decision-making processes of the target audience is crucial in terms of tailoring the message and encouraging them to make a purchase. The evolution of the internet and digital technologies has created a highly interconnected world where information is readily accessible from any location at any time. This accessibility allows businesses to gain insights into the behavior and interests of their target customers and track the effectiveness of their marketing activities. From the customer's perspective, this transparency provides more opportunities to gather necessary information, compare offers and make purchasing decisions based on the best value for their money.

Social media and online platforms have become widely accessible to the public and serve as influential sources of information for higher education institutions to promote their educational programs, build a strong and desirable brand image and target various groups (Bamberger et al. 2020). Utilizing digital marketing promotion enables universities to reach a wider audience, including international students, and increase the visibility and digital presence of their summer school programs on social media. Additionally, it is an effective method of informing potential students and partner universities about program offerings. With the availability of information on the internet, customers can easily research products and services, and compare different offerings before making a purchase. Nowadays, they have access to multiple channels to obtain the necessary information, such as official company websites, social media accounts, consumer reviews and recommendations from friends and influencers. From a business perspective, there are ten dimensions of digital marketing that companies can utilize to establish closer relationships with their customers and promote their offerings (Gunawan et al. 2020). Each of the dimensions presented plays an important role in establishing communication with and providing necessary information to the target audience:

1) *Website*: This plays a crucial role in promoting offers, especially educational programs, to prospective students. It provides detailed information on the programs offered, helping students understand if a certain program would be the right choice for them. This information typically includes program requirements, course descriptions and learning outcomes, admission procedures and contact information. Testimonials from current and past participants can also be showcased to highlight the benefits of the educational programs and lend credibility to the program.
2) *Marketing analytics*: This allows universities to track the effectiveness of online marketing activities and user behavior at a detailed level. It provides insights into metrics such as the number of times a link in an email or web page was opened and the amount of time users spent on a certain page. This information, gathered through various software tools, helps comprehend if user interaction can be improved and whether marketing campaign goals are being achieved.
3) *Search Engine Optimization (SEO)*: This concerns the use of the most frequently searched and relevant keywords, the improvement of the website's visibility and user-friendliness, cross-linking and many more aspects (Almukhtar et al. 2021). All in all, it is about making the website easier for users to find on search engines and more appealing, credible, and relevant for finding necessary information and achieving desired actions, such as learning about an educational program in detail and applying, contacting the International Office, etc.
4) *Online advertising*: this is a marketing tool that can be used to promote educational programs online using different formats, such as visual display ads on third-party websites, targeting the most relevant audience based on socio-demographic characteristics, interests, and behavior. It requires financial investments in the creation and running of the campaigns but, the payoff is an increase in targeted traffic and greater awareness of the promoted offers.
5) *Email marketing*: This is an efficient way to send important promotional materials and offers, providing personalized messages and newsletters. For universities, this method is applied not only to communicate with potential students but also with partner and non-partner universities who may be interested in sending their students on exchange programs.
6) *Online public relations*: this involves creating and maintaining a credible and positive image for the company through various media, including forums and blogs.
7) *Social media marketing*: This is a powerful activity that universities invest in to create and maintain relationships with consumers and build virtual brand communities by sharing developed content (Motta and Barbosa 2018) and engaging with prospective consumers (Bamberger et al. 2020).
8) *Content marketing*: This effectively promotes educational offers by creating and sharing valuable and informative content relevant to the needs and interests of

potential students. It can be done through blog posts, newsletters, videos and social media posts. The goal is to establish trust with the audience, increase brand awareness and ultimately increase enrollments.

9) *Affiliate marketing*: This involves activities organized in partnership with other organizations, companies, individuals and influencers to promote educational offers and achieve mutual benefits. Utilizing the popularity and established audience of experts or influencers in certain fields, the collaboration helps to increase awareness of products or services and build trust in them through recommendations.
10) *CRM (Customer Relationship Management)*: This helps higher education institutions establish and manage relationships with all their customers, including students, corporate partners, alumni and faculty.

Higher education institutions are becoming actively engaged in the creation of multi-channel communication and marketing strategies, providing their own content on social media, collaborating with influencers and monitoring brand reputation on forums and blogs. With the increased availability of information, customers now face the challenge of finding trustworthy resources where the most relevant and transparent information about educational offers is presented. This is especially important for offers that may be considered expensive, as accurate and detailed information is needed to ensure value for money.

3. Paradigm Shift in Customer-Brand Interactions and the Relevance of Marketing 4.0 in Promoting Educational Programs to Generation Z

More and more customers are being influenced by recommendations from their friends, family and influencers rather than traditional marketing communication from brands. As a result, the nature of communication between customers and brands is shifting from simply selling products to actively engaging with the audience. Building strong and meaningful connections based on trust with past, current and potential customers allows the brand image to become more reliable, turning clients into not just an audience but also friends and advocates of the brand. This opens up new opportunities for brands to promote their offers, communicate with their audience and collaborate with them. To address these changes, Kotler et al. (2020) identified a new, more digitally oriented and human-centered dimension, emphasizing the use of a multi-channel marketing strategy that combines offline and online interactions to attract customers and maintain strong relationships with them (Kotler and Keller 2016). According to this perspective, in the era of digital connectivity, the traditional 4P marketing mix (product, price, placement and promotion) transforms into the 4C marketing mix. This new consumer-oriented mix focuses on greater client involvement in communication (Kotler et al. 2020), treating them as peers and friends rather than mere buyers. The 4C marketing mix includes the following components. First, 'co-creation' as clients now participate alongside the brand in the creation of new products by providing feedback and new ideas for development.

This allows for personalized offerings and increased value, setting the brand apart from competitors. Second, 'currency': companies should prioritize providing higher value and an experience that consumers truly need, and this should not be traded for a lower cost. The total cost should include not only the price set by the seller but also any additional costs that may arise at any stage of the consumer experience. Third, 'communal activation' refers to the convenience with which customers can obtain information about the product, make a purchase and have it delivered at the right place and time. Finally, 'conversation' because communication with customers has traditionally focused on conveying messages and influencing them to make a purchase. However, in today's context, it goes beyond that and centers on building stronger and more meaningful relationships with customers (Paul and Bihani 2014), resulting in increased brand loyalty.

According to Yassine (2023), a digital marketing strategy has a positive impact on customer satisfaction, engagement and loyalty, highlighting the need to consider potential effects when building such strategies. Geçit and Kiyak (2021) point out that marketing mix concepts simply serve as a philosophical framework that guides key decisions and the development of long-term and short-term operational activities. They emphasize that the use of an omni-channel marketing approach, where the methods of both traditional and digital marketing are used, provides uninterrupted experience. According to Kotler et al. (2020), companies that provide services both digitally and physically can benefit from using a combination of traditional and digital marketing to deliver the best customer experience. They tell us that digital marketing is more focused on building relationships and interactions with clients, thanks to the ease of tracking and evaluating results, and identify five stages in the client path in the era of connectivity: awareness, selection, asking for more information, act and advocacy. It begins with clients becoming aware of various brands through past experiences, marketing communication and word-of mouth advocacy. Customers then process all the messages they have received from brands and select a shortlist of those that appeal to them. Once they have made this selection, customers ask for more information by checking with their friends, family and colleagues, searching online, on social media or directly through the brand. If this experience goes well, they can then move onto the Kotler's act stage, which can include either a transaction, subscription or trial period. Depending on their satisfaction with the purchase, usage and services rendered, consumers may or may not move onto the Kotler's advocate stage. Here, the consumer continues to use the brand, stays loyal and recommends it to others.

Some authors emphasize the need for universities to position themselves and manage their brands like corporate brands, utilizing digital marketing tools to construct a positive organizational image and influence how they are perceived and evaluated. According to Nguyen and Tran (2021), to increase the effectiveness of marketing 4.0 in universities, they should:

1) Constantly ensure they provide accurate, reliable and relevant information about their educational programs, as this plays a crucial role in the decision-making process of prospective students comparing different offers.

2) Carefully select content to align with the desired image of the university, considering tone, subject matter and the quality of images and videos used.
3) Continuously engage in communication with the target audience, defining attractive and popular content through surveys and specific analytical tools, while also improving participative activities.
4) Invest in providing a user-friendly mobile design for the university's website, considering that phones have become the primary means for potential students to learn about universities and their offerings.

Raj et al. (2013) suggest that there may be gaps in educational services between universities and customers, which educational institutions need to analyze and address to provide the best possible customer experience. According to the authors, to reduce these gaps universities must understand the expectations of students; ensure that the design and standards of the desired services meet the needs and requirements of students and that the expected quality is delivered; and align their performance with the promises communicated to students.

These authors highlight five pillars of educational services that should guide the creation of a digital marketing strategy: make it easy to find necessary information in a limited amount of time; make the communicated content relevant to the needs of students; keep the content and visuals fresh to maintain attention; manage the interaction of the target audience and their user behavior; and measure defined goals through analytical services.

In the process of creating a marketing strategy, it is important to consider the characteristics of the target audience, including their behavior, communication preferences and the offers they are interested in. The strategy can thus be tailored to attract attention and establish effective communication with potential clients. One commonly used approach is the theory of generations, which suggests that each generation has unique expectations, experiences, lifestyles, values and demographic characteristics that should be taken into account when adapting a marketing strategy (Williams and Page 2011). When it comes to short-term educational programs like winter and summer schools, the main target audience is currently undergraduate students, which corresponds to Generation Z.

Generation Z, also known as 'Gen Z' or the 'iGen', generally refers to individuals born between the mid-1990s and mid-2010s. According to studies by Bamberger et al. (2020) and Giunta (2020), Generation Z represent a significant consumer market, with a global spending power of $143 billion and accounting for 40% of global consumers, particularly in the United States. While the generational approach may overlook important regional, ethnic and national differences, it provides insight into common trends among different age groups, which can serve as the basis for a marketing strategy. However, as most Generation Z individuals are currently pursuing education and just starting their careers, they are often dependent on their parents, who play a crucial role in the decision-making and buying processes. Educational institutions such as universities and colleges also serve as sources of sponsorship. This is especially relevant for participation in short-term educational programs like summer and winter schools, where program fees are typically high for in-person attendance. Several characteristics are attributed to Gen Z. They are considered digital natives, having grown up in a world where technology has always been a part of every aspect of life. According to Fromm and Read (2018), Generation Z enjoy using social media to create extensive networks, share their own lives and gain visibility into the lives of others. They tend to have lower power distance preferences, expressing their thoughts openly on various social media platforms (Giunta 2020). This technology self-efficacy has made Generation Z part of the culture of connectivity (Brahnam 2017) and the 'selfie culture', where consumers are influenced by social media, influencers, friends and family. Being highly connected to the world and people, they seek transparent and authentic information about educational programs. Trust in relationships with brands is important to them, and they are more likely to pay attention to advertisements and recommendations shared by people they trust (Munsch 2021). Word of mouth, product reviews and user-generated content significantly influence their decision to purchase or participate in something. Generation Z are driven by a sense of purpose and motivation to make a positive change in the world. Growing up in times of economic hardship and global conflicts, they are pragmatic and realistic about career and financial prospects (Rue 2018). When developing marketing campaigns for summer schools, it is important to emphasize the practical relevance of the skills they can acquire and their alignment with desired workplace skills (Fromm and Read 2018). Interaction with both the product/service and the brand online is a crucial part of the customer experience for Generation Z. Direct communication with the brand helps them feel connected and fosters loyalty. They are willing to participate in co-creation and recommend offerings to others if they have had a positive experience. Moreover, as discussed pointed out by Rue (2018), they usually have high expectations about the digitalization of communication to provide better service, engagement and personalization. Digital marketing communication has a higher chance of capturing the attention of Generation Z if advertisements are short (around 15 seconds), deliver concise messages, evoke emotions and utilize popular songs (Munsch 2021). As Generation Z are technologically proficient, digital marketing should be optimized for various devices they may use. Storytelling, high-quality digital visual ads and relatability in the message conveyed are effective ways to appeal to the emotions of Generation Z (Ninan et al. 2020). Short video formats, often promoted through platforms like YouTube Shorts and Instagram Reels, are popular methods of engaging this audience. To summarize, Generation Z have distinct characteristics compared to other generations, including a focus on career-oriented education, high technical proficiency, active use of social media and increased expectations for communication with organizations. This generation wields significant influence over the market, particularly in the digital realm.

In order to meet the expectations of this consumer generation, educational institutions need to reach certain goals; for example, establish a strong digital presence across multiple channels to ensure that Generation Z can easily access the necessary information about educational programs. It is also important to provide transparent, authentic and engaging content with an appropriate communication style to build trust with the audience. Understanding the consumer experience, identifying touchpoints and pain points and conveying the right message at each stage are crucial for relevant content. Moreover, educational institutes can foster engagement and meaningful interactions that align with the values and goals of the target audience. Maintaining communication with both current and prospective students and creating opportunities for them to exchange and share their experiences are important for building trust, loyalty and a sense of community, all of which are sought by Generation Z. Educational institutions can encourage students to share their experiences on social media and tag official institution accounts, as well as feature and promote user-generated content through various channels. Another effective method is to invite students to participate in co-creation by incorporating their feedback, ideas and testimonials into the content. Basha (2019) highlights the advantages of social media as a cost-effective and measurable marketing tool for universities, given that 99% of the student population is present on social media. While this study focused on a few educational institutions in Bangalore and may not be sufficiently broad, it supports the idea that digital marketing has an impact on the way students select educational institutions. Ikatrinasari (2020) proposes the use of the SWOT method for choosing the right digital marketing strategy for higher education institutions, based on questionnaire responses from staff involved in strategy development. Other researchers examine the role of specific digital tools, such as SEO, in helping universities achieve a stronger international presence (Iddris 2018). Kusumawati (2019) discusses how digital marketing engagement on websites and social media positively influences student decision-making, identifying key factors such as institution reputation, academic programs, facilities, location and cost.

4. Unveiling Generation Z Motivations: Outcomes in International Summer Programs

Overall, research efforts have explored the benefits of digital marketing strategies for universities, including the analysis of strategies implemented by specific educational institutions. However, there is a lack of research specifically focused on developing digital marketing strategies for European summer schools by considering the motivations, interests and consumer behaviors of Generation Z as the target group. Even though the literature provides valuable insights into the relevance, development and evaluation of the effectiveness of digital marketing strategies for higher education institutions, most of the research focuses on either the analysis of trends in creating such strategies in the education sector or the promotion of educational programs at HEIs in general. The analysis and adaptation of digital marketing strategies to summer schools with the aim of understanding their relevance to recent trends and correspondence to the consumer behaviors, preferences and motivations of their target audience, mostly Gen Z, is noticeably absent from the scientific literature. This gap is the research focus of our research, following the directions offered by Torenbeek and Van Rest (2014) for further research on students' motivations to enroll in summer schools. This allows us to explore the holistic experience for students from Generation Z of international university summer programs.

Table 1. Our sample.

#	Respondent's name	Age	Gender	Continent of origin
1	Maximiliano	23	Male	South America
2	Georgia	21	Female	Oceania
3	Zuri	23	Female	North America
4	Eileen	21	Female	North America
5	Isabella	22	Female	Asia
6	Yazmin	21	Female	North America
7	Kaitlyn	20	Female	North America
8	Emily	22	Female	North America
9	Maria	23	Female	North America
10	Anumita	19	Female	Asia

For our exploratory research, qualitative research was conducted using semi-structured interviews with past and future participants of a European summer program in a French university. Semi-structured interviews were employed to gain deeper insights and analysis of students' motivations for participating in a summer school, their perceptions of current marketing efforts and their needs and expectations from the social media accounts of the program. This qualitative approach allows for a balance between a structured research design and flexibility in exploring perspectives and experiences and gaining an in-depth understanding. A total of 10 participants from Generation Z (Table 1) were selected for interviews, representing 10 different universities and 8 countries. The criteria for choosing interviewees were based on recency and the diversity of experiences, including students from different higher educational institutions and nationalities to provide a range of perspectives on the program.

The semi-structured interviews consisted of a set of predetermined questions and were divided into three parts. The first part focused on their decision to study abroad in a summer school, specifically in this French program. The second part aimed to uncover students' experiences with digital marketing methods, such as the website and social media, during their time as a student, as well as after completing the program as an alumnus. The third part aimed to identify students' most memorable experiences in the program. It is worth noting that depending on the flow of the conversation, additional questions were asked to delve deeper into the subjects discussed when more clarity and detail were needed (Arsel 2017). The answers provided valuable insights into what makes the program special to students, identifying key themes and aspects of the holistic experience that are valuable for the development of a digital marketing strategy to promote the program. Thematic analysis was employed to analyze the interview data. This method involved organizing the data into meaningful groups based on common content, identifying patterns, refining themes, and naming them. Only themes that contributed to the exploration of the research problem were used.

Three main themes emerged from the results of the interviews:

a) A multicultural social experience. Students were driven by their personal aspirations, curiosity for cultural exploration and the desire to improve their language proficiency. Maximiliano: "*I wanted to experience how life abroad works, student life in university. I had an exchange semester abroad before with a Spanish university, but virtually. Now I really wanted to live it*". The intrinsic motivations go together with a keen pursuit of academic enrichment, where summer schools represent an opportunity to earn transferable credits and fulfill the requirements of home universities for having international experiences before graduation. Yazmin explains: "*So I felt like this was the program for me because, one, it was in a place where I could practice my French, and two, I would be getting credit for my degree, which is important*". Another expectation and evident outcome of these programs relates to social and interpersonal aspects, as for Zuni: "*I like the program because I feel like it was a good way to meet new people*". International summer programs serve not merely as academic endeavors, but also as a platform for a vibrant and multicultural social experience. They offer the chance to connect globally and make friends from all over the world, extending the networks across different nationalities. As representatives of Generation Z, our interviewees showed a common pattern of wanting to learn a new culture by living in a new environment and interacting in person with people from it. They not only create connections with students, but also seek to extend career opportunities through communication with professors and professionals who teach in the programs. For many participants, attending international summer school is a vibrant and socially dynamic journey. For others, it serves as an initial personal experience in travelling abroad and living on their own, in a safe environment and academic context. Another common pattern was the view of the program as a chance to experience education in a certain country, before deciding whether to pursue long-term graduate studies abroad or even at the same university.

b) A connected social media experience enriched by WOM. Navigating through the informational landscape reveals a complex mix of both digital and traditional communication and means of recommendation that are utilized by Gen Z to learn more about summer programs and communicate with universities. The pivotal role of home and host university and program websites as primary informational touchpoints is complemented by the explorative and rich visuals offered by social media and other digital platforms. Anumita explains: "*I went to the university website, the courses that were offered. Because I, again, I was looking at the prospect of doing a masters. So, I was just like, let me see how this university ranks in doing a masters*". Furthermore, traditional mediums and personal interactions continue to exercise significant influence: "*I searched for the Instagram social media. There was a student [...]. She was [from] Argentine. I don't remember where she was, but she was studying abroad in the same city, and she shared 'like a day with me', or questions about how it feels to study abroad in this country. So I followed her, and it was amazing because I felt like empathy and closeness*" (Eileen). Pivotal touchpoints cited included the

International Relations Offices of the home universities, as well as friends and professors who once participated in the same program and now recommend it to others. Kaitlyn said: "*Our professor, he had been there a bunch in the past cause I think he's worked with M. (coordinator of the Programs) and maybe like taught there. So, he was a great source of information. He gave recommendations on the weekend programs. He was like, okay, definitely do Normandy*". This emphasizes the importance of word of mouth nowadays for such complex and international educational programs, as already mentioned. In addition to this, our primary sources of information were in-person and virtual Study Abroad Fairs, printed promotional materials distributed between universities and on social media such as Instagram and YouTube. The use of social media varies among participants. Some rely heavily on it, while others use a mix of online information, personal stories and traditional methods. After the program ends, many use social media to stay connected and reminisce "*Because it reminds me of that beautiful moment. I really enjoy seeing the photos. Because even for us, it brings this feeling of nostalgia when students are leaving comments or just putting like on the post when we publish something like that's so nice to still keep in touch in this way*" (Maria). They like to see updates and connect with fellow alumni on platforms like Instagram and Facebook. Participants expressed a desire to keep in touch with the program and the organizers via Instagram, Facebook and newsletters to be able to see the changes made to the program and new students, look back at their memories to experience nostalgia and communicate with other alumni. Isabella explains: "*I think I would like to see, like, Instagram Reels, like, videos, like, the experiences of the students... I think having different perspectives would help. So, like, testimonials from students on their experience, professors and what kind of things they're teaching, so more of the classroom setting, and then also the interns.*"

5. Theoretical and Managerial Contributions

This research serves as a pivotal addition to existing knowledge on international summer schools. It introduces novel ideas and enhances established academic insights in several crucial ways.

Theoretically, the results unveil an element not explicitly covered in the research by Helsky-Lehtola (2015): the expectation of creating lasting international connections. As mentioned by interviewees, what made the program and all the moments so special are the people with whom they spent them and with whom they still keep in touch. Whether staying in contact on social media, going on trips together even after the end of the program, or hoping to meet in the future again, it seems the summer school experience fosters more than temporary connections, but rather provides great opportunities for networking and shared experiences. Torenbeek and Van Rest (2014) acknowledge the possibility of obtaining academic credits and discovering other cultures, but this study goes further in the exploration of the social experience students can have from participation in summer programs. Denton (2002) and Borman (2000) discuss the elements that contribute to a successful summer school program. This study goes further and offers real practical observations on how programs should be designed based on the social experience of the students in order to resonate with them, beyond focusing solely on a dynamic alumni network, as proposed by Helsky-Lehtola (2015).

Our managerial contribution can be summarized in five digital strategies:

1) User-generated content to foster collaboration in content creation. Student engagement can foster a sense of ownership. Generation Z, being driven by a desire for constant changes and improvements for a greater experience, are willing to actively engage when there is an opportunity to do so. They are highly influenced by user-generated content, which is perceived as more meaningful. Such participation could take the form of testimonials, interviews or shared experiences.
2) Storytelling for more personal and trustworthy promotion. Generation Z prefer to hear the firsthand experiences of students, professors and the organization team. Using storytelling in a digital marketing strategy is a specific way to forge such relationships with Generation Z and give students a more comprehensive view of educational programs and outcomes. This method also serves as a powerful emotional marketing tool, which offers real and relatable experiences and insights into program participation. This could help students to visualize the experience they might have if they apply. By fostering an emotional connection, it is possible to increase audience engagement and contribute positively to decision-making.
3) Interactive and engaging content. Providing virtual tours, quizzes and interactive FAQs, as well as inviting followers to join the discussion and share their experiences can help to increase student engagement. This not only improves the consumer experience, with participants receiving the necessary information at different stages of the consumer cycle, but also improves their understanding of the program.
4) Importance of virtual representation. Generation Z, as digital natives, prefer visual content when processing information. The introduction of reels and stories on Instagram contribute to this, as well as YouTube videos about the university. By enhancing the digital experience with visually appealing content for the current generation of students, international summer programs can create an environment for more enjoyable and informative exploration of what is on offer.
5) Utilization of multiple marketing methods and channels. From the digital marketing perspective, Generation Z use multiple platforms to find relevant information about educational programs, communicate with the administration and participants, and share their experience. The findings of this research show the necessity for international summer programs to have a strong digital presence through their website, social media accounts, newsletters and communication via emails.

More specifically, we recommend using social media as a channel not only to provide official information but especially as a tool to spread stories of personal and in-class experiences. This would give prospective students a kind of pre-immersion in the experience, while alumni would have access to memories and be linked to the university and the other participants.

Limitations of the research relate to the fact that it is a single case study and the number and diversity of interview participants. For a broader perspective on promoting international summer programs, traditional and digital marketing methods and the preferences and perceptions of other stakeholders could usefully be investigated.

References

Ait Yassine, F.A. 2023. The effect of digital marketing strategy on customer outcomes. Marketing and Management of Innovations 13: 45–54.

Almukhtar, F., Mahmoodd, N. and Kareem, S. 2021. Search engine optimization: a review. Applied Computer Science 17(1): 70–80.

Arsel, Z. 2017. Asking questions with reflexive focus: A tutorial on designing and conducting interviews. Journal of Consumer Research 44(4): 939–948.

Bamberger, A., Bronshtein, Y. and Yemini, M. 2020. Marketing universities and targeting international students: A comparative analysis of social media data trails. Teaching in Higher Education 25(4): 476–492.

Basha, A. 2019. A study on effective digital marketing strategy in education sector at Bangalore City. International Journal of Research and Analytical Reviews 6(1): 161–169.

Borman, G.D. 2000. The effects of summer school: questions answered, questions raised. Monographs of the Society for Research in Child Development 65(1): 119–127.

Brahnam, C. 2017. The culture of connectivity: A critical history of social media. Book Review. Journal of Business and Technical Communication 31(2): 265–268.

Cooper, H., Charlton, K., Valentine, J.C., Muhlenbruck, L. and Borman, G. 2000. Making the most of summer school: a meta-analytic and narrative review. Monographs of the Society for Research in Child Development 65(1): i–127.

Datareportal. 2023. Digital Around the World. Retrieved from Datareportal: https://datareportal.com/global-digitaloverview#:~:text=A%20total%20of%205.16%20billion,of%20the%20world's%20total%20population.

Denton, D.R. 2002. Summer School: Unfulfilled Promise. ERIC, Atlanta.

Fromm, J. and Read, A. 2018. Marketing to Gen Z: The Rules for Reaching This Vast – and Very Different - Generation of Influencers. AMACOM, New York.

Geçit, B.B. and Kıyak, Ö. 2021. The positive influences of financial omni-channel marketing approach on customer satisfaction. pp. 223–236. *In*: Dinçer, H. and Yüksel, S. (eds.). Financial Strategies in Competitive Markets: Multidimensional Approaches to Financial Policies for Local Companies. Springer Cham, Berlin.

Giunta, C. 2020. Digital marketing platform tools, Generation Z, and cultural considerations. Journal of Marketing Development and Competitiveness 14(2): 63–75.

Gunawan, I., Fung, T. and Silaswara, D. 2020. Digital marketing study, through Instagram media case study of private Universities in the Tangerang region. Primanomics: Jurnal Ekonomi & Bisnis. 18(2): 1–10.

Helsky-Lehtola, U. 2015. A Marketing Strategy for International Summer School. Ph.D. Thesis, Tampere University of Applied Sciences, Tampere, FI.

Iddris, F. 2018. Search Engine Optimization (SEO) As Digital Marketing Strategy for Internationalisation of Higher Education. Proc. of the he 22nd McGill International Entrepreneurship Competition. Sweden: 1–13.

Ikatrinasari, Z.F., Tyas, S.K., Cahyana, B.J. and Purwanto, P. 2020. Development of digital marketing strategy in the education industry. International Review of Management and Marketing 10: 63–67.

Köster, M., Passi, S.R., Bitterer, F., Vuorinen, U. and Karaoglu, N. 2022. Virtual summer schools: Experiences from Finland and Germany. Journal of Virtual Exchange 5: 144–154.

Kotler, P. and Keller, K.L. 2016. A Framework for Marketing Management. Pearson, Boston, MA.

Kotler, P., Kartajaya, H. and Setiawan, I. 2020. Marketing 4.0: L'éré du digital. De Boeck Supérieur, Louvain-la-Neuve.
Kusumawati, A. 2019. Impact of digital marketing on student decision-making process of higher education institution: a case of Indonesia. Journal of e-Learning and Higher Education 1–10.
Motta, J. and Barbosa, M. 2018. Social media as a marketing tool for european and north american universities and colleges. Journal of Intercultural Management 10(3): 125–154.
Munsch, A. 2021. Millenial and Generation Z digital marketing communication and advertising effectiveness: a qualitative exploration. Journal of Global Scholars of Marketing Science 31(1): 10–29.
Ninan, N., Roy, J.C. and Cheriyan, N.K. 2020. Influence of social media marketing on the purchase intention of Gen Z. International Journal of Advanced Science and Technology 29(1): 1692–1702.
Nguyen, D.N. and Tran, L.X. 2021. Applying Marketing 4.0 in Formal University at Vietnamese Universities. European Journal of Business and Management Research. 7(1): 186–189.
Paul, T. and Bihani, P. 2014. Expectation based customer oriented marketing mix. International Journal on Research and Development - A Management Review 3(1): 53–60.
Raj, D.M., Raguraman, M. and Veerappan, R. 2013. Marketing of educational services: a new strategy for customer satisfaction. International Journal of scientific research and management 1(8): 435–440.
Romanovska, A. 2021. Enhancing the Youth' Participation in Research and Promoting Tolerance: Experience of Organizing a Summer School. Proc. of ICERI2021 Conference. Spain: 4551–4557.
Rue, P. 2018. Make Way, Millenials, Here Comes Gen Z. About Campus 23(3): 5–12.
Torenbeek, J. and Van Rest, E. 2014. Summer Schools in Europe: The culmination of a trend or the start of another? European Association for International Education (EAIE), Amsterdam.
Williams, K. and Page, R. 2011. Marketing to the Generations. Journal of Behavioral Studies in Business 3(1): 37–52.

CHAPTER 8

The Intersection of the AMO Model and Sustainable Human Resource Management. A Systematic Literature Review and Research Agenda

Michela Floris and *Roberta Pinna**

1. Introduction

In this historical period, the growing pressure on economic, environmental and social sustainability has made the need for organizations to incorporate sustainability as core activities into their corporate policies and strategies to take a proactive role in controlling the impact of business life on the natural, social and human environments. In general, sustainability includes:

- coping with economic and social changes,
- committing to operating according to ethical and socially responsible practices,
- providing high-quality products and services,
- implementing methods to determine if the organization satisfies its stakeholders' needs.

Department of Economics and Business, University of Cagliari.
* Corresponding author: pinnar@unica

For a long time, organizations have focused on the potential of sustainability to reduce the organization's ecological impact or the consumption of resources and energy. Only a few have considered what sustainability means when dealing with people within their organizations. As emphasized by Bal and Brookes (2022), numerous organizations underscore the significance of sustainability in HRM, and it is evident that status quo approaches to HRM continue to dominate.

Sustainable HRM refers to the creation of HRM systems that simultaneously help a firm achieve its environmental, social and economic goals while recognizing that a firm's HRM system itself has a significant social impact on its employees and the communities they live in (Pfeffer 2010) and that there can be inherent tensions in trying to balance all of its Sustainable HRM objectives.

Several Sustainable Development Goals (SDGs) are relevant for HRM function, such as "Good Health and wellbeing" (SDG 3), "Gender equality" (SDG 5), "Decent work and economic growth" (SDG 8), "reduce inequalities" (SDG 10) and "responsible consumption and production" (SDG 12). Therefore, a SHRM entails considering the economic, ecological and social aspects of company objectives while implementing the human resource function. As some scholars point out (Ehnert 2014), people have an important role in sustainability. HRM's relevance in developing sustainable organizations has often been overlooked in the past and is still mostly ignored today.

HRM aims to explore and design suitable practices for achieving organizational goals and provide suggestions about involving and committing individuals, groups, or managers to ensure their ability and willingness to contribute to organizational goals efficiently and effectively over the long term. Sustainable HRM leads to improved employee engagement, increased employee satisfaction and the protection and promotion of the dignity of the people inside and outside the organizations. What has just been mentioned becomes even more relevant when considering that in recent years, the phenomenon of "quiet quitting" has been increasingly emerging in contemporary organizational contexts (Harter 2022). This event involves avoidance behaviors by employees, which consist of distancing themselves emotionally and cognitively from their work by limiting the resources dedicated to it. For example, they refuse to take on optional tasks, take breaks when necessary, work less intensely and be absent whenever their life commitments require it, even when it may impact the company's objectives, all while still fulfilling their formal duties. In their reflection on the causes of "quiet quitting," Mahand and Caldwell (2023) attribute the reasons for this "silent abandonment" to the organization's inability to meet some of the employees' expectations regarding professional development and career advancement, the ability to autonomously decide how, where, and when to perform their work, exclusion from decision-making processes and the circulation of information, factors that contribute to a sense of disconnection and estrangement from the organization, the organization's indifference to the material and psychological difficulties faced by employees and insensitivity towards them.

Hence, understanding how Sustainable Human Resource Management (SHRM) practices affect employee motivation for engaging in sustainability initiatives and how organizations cultivate capabilities and provide opportunities for employees to participate in sustainability management and individuals' perspectives on their quality of working life becomes crucial. As a result, HR executives must contemplate the sustainability of their HRM systems and its implications for HR practices and strategies.

Considering these factors and the significance of the Ability Motivation Opportunity model (AMO) in HR literature, this chapter sustains that the AMO framework needs to be investigated under the lens of SHRM. Specifically, exploring the AMO model within sustainability issues allows for understanding how organizations currently employ and apply human resources to ensure business and human sustainability. While the Ability Motivation Opportunity (AMO) model has been used as a guiding framework for firms in their selection of HR practices in HRM literature in recent decades (Bos-Nehles et al. 2013), there is a notable absence of empirical studies that delve into how the sustainability vision has been integrated into the AMO model. Indeed, the existence and nature of this relationship have remained unexplored and undisclosed. This chapter, intending to fill this gap, carries out a Systematic Literature Review of the intersection between the AMO model and the SHRM, highlighting the state-of-the-art and proposing a rich research agenda. To our knowledge, scholars still need to propose literature reviews on this topic. Findings show interesting insights and shed light on new unexplored streams of study.

The chapter is organized as follows: the first section introduces the AMO model; the second shows the relationship between SHRM and the AMO model; and the third explains methods, findings, contributions and limitations.

2. The Ability, Motivation and Opportunity Model

The AMO model is a framework used in organizational psychology and management to understand and analyze employee performance and behavior (Appelbaum et al. 2000, Boxall and Purcell 2003, Boselie et al. 2005, Ehrnrooth and Björkman 2012). Appelbaum et al. (2000) developed the AMO framework based on a model proposed by Bailey (1993), and it suggests that an employee's performance and behavior can be influenced by three key factors, employee's ability, motivation and opportunity to participate.

The **ability** dimension refers to the physiological and cognitive capabilities that enable an individual to perform a task effectively, and it is defined by the acronym KSA (knowledge, skills and abilities). In the AMO model framework, when employees possess the required knowledge, skills and competencies to carry out their job responsibilities effectively, it raises the probability of them attaining the desired performance results. Specifically, "ability" plays a crucial role in performance, as employees with more excellent abilities generally exhibit superior performance levels. Thanks to their ability, the employees excel in acquiring and applying job-specific knowledge compared to those with lower ability levels (Kim et al. 2015).

The **motivation** dimension encompasses the psychological factors that inspire an employee's eagerness and dedication to perform their job and achieve specific objectives effectively. It can be viewed as a driving force that guides, energizes and sustains behavior, reflecting the willingness and eagerness of employees to complete tasks (Bos-Nehles et al. 2013). Employees with high levels of intrinsic or extrinsic motivation are more inclined to invest effort, remain engaged and persist in their tasks, leading to enhanced performance. While the ability component underscores employees' capabilities to make a meaningful contribution, motivation revolves around the extent to which they are enthusiastic about utilizing those capabilities.

The **opportunity** dimension, as defined by Blumberg and Pringle (1982), encompasses the external factors and resources outside an individual's direct control. These factors include some work environment factors such as working conditions, leader behavior, open communication, organizational support and individual factors such as autonomy, task significance and the impact employees perceive they have at work. These factors reflect employees' chances to apply their skills and contribute to the firm's success (Ehrnrooth and Björkman 2012). Without suitable opportunities to utilize their abilities and motivation at work, employees will likely make fewer contributions than those provided with such opportunities.

All three elements (opportunity, capacity and willingness) must be present for performance to occur. According to the model, individuals excel in their performance when they possess the necessary capabilities, maintain appropriate motivation and work within an environment that offers opportunities for engagement (Boxall and Purcell 2003, Choi 2014).

3. The AMO Model and Sustainable Human Resource Management

In recent decades, research has made significant progress in applying sustainability principles to social aspects. However, these perspectives often overlook the significance of social resources within organizations and the necessity of planning sustainable work systems from a human factors perspective. In particular, the "quit quitting" phenomenon has made the transition to sustainable HRM even more urgent in the last decade. Quiet quitters are disengaged at work and do not intend to go above and beyond their line of duty. This behavior reflects the organization's inability to create a meaningful relationship with its employees (Zenger and Folkman 2022). Consequently, quiet quitting employees limit their effort at work, often to maintain personal work/life balance or to maintain health and well-being in a high-pressure work environment (Landin et al. 2023).

Among the principal drivers of quiet quitting, there needs to be more feeling cared about, opportunities to learn and grow and connection with the organization's purpose (Harter 2022). The fundamental cause of dissatisfaction of those actively disengaged is that their work needs need to be met. The lack of empathy and compassion toward the employees and toward work-life balance undermines the employee relationship. It conveys that employees need to take second place in organization priorities. Second, the lack of opportunities to learn and grow points to a need for alignment with fundamental values common to most employees, especially GenZ and Millennials. Third, lack of professional fulfillment and meaningfulness of work point to a lack of connection with the organization's purpose, which inevitably leaves employees confused and disengaged, wondering why they are part of that organization. In other words, it lowers their sense of belonging and overall interest and commitment. When employees feel that their organization helps change the world for the better by actively caring about issues that are important to them, it brings meaning and purpose to their work and are fulfilled by the contributions they are making to the company and society.

Consequently, a Sustainable HRM must set three objectives regarding people: to increase work engagement, promote individuals' physical and psychological well-being through a balance between job demands and available resources and promote the work-life balance. Consequently, determining which practices are best suited for exploring the linkage between HRM practices and sustainability remains challenging. Designing sustainable work systems from a human factors perspective necessitates consideration of various elements, including social resources within organizations, employee capacity development and environmental goals. Beyond this core idea, the sustainable work system perspective affirms that a sustainable firm must be engaged in balancing the quality of the working life and organizational performance with sustainable change processes and employment (Docherty et al. 2009). Consequently, employee needs and well-being become an integral part of an organization's human and social goals.

As mentioned in the previous section, the AMO model emphasizes the relevance of employees' capabilities, motivation and opportunities to achieve organizations' goals and to promote a sustainable work environment. The AMO model and SHRM intersect in their shared focus on enhancing employee capabilities, motivation and opportunities, all of which contribute to improved organizational performance and sustainability. However, this intersection appears to be under investigated, and often, scholars who study the AMO model refer to GHRM, mainly focusing on green and, thus, environmental sustainability rather than including economic and social sustainability. To understand which practice can affect sustainable behavior and what factors can be leveraged to encourage more sustainable decision-making, the AMO model could guide the design of interventions to promote a sustainable organizational environment and behaviors. For example, regarding ability improvement, the AMO model underlines the importance of employees' skills, which aligns with SHRM's goal of developing employees' skills and knowledge to foster sustainability within the organization.

Regarding the motivations dimension, SHRM strives to design a work environment that encourage employee engagement and commitment, contributing to performance and sustainability. Motivation-enhancing practices foster employees' efforts to achieve goals and achieve high performance. The design of working conditions, delivery of work pressure in work performance, learning at work, autonomy and work enrichment all contribute to workability and the sustainable success of individuals and the organization. These factors link with non-financial rewards, employee engagement, learning and development and are fundamental to a sustainable organization (Harry 2014).

Opportunity-enhancing HRM practices are used to boost 'employees' opportunities to perform, such as taking part in the decision-making process, horizontal communication, knowledge sharing and job enrichment (Schimansky 2014). In addition, autonomy-enhancing practices are specifically devised to decentralize decision-making processes and grant employees greater autonomy within their work environment (Sarikwal and Gupta 2013).

Taking into account sustainable values in three dimensions of AMO model means not only supporting the organization's sustainable development strategy, but also contributing to develop the skills and trust of employees, and increasing their engagement in sustainable development; emphasizing fair treatment, development, and the well-being of employees; focuses on the well-being of the employees and external stakeholders; and to supports environmentally-friendly organizational practices.

In conclusion, if until now, HR managers have adopted a mass approach to the management of human resources, from the perspective of sustainability, it becomes necessary to have an approach that places the individual as a whole at the center, regardless of gender, ethnicity, disability, religious or political belief, age and sexual orientation. Through the implementation of the SHRM approach, it is possible to have the support of highly qualified employees who understand and apply the principles of sustainable development in their work.

4. Methods

This study adopts a Systematic Literature Review (SLR) because it provides a comprehensive overview of literature related to the aim of this study and synthesizes previous work to strengthen a particular topic's foundation of knowledge while adhering to the concepts of transparency and bias reduction (Pittway 2008, Tranfield et al. 2003). Based on the combination of SCOPUS and Google Scholar databases, which include many leading journals, this study analyzes the articles from 2016 to 2022 in the field of Social Sciences with research that directly or indirectly applies the AMO model in their studies.

4.1 Data Collection

The search was made in SCOPUS and Google Scholars using the following keywords and phrases in Title, Abstract and Keywords: "Sustainability" or "Sustainable Human Resource Management," or "Green Human Resource Management", and "AMO model" or "Ability-motivation-opportunity model" or "ability", "motivation", "opportunity". Moreover, we included only English language articles published in academic journals and collected on the subject of Social Science. Table 1 synthesizes inclusion and exclusion criteria.

A total of 474 scientific papers were collected. Consequently, duplicates were eliminated, resulting in 381 remaining articles. Next, the abstracts were analyzed to determine their relevance to our research objectives. Following this refinement process, the total number of articles was reduced to 170. Lastly, a comprehensive

Table 1. Inclusion and exclusion criteria.

Inclusion criteria	Exclusion criteria
- Scientific papers in journals indexed in *Scopus* or *Google Scholar*. - Articles or reviews published from the year 2016 to 2022, in the field of Social Sciences, especially those related to the sustainability and human resources management. - Articles written in English. - Research that directly or indirectly (linking ability, motivation or opportunity practice) apply the AMO model in their analysis.	- Articles or reviews published before 2016. - Articles written in languages other than English. - Research not related to human resources management. - Research that does not apply the AMO model in their analysis. - Research related to AMO framework for explaining consumption patterns, consumer behavior, consumer psychology, advertisement strategies or marketing approaches.

review of the full papers was conducted, leading to the identification of 94 publications (Table 2 in Appendix) that met the criteria for inclusion in our study.

5. Findings

Findings reveal the existence of an underdeveloped field of research. As expected, we found that the number of articles could have been higher. Moreover, the selected papers refer mainly to the environmental dimension of sustainability, highlighting that sustainability is still approached as a "green" side of society and organizations.

Regarding the geographical affiliation of the authors of the publications, it is notable that in Asia, there is a significantly higher number of articles compared to other continents, especially in China, Malaysia, and Pakistan. These countries have seen a continuous increase in entrepreneurial development, paralleled by businesses' growing focus on sustainability across their three dimensions (economic, environmental and social). In the European context, however, there is a more even distribution of articles compared to the Asian context. In the remaining continents and the Middle East, the geographical distribution of articles appears well-balanced. Limited interest is apparent among scholars from the American and Oceanic contexts.

Concerning the journals, the 94 selected articles have been published in internationally renowned journals. There is a higher presence of articles from two particular journals: "Sustainability" with 17 articles, and "Journal of Cleaner Production" with six articles. The former is an international, interdisciplinary, peer-reviewed and open-access journal that focuses on human beings' environmental, cultural, economic and social sustainability. The latter is an international journal that concentrates on research related to environmental and sustainability issues in businesses, institutions and societies. Additionally, a substantial number of articles originate from the journals *Corporate Social Responsibility and Environmental Management* and *International Journal of Research in Human Resource Management*. The latter is a peer-reviewed journal that analyzes the growing role of strategic human resource management in a rapidly evolving global environment. Lastly, the scientific journal *International Journal of Environment Research and Public Health*, which is open-access, contributes significantly to examining all aspects related to environmental and public health.

Regarding the research methodology, quantitative methods are prevalent. However, there are differences in the research approach. In 34 articles, some researchers conducted quantitative analyses using surveys and questionnaires, interpreting the results without resorting to statistical tools. In contrast, others (42 articles) employed statistical software, such as Smart PLS-SEM, for their analyses.

A substantial number of articles, totaling 20, emerged from applying various theories in real business contexts. Finally, the last three categories feature a similar number of articles: 10 articles using a mixed methodology (combining both qualitative and quantitative analysis), 13 articles resulting from literature reviews and 11 articles derived from the analysis of business cases, primarily through a multi-case approach, with data gathered through semi-structured interviews and meticulous document analysis.

Lastly, the final aspect analyzed pertains to the theories adopted. Thirty-eight out of the total 121 articles rely on well-known theories. Just under half of them (15 articles) base their studies on the AMO framework. Additionally, four articles are grounded in the Resource-Based View theory, which posits that a firm's internal resources are crucial to achieving sustainable and enduring competitive advantage. The remaining articles draw on various diverse theories, among which the Stakeholder theory is worth mentioning. Another point of interest is the use of two theories in the same scientific research article, which is observed in six articles where the AMO model is employed alongside other theories.

5.1 The Main Themes

This section presents the results of the content analysis of the selected articles. Three main thematic areas were identified, each with further sub-themes, as summarized in Table 3.

5.1.1 Green HRM Impact and Effects on Employees and Organizations

The first thematic area comprises 44 articles, divided into numerous sub-themes, focusing on the impact of Green Human Resources Management practices on employees and organizations. Among these, 30 articles delve into the detailed examination of employee behavior within the organization. Researchers (Dumont et al. 2017) have defined this behavior as combining individual actions to reduce adverse environmental effects. However, as organizations often define social objectives alongside environmental ones, it is crucial to include this dimension in the sustainable organizational change process. Employee behavior, therefore, is identified as a pro-social attitude adopted by employees that contributes value to the organization. This behavior is further divided into two aspects: sustainable behavior within one's job role and voluntary sustainable behavior beyond one's job duties. The former concerns sustainable actions taken by employees following contractual

Table 3. The main themes.

Theme	Sub-themes	Articles	Tot. Articles
Green HRM impact and effects on employees and organizations	Green HR practice	2, 4, 5, 8,13, 19, 22, 24, 31, 32, 33, 36, 37, 40, 42, 43, 45, 47, 54, 61,63, 64, 66, 71, 75, 76, 77, 78, 81, 82, 83, 84, 89, 93	44
	Engagement and satisfaction	1,6, 44	
	Sustainable performance	35, 57, 58, 60, 73	
	Organizational climate	25, 29	
Evolution of the AMO model for a sustainable work systems	Ability, Motivation and Opportunity practices	11, 12, 14,15, 16,17, 18, 20, 21, 23, 26, 27, 28, 30, 39, 41, 46, 48, 49, 50, 51, 55, 56, 59,62, 65, 67, 68, 70, 72, 74, 85, 86, 87, 88, 90, 94	37
Other drivers of sustainability	Creativity and Innovation	3, 38	13
	Corporate Social Responsibility	7, 9, 10, 34, 52, 53, 69,79, 80, 92, 91	

and organizational constraints specific to their roles. The latter involves spontaneous actions in favor of sustainability that go beyond their job requirements, even though they are not explicitly required. As highlighted in Articles 24 and 75, Green HRM practices significantly influence the development of employees' environmental values and, consequently, their behavior in the workplace. These practices encompass activities such as efficient resource use, waste reduction, proper disposal, energy savings and recycling. They also involve employee engagement in corporate social responsibility initiatives, positive attitudes towards workplace diversity and proactive involvement in sustainability-related actions (Articles 36, 37, 70, 78). In this way, employees are empowered to recognize and rectify negative behaviors related to sustainability, benefiting both the organization and society by preventing further problems. In Article 77, it is suggested that limited sustainable knowledge among employees can hinder the establishment of a long-term relationship between employees and the organization. To prevent this, Article 40 asserts that employees can share their knowledge, enabling the organization to gain a sustainable competitive advantage. As highlighted in Article 42, the benefits are substantial, as recruiting and selecting potential candidates with significant sustainability knowledge facilitates the achievement of organizational strategic objectives.

Another extensively analyzed aspect is employee engagement and job satisfaction from adopting Green HRM practices. Regarding engagement, several articles consider that implementing customized training programs and compensation systems that reward sustainability actions can motivate employees to achieve the organization's sustainable objectives. Employees are also more likely to participate in company initiatives related to sustainability and address any related organizational issues. Another factor fostering their involvement is the support employees perceive from the company. Articles 1 and 44 suggest that organizations showing greater interest in employees' sustainable activities lead to increased engagement. Engaged employees tend to spontaneously engage in sustainable behavior at the workplace, going beyond their job roles and without seeking additional benefits. Job satisfaction of employees plays a crucial role in the organization's competitive advantage. Green HRM practices certainly contribute to increased employee happiness, as stated in Article 6, where motivated employees take pride in actively participating in the sustainable change process. However, employee well-being and productivity are most correlated when employees' ethical and sustainable ideals align with the companies. Therefore, clarifying the company's sustainable objectives to employees fosters improved performance for both employees and the organization.

Moreover, seven articles explore the role of Green HRM practices in achieving sustainable performance, both by employees and the organization. According to scholars (Roscoe et al. 2019), sustainable performance is the perception of employees effectively executing actions to protect the environment and contribute to organizational goals. Researchers in the analyzed articles concur that effective human resource management, when carried out correctly, is one of the best business strategies to achieve high sustainable performance. As stated in Article 64, the advantages are significant for the organization, leading to lower costs, increased efficiency, and better employee retention. Subsequently, it benefits society as a whole, as engaged employees dedicated to the change process activate behaviors aimed at resource conservation or material recycling, thereby eliminating inefficient activities.

The last sub-theme, explores the influence of organizational climate on employees' sustainable behavior. Researchers argue that a positive and sustainability-oriented organizational climate can psychologically and socially influence employees' behavior toward efficient performance, leading them to work with utmost dedication. Well-defined sustainable human resource management practices facilitate this.

5.1.2 Evolution of AMO Model for Sustainable Work Systems

In this thematic area are 37 articles based on the evolution of the Ability, Motivation, Opportunity (AMO) model to promote sustainable work systems. These articles have been categorized into three sub-themes.

The first sub-theme focused on the Ability dimension, examining the role played by recruitment and selection process, training and development programs. Recruitment and selection process play a crucial role because the problem is to hire the best candidate who best fit the organization's needs over the long term (Article 65). The recruitment process ensures that potential candidates understand and share the company's values. To be more sustainable over the long term the main problem for HRM professionals will have to be carefully choose and nurture human resource. Therefore, organizations must build a reliable sustainability reputation to attract candidates who contribute to its culture. A more sustainable approach to HRM management calls for developing and enthusing new hires—that is, getting them "engaged" with the goals of the company and showing them that they are excited about working for just and sustainable companies. Building trust and having open lines of communication are the keys to getting employees interested in their employer's goals, particularly the long-term ones, and sustainability. For employees of generation Y, who have only recently entered the workforce, this participation is especially crucial. Workers may feel that their efforts are the result of the labors of those who came before them in the organization if they are engaged and driven in this way. Additionally, the organization's website and other informational channels should prominently display its environmental strategy and policies, allowing potential candidates to see its commitment to sustainability and be more attracted. Therefore, sustainable recruitment is about communicating the organization's environmental values and implementing practical methods to minimize environmental impact. The scholars show that sustainable recruitment can help organizations achieve growth goals quickly, benefiting employers and employees. Almost all researchers in the selected articles consider the set of practices related to training and development as the most important, as it allows the organization to compete in a changing environment and change the behavior of both managerial and non-managerial staff. HRM will place a lot more emphasis on actual learning and human capital development if it is to be sustainable. Articles 55 based on the AMO model, has highlighted that organizations in order to be able to adapt to change and create new ways of working, they must support and encourage individuals who are able to learn and come up with new ideas. Because of this, a key component of strategy must be sustainability in order to ensure that innovation and development are centered on people and directly relate to broader societal and environmental issues. By utilizing education, expertise, pre-existing infrastructure and capabilities, organizations can maintain their competitive edge and contribute to the economic and social stabilization of society. Articles 88 and 89 note that training alone cannot rapidly advance employees' professional growth. It becomes necessary to motivate employees to achieve better performance and encourage them to acquire new knowledge and skills applicable in the present and future. Through sustainable training, employees understand the importance of proactively addressing sustainability issues. However, only some organizations implement training and development programs that guide employees toward sustainable management of their job roles while cultivating their skills and professional competencies. The resulting benefits are evident: it significantly increases employees' attention to sustainability issues in the workplace and daily life (Article 41) or enhances the performance level of organization members, employees and managers. HRM may go beyond corporate boundaries by showcasing the advantages of applied inventive creativity and educating both current and prospective employees on how learning can lead to prosperity and well-being.

From the Motivation dimension perspective, the most important practices are usually based on compensation and performance management, job security, internal promotions and incentives. Organizations must integrate benefits into the organizational compensation system to promote sustainable employee behaviors and reward employee activities (Articles 62 and 90). Companies should include sustainable objectives and regular performance goals to provide feedback on employees' progress and ensure the actual effectiveness of the organizational sustainability policy (Articles 16, and 62). HRM may create systems of active performance management that cascade from strategic direction to individual employees, clearly defining the organization's sustainability goals beyond just financial ones. The benefit may be closely related to non-financial domains like chances for skill development, learning and development opportunities (including lateral career movements), or opportunities to participate in community or environmental protection initiatives. HRM play an important role in order to guarantee that people wellbeing and maintenance of a sustainable workforce is central to the HRM vision and strategy. The redesign of working conditions, autonomy and work enrichment and learning at work all contribute to workability and the sustainable success of individuals and the organization. These factors link with non-financial rewards, employee engagement, learning and development and are fundamental to the sustainable organization. These elements are interconnected with non-monetary incentives, employee involvement, learning and development and form the cornerstone of a sustainable company. Consequently, a SHRM practice that establish workplace resources for employees in term of job resources (autonomy, task variety, training, compensation schemes and performance feedback) helps grow personal resources (competence and resilience) and mitigate feelings of discomfort, reduce stress and enhance well-being and individual performance.

The last dimension of the model is Opportunity. To achieve better performance and adhere to their sustainable strategy, companies must involve employees in decision-making and empower them to make such decisions. Delegating decision-making from the top hierarchical level to the low level through autonomy and information sharing is Opportunity enhancing for the employees within an organization. (Article 86). In this way, it can increase employee commitment, satisfaction and sense of belonging to the company, facilitating sustainable organizational management. Employee's involvement in the decision-making indicates top management's trust in them, which enhances employee satisfaction and leads to better organizational outcomes. Employee participation and involvement in workplave affect the employee's job performance because when they are close up to the organization's work, they are skilled and most competent to make suggestions for the success of the organization. Consequently, top management should be authorized and allowed to increase their participation in the organization's decision-making (Article 55). A sustainable work system and employee participation encourage and promotes business sustainability. Based on the above arguments, it is clear that employee participation plays a significant role in job performance

(Article 55). Factors such as organizational support atmosphere positively impact employees' behavior, encouraging employees to participate more in organizational extra-role behaviour relating organization's sustainable goal, and inspiring employees to promote more sustainable ideas (Articles 51 and 39). Supportive supervision embodies the chance to excel, whereas Opportunity signifies the invitation to engage and actively participate. Through their conduct, leaders can foster opportunities that promote employees' personal and professional development, facilitate the enhancement of employees' skills and cultivate avenues for active participation. In a supportive supervision setting, the work environment offers support to team members. As some scholars point (Article 48) out, when an employee believes that her or his supervisor or organization is supportive, the employee will demonstrate more favorable work-related attitudes and behaviors. Supervisory support manifests through diverse behaviors, including fostering participation opportunities, enhancing the collective skills and methods of the group, defining purpose and objectives, cultivating dedication, eliminating externally imposed barriers and creating platforms for performance.

5.1.3 Other Drivers of Sustainability

The final thematic area delves into other factors that, as noted by the authors of the selected articles, can impact the cultivation of sustainable behavior within organizations. In this segment, we have 21 articles, with seven exploring the role of innovation, while the rest concentrating on Corporate Social Responsibility (CSR).

Concerning the seven articles that examine the influence of innovation, researchers have collectively observed a relatively limited number of studies investigating how human resource management practices affect a company's innovation capacity. For instance, in Articles 15, 27 and 46, the research explores the impact of sustainable innovation and workplace creativity on Green HRM practices and organizational performance. The scholars affirm that the generation of sustainable idea created through the interaction between employees and situational factors will inevitably be influenced by AMO factors. In this thematic area, most articles have underscored that the Ability, Motivation, Opportunity (AMO) model linked to sustainable innovation positively influences corporate performance. For example, Article 3 emphasizes that the Ability dimension, rooted in innovation, contributes the most to sustainable organizational performance compared to other dimensions. On the other hand, Articles 93, 105 and 110 highlight the scarcity of research into how HRM practices influence employees as a source of innovation. Researchers consider it crucial to understand the impact of these practices on employees as it leads to increased job satisfaction. Recognition, self-fulfillment, career advancement and other job aspects significantly influence how employees perceive their roles.

The remaining articles focus on the impact of Corporate Social Responsibility (CSR) on sustainable organizational performance and human resource management. Articles 50 and 67 investigate this topic using the AMO model, highlighting that a company with robust Green HRM practices achieves superior performance and fosters a more favorable reputation for stakeholders and customers. In this regard, Articles 24, 73, 101 and 125 concur that employees prefer working for companies that champion sustainability and thus possess a strong sustainable culture. Sustainable culture is defined by researchers as a set of beliefs and knowledge about the environment held by employees, as well as actions aimed at minimizing negative environmental impacts. In particular, the article 52 highlight that to support employees in addressing the big challenges it is more important for organizations to develop an approach to SHRM practice based on common value, such as dignity, solidarity, and reciprocity. The SHRM regards employee welfare and interests as crucial components of an organization's human and social objectives. Accomplishing these facets establishes the groundwork for HRM to assist organizations in achieving their broader goals. Consequently, the probability of employees exhibiting virtuous behavior is significantly higher within such a context.

The remaining articles reveal that, in the past, there needed to be more understanding of how Green HRM practices could influence employee performance. Therefore, researchers have discovered that such practices can amplify the impact of CSR on employees' sustainable behavior. In Article 127, scholars assert that employee well-being is linked to Social Responsibility. Aligning corporate objectives with these aspects could optimize organizational efficiency, impacting employees' sustainable behavior and overall organizational performance.

6. The Research Agenda

The findings suggest that understanding how SHRM practices influence employee motivation to become involved in sustainability activities needs to catch up to how organizations develop abilities and provide employees with opportunities to be involved in sustainability management and organizational efforts. The Systematic Literature Review provides interesting points for reflection and numerous suggestions for future research. In this regard, below are several themes on which new lines of research could be developed, along with numerous research questions to which scholars are invited to propose interesting answers.

Themes:

- Exploring the influence of sustainability in adopting human resource management practices within an organization.
- Evaluating how sustainable HRM practices can impact the behavior and social and psychological well-being of employees.
- Enlarging the study by analyzing a larger sample and considering other geographic, corporate or industry contexts related to the research topic.
- Investigating all GHRM practices to understand the phenomenon and its implications comprehensively.

- Considering the role of all organization members in achieving sustainable organizational goals.
- Studying the AMO model in less-developed countries to generalize research results and identify the most effective sustainable practices for employees and organizations.
- Investigating the impact that technological advancements can have on SHRM practices.
- Exploring whether there are additional sustainable AMO model practices that may have a more significant effect than current ones.
- Exploring the role played by employees' values and perceptions of sustainable practices and the corporate innovation process to understand how to enhance sustainable organizational performance.
- Proposing comparative studies of contexts where SHRM practices are present with contexts where they are not to demonstrate the advantages of organizational and social performance.

Research questions:

- Does the individual have the necessary information and understanding of sustainable behavior?
- Does the individual possess the required skills to carry out the behavior effectively?
- Does the individual have access to the physical, financial and social resources necessary for sustainable behavior?
- Is this the internal desire or sense of satisfaction from engaging in sustainable behavior?
- Could it be a personal belief in sustainability's importance or the behavior's intrinsic rewards?
- Do incentives exist that encourage sustainable behavior (financial, recognition, social approval)?
- Does the physical environment exert pressure on sustainable behavior?
- Does it support or hinder the behavior?
- Do social norms, peer influences or community represent support for sustainable behavior?
- Are there laws or regulations that encourage or discourage sustainable behavior?

7. Conclusions

This chapter has conducted a Systematic Literature Review of the intersection between the AMO model and SHRM. Even if focused on GHRM, the comprehensive examination of prior research has shed light on the fundamental interrelationships among employee capabilities, motivation and opportunity, as delineated in the AMO model and the principles of SHRM. The review of the existing literature indicates that the AMO model is used to justify research rather than guide research.

The analysis has emphasized the importance of integrating human resource practices with sustainability targets, acknowledging the crucial contribution of employees in attaining organizational performance and sustainability goals. The convergence of these two paradigms highlights the significance of establishing a conducive work environment that cultivates employee engagement, growth and ethical leadership while simultaneously advocating for sustainable practices.

The incorporation of the AMO model into SHRM presents a promising opportunity for organizations to improve their performance, encourage sustainable practices and cultivate a workforce that is both competent and motivated to contribute to a more sustainable future. This study will be a helpful resource for scholars, practitioners, and policymakers interested in investigating and adopting SHRM management solutions that the AMO model guides. We advocate for additional empirical research and case studies to explore the practical ramifications of this intersection. These investigations will ultimately contribute to advancing sustainable organizational practices, improving employees' well-being and preserving the environment.

References

Ababneh, O. 2021. How do green HRM practices affect employees' green behaviors? The role of employee engagement and personality attributes. Journal of Environmental Planning and Management 64(7): 1204–1226.

Abbas, Z., Khan, A.G., Smaliukienė, R., Zámečník, R., Hussain, K. and Mubarik, S. 2022. Green HRM pursuit of social sustainability in the hotels: AMO theoretical perspective. Calitatea 23(190): 41–50.

Aboradan, M. 2022. The effect of green HRM on employee green behaviors in higher education: the mediating mechanism of green work engagement, International Journal of Organizational Analysis 30(1): 7–23

Abu Elnasr, E.S., Ahmed, H. and Ibrahim, E. 2020. Influences of green human resources management on environmental performance in small lodging enterprises: the role of green innovation. Sustainability 12(24): 10371.

Adeel, M., Mahmood, S., Khan, K. and Saleem, S. 2022. Green HR practices and environmental performance: The mediating mechanism of employee outcomes and moderating role of environmental values. Frontiers Environmental Sciences 10: 1001100.

Adjei-Bamfo, P., Bempong, B., Osei, J. and Kusi-Sarpong, S. 2020. Green candidate selection for organizational environmental management. International Journal of Manpower 41(7): 1081–109.

Ahmed, M., Guo Q., Qureshi, M.A., Raza, S.A., Khan, K.A. and Salam, J. 2021. Do green HR practices enhance green motivation and proactive environmental management maturity in hotel industry? International Journal of Hospitality Management 94, art. NO. 10285.

Aizgool Mahmoud, R.H. 2020. Nexus between green HRM and green management towards fostering green values. Management Science Letters 11.2.

Alenzi Mohamad, A.S., Jaaffar, A.H. and Khudari, M. 2022. The mediating effect of organisational sustainability and employee behaviour on the relationship between GHRM and sustainable performance in Qatar. WSEAS Transactions on Business and Economics 19: 1430–1442.

Ali Ababneh, O.M. 2021. How do green HRM practices affect employees' green behaviors? The role of employee engagement and personality attributes. Journal of Environmental Planning and Management 64(7): 1204–1226.

Andjarwati, T., Budiarti, E., Audah, A.K., Khouri, S. and Rębilas, R. 2019. The impact of green human resource management to gain enterprise sustainability. Polish Journal of Management Studies 20(2): 93–103.

Ansari, N.Y., Farrukh, M. and Raza, A. 2021. Green human resource management and employees pro-environmental behaviours: Examining the underlying mechanism. Corporate Social Responsibility and Environmental Management 28(1): 229–238.

Anwar Nosheen, Mahmood Nik Hasnaa, Yusoff Yusliza and Khalid Waqas. 2018. Review of green human resource management: from the lens of ability-motivation-opportunity framework. Advanced Science Letters 24(4): 2507–2510.

Appelbaum, E., Bailey, T., Berg, P. and Kalleberg, A. 2000. Manufacturing Advantage: Why High-performance Work Systems Pay Off. Ithaca, NY: Cornell University Press.

Asghar Afshar, J., Tahereh, M. and Najla, S. 2021. Employees' environmentally responsible behavior: the critical role of environmental justice perception. Sustainability: Science, Practice and Policy 17(1): 1–14.

Awan, F.H., Dunnan, L., Jamil, K. and Gul, R.F. 2022. Stimulating environmental performance via green human resource management, green transformational leadership, and green innovation: a mediation-moderation model. Enviromental Science and Pollution Research 30: 2958–2976.

Aykan, E. 2017. Gaining a competitive advantage through green human resource management. Corporate Governance and Strategic Decision Making. IntechOpen.

Bahrami, L., Safaie, N. and Hamidi, H. 2021. Effect of motivation, opportunity and ability on human resources information security management considering the roles of attitudinal, behavioral and organizational factors. International Journal of Engineering 34(12): 2624–2635.

Bailey, T. 1993. Discretionary effort and the organization of work: Employee participation and work reform since Hawthorne. Teachers College and Conservation of Human Resources, Columbia University.

Bano, S., Aijaz, U. and Athar, A. 2022. High performance work system (HPWS) in the IT sector of Pakistan: An application of ability-motivation-opportunity model. Human Nature Journal of Social Sciences 3(3): 361–387.

Blumberg, M. and Pringle, C.D. 1982. The missing opportunity in organizational research: Some implications for a theory of work performance. Academy of Management Review 7(4): 560–569.

Boselie, P., Dietz, G. and Boon, C. 2005. Commonalities and contradictions in HRM and performance research. Human Resource Management Journal 15(3): 67–94. http://dx.doi.org/10.1111/j.1748-8583.2005.tb00154.x.

Bos-Nehles, A.C., Van Riemsdijk, M.J. and Kees Looise, J. 2013. Employee perceptions of line management performance: applying the AMO theory to explain the effectiveness of line managers' HRM implementation. Human Resource Management 52(6): 861–877.

Bombiak, E. and Marciniuk-Kluska, A. 2018. Green human resource management as a tool for the sustainable development of enterprises: polish young company experience. Sustainability 10(6): 1739.

Boxall, P. and Purcell, J. 2003. Strategy and Human Resource Management. London: Palgrave Macmillan.

Chen, S., Wanxing, J., Xin, Li and Han, G. 2021. Effect of employees' perceived green HRM on their workplace green behaviors in oil and mining industries: based on cognitive-affective system theory. International Journal of Environmental Research and Public Health 18(8): 4056.

Choi, J.-H. 2014. The HR-performance link using two differently measured HR practices. Asia Pacific Journal of Human Resources 52(3): 370–387. http://dx.doi.org/10.1111/1744-7941.12009.

Cuifang, L. and Rui, W. 2019. Research on the influencing factors of employees' green behavior from the perspective of AMO. In 4th International Social Sciences and Education Conference (ISSEC 2019), China.

Cummings, L.L. and Schwab, D.P. 1973. Performance in Organizations. Scott, Foresman and Company, Glenview, IL.

Dahlin, K.B., Chuang, Y.T. and Roulet, T.J. 2018. Opportunity, motivation, and ability to learn from failures and errors: Review, synthesis, and ways to move forward. Academy of Management Annals 12(1): 252–277.

Dasí, À., Pedersen, T., Barakat, L.L. and Alves, T.R. 2021. Teams and project performance: An ability, motivation, and opportunity approach. Project Management Journal 52(1): 75–89.

Docherty, P., Forslin, J. and Shani, A.B. 2002. Creating sustainable work systems: emerging perspectives and practice.

Dumont, J., Shen, J. and Deng, X. 2017. Effects of green HRM practices on employee workplace green behavior: the role of psychological green climate and employee green values. Human Resources Management 56(4): 613–627.

Edgar, F., Blaker, N.M. and Everett, A.M. 2021. Gender and job performance: linking the high performance work system with the ability–motivation–opportunity framework. Personnel Review 50(1): 47–63.

Ehnert, I., Harry, W. and Zink, K.J. 2013. Sustainability and HRM: An introduction to the field. pp. 3–32. In Sustainability and Human Resource Management: Developing Sustainable Business Organizations. Berlin, Heidelberg: Springer Berlin Heidelberg.

Ehnert Ina, Parsa Sepideh, Roper Ianc, Wagner Marco and Muller-Camen Michael. 2016. Reporting on sustainability and HRM: a comparative study of sustainability reporting practices by the world's largest companies. The International Journal of Human Resource Management 27(1).

Ehrnrooth, M. and Björkman, I. 2012. An integrative HRM process theorization: Beyond signalling effects and mutual gains: An integrative HRM process theorization. Journal of Management Studies 49(6): 1109–1135.

Elshaer Ibrahim, A., Abu Elnasr, E. Sobaih, Meqbel Aliedan and Alaa M.S. Azazz. 2021. The effect of green human resource management on environmental performance in small tourism enterprises: mediating role of pro-environmental behaviors. Sustainability 13(4): 1956.

Engin Ari, Osman M. Karatepe, Hamed Rezapouraghdam and Turgay Avci. 2020. A conceptual model for green human resource management: indicators, differential pathways, and multiple pro-environmental outcomes. Sustainability 12(17): 7089.

Ercantan, O. and Eyupoglu, S. 2022. How do green human resource management practices encourage employees to engage in green behavior? Perceptions of university students as prospective employees. Sustainability 14(3): art. N. 1718.

Faezah Juhari Noor, Yusliza Mohd Yusoff, Maometto Zikri and Fawehinmi Olawole. 2022. Promoting employee ecological behavior through green initiatives. International Journal of Sustainable Development and Planning 17(1): 41–49.

Fang, L., Shi, S., Gao, J. and Li, X. 2022. The mediating role of green innovation and green culture in the relationship between green human resource management and environmental performance. Plos One 17(9).

Fawehinmi, O., Yusliza, M.Y., Wan Kasim, W.Z., Mohamad, Z. and Sofian Abdul Halim, M.A. 2020. Exploring the interplay of green human resource management, employee green behavior, and personal moral norms. Sage Open 10(4): 2158244020982292.

Fiza Amjad et al. 2021. Effect of green human resource management practices on organizational sustainability: the mediating role of environmental and employee performance. Environmental Science and Pollution Research 28: 28191–28206.

Gallup, State of the Global Workplace: 2022 Report.

Garavan, T., Ullah Irfan, O'Brien Fergal, Darcy Colette, Wisetsri Worakamol, Afshan Gul and Mughal Yasir Hayat. 2022. Employee perceptions of individual green HRM practices and voluntary green work behaviour: a signalling theory perspective. Asian Pacific Journal of Human Resources.

Guerci, M., Montanari, F., Scapolan, A. and Epifanio, A. 2016. Green and nongreen recruitment practices for attracting job applicants: exploring independent and interactive effects. The International Journal of Human Resource Management 27(2): 129–150.

Gull, S. and Idrees, H. 2022. Green training and organizational efficiency: mediating role of green competencies. European Journal of Training and Development 46(1/2): 105–11.

Harter, J. 2022. Is quiet quitting real. Gallup. com.

Harry, W. 2014. The relevance of the vision of sustainability to HRM practice. pp. 401–419. In Sustainability and Human Resource Management: Developing Sustainable Business Organizations. Berlin, Heidelberg: Springer Berlin Heidelberg.

He Jie, Alastair M. Morrison and Hao Zhang. 2021. Being sustainable: The three-way interactive effects of CSR, green human resource management, and responsible leadership on employee green behavior and task performance. Corporate Social Responsibility and Environmental Management 28.3: 1043–1054.

Hosna, H. and Kaoutar, E. 2022. Green Human Resource Management: An Exploratory Study from Moroccan ISO 14001 Certified Companies, Corporate Social Responsibility.

Hu, X., Khan Shumaila, M., Huang, S., Abbas, J., Matei Mirabela, C. and Badulescu, D. 2022. Employees' green enterprise motivation and green creative process engagement and their impact on green creative performance. International Journal of Environmental Research and Public Health 10(19).

Hughes, J. 2007. The ability-motivation-opportunity framework for behavior research in IS. 40th Annual Hawaii International Conference on System Sciences (HICSS'07) 1–10. http://dx.doi.org/10.1109/hicss.2007.518.

Huo, X., Arooj, A., Nabeel, R. and Nauman, M. 2022. The role of green human resource management practices in driving green performance in the context of manufacturing SMEs. Sustainability 14(24): 16776.

Iftikar, T., Hussein, S., Malik, M.I., Hyder, S., Kalem, M. and Saqib, A. 2021. Green human resource management and pro-environmental behaviour nexus with the lens of AMO theory. Cogent Business and Management 9.

Irani, F. and Kilic, H. 2022. An assessment of implementing green HRM practices on environmental performance: The moderating role of green process innovation. Journal of Global Hospitality and Tourism 1(1): 16–30.

Jia, J., Huanxin, L., Tachia, C. and Dongqing, H. 2018. The continuous mediating effects of GHRM on employees' green passion through transformational leadership and green creativity. Sustainability 10(9).

Kalimullah, K., Muhammad Shahid, S., Qaisar Khan Sher, A. and Murtaza, M.N. 2022. Organizational Psychology, Frontiers in Psychology Relationship Among Green Human Resource Management, Green Knowledge Sharing, Green Commitment, and Green Behavior: A Moderated Mediation Model. Original Research.

Kang Ya, C., Hsiao Hsien-Sheng and Ni Jia Yi. 2022. The role of sustainable training and reward in influencing employee accountability perception and behavior for corporate sustainability. Sustainability (Svizzera) 14(18).

Kanika, S. 2016. Conceptualization of green HRM and green HRM practices: commitment to environment sustainability. International Journal of Advanced Scientific Research and Management 1(8), August.

Kaur, S., Sehgal Jagdish, K. and Grima, S. 2022. Virtual hiring: an effective green human resource management practice. International Journal of Sustainable Development and Planning 17: 1699–1704.

Khan, A.J., Ul Hameed, W., Iqbal, J., Shah, A.A., Tariq, M. and Bashir, F. 2022. Green HRM and employee efficiency: The mediating role of employee motivation in emerging small businesses. Frontiers Environmental Sciences 10: 1044629.

Khan, N.U., Rasli, A.M. and Qureshi, M.I. 2017. Greening human resource management: A review policies and practices. Advanced Science Letters 23(9): 8934–8938.

Kim, T. 2022. Assessing the impacts of individual and organizational factors on south Korea hotels' green performance using the AMO model. International Journal of Environmental Research and Public Health 19(16): 10440.

Kim, Y.J., Kim, W.G., Choi, H.-M. and Phetvaroon, K. 2019. The effect of green human resource management on hotel employees' eco-friendly behavior and environmental performance. International Journal of Hospitality Management, Parte A 76: 83–93.

Kim, K.Y., Pathak, S. and Werner, S. 2015. When do international human capital enhancing practices benefit the bottom line? An ability, motivation, and opportunity perspective. Journal of International Business Studies 46(7): 784–805. http://dx.doi.org/10.1057/jibs.2015.10.

Krapež Trošt, J., Škerlavaj, M. and Anzengruber, J. 2016. The ability–motivation–opportunity framework for team innovation: efficacy beliefs, proactive personalities, supportive supervision and team innovation. Economic and Business Review 18(1): 4.

Kundu, S.C. and Gahlawat, N. 2018. Ability–motivation–opportunity enhancing human resource practices and firm performance: Evidence from India. Journal of Management & Organization 24(5): 730–747.

Landin, S., Hadzic, S. and Biregeyi, J. 2023. Beyond the Pandemic: Exploring Quiet Quitting and Job Satisfaction: A qualitative research exploring job satisfaction in "the new workplace".

Lee-Chin, T., Fee-Yean, T. and Khulida Kirana, Y. 2017. The power of ability-motivation-opportunity enhancing human resource management practices on organizational ethical climate. International Journal of Business and Society 18(3): 547–562.

Lu, Y., Zhang, M.M., Yang, M.M. and Wang, Y. 2023. Sustainable human resource management practices, employee resilience, and employee outcomes: Toward common good values. Human Resource Management 62(3): 331–353.

Mahand, T. and Caldwell, C. 2023. Quiet quitting–causes and opportunities. Business and Management Research 12(1): 9–19.

Malik Saqib Yaqoob, Yasir Hayat Mughal, Tamoor Azam, Yukun Cao, Zhifang Wan, Hongge Zhu e Ramayah Thurasamy. 2021. Corporate social responsibility, green human resources management, and sustainable performance: is organizational citizenship behavior towards environment the missing link? Sustainability 13(3): 104.

Malik, S.Y., Yukun, C., Yasir, H.M., Ghulam, M.K., Mudassir, H.M. and Ramayah, T. 2020. Pathways towards sustainability in organizations: empirical evidence on the role of green human resource management practices and green intellectual capital. Sustainability 12(8): 3228.

Manzoor, F., Longbao, W., Tamás, B., Mohammad, N. and Qazi Abdul, S. 2019. An examination of sustainable HRM practices on job performance: an application of training as a moderator. Sustainability 11(8): 2263.

Marin-Garcia, J.A. and Martinez Tomas, J. 2016. Deconstructing AMO framework: A systematica review, Intangible Capital 12(4): 1040–1087 – Online ISSN: 1697-9818 – Print ISSN: 2014-3214 http://dx.doi.org/10.3926/ic.838.

Martins, J.M., Aftab, H., Mata, M.N., Majeed, M.U., Aslam, S., Correia, A.B. et al. 2021. Assessing the impact of green hiring on sustainable performance: Mediating role of green performance management and compensation. International Journal of Environmental Research and Public Health 18(11): 5654.

Mateus, J.H., de Lacerda, T.C. and Henriques Paulo Lopes. 2020. From Sustainable HRM to Employee Performance: A complex and intertwined road. European Management Review 17(4).

McCarthy, G. and Milner, J. 2020. Ability, motivation and opportunity: managerial coaching in practice. Asia Pacific Journal of Human Resources 58(1): 149–170.

Mirčetić, V., Ivanović, T., Knežević, S., Arsić, V.B., Obradović, T., Karabašević, D. et al. 2022. The innovative human resource management framework: impact of green competencies on organisational performance. Sustainability 14(5): 2713.

Mousa, S.K. and Othman, M. 2020. The impact of green human resource management practices on sustainable performance in healthcare organisations: A conceptual framework. Journal of Cleaner Production 243: 118595.

Mwita, K. and Stella, M.K. 2018. The role of green recruitment and selection on performance of processing industries in tanzania: a case of tanzania tobacco processors limited (TTPL). International Journal of Human Resource Studies 8(4).

Mwita, K. 2019. Conceptual review of green human resource management practices. East African Journal of Social and Applied Sciences 1(2): 13–20.
Nauman, M., Arooj, A., Huo, X. and Nabeel, R. 2022. The role of green human resource management practices in driving green performance in the context of manufacturing SMEs. Sustainability 14(24): 16776.
Obaid, S., Ahmad, S.F. and Mumtaz, F. 2022. Ability-motivation-opportunity framework: An analysis of interrelated effects of HRM practice and leadership style on organizational outcomes. International Journal of Asian Business and Information Management (IJABIM) 13(1): 1–26.
Ong, J.O. and Mahazan, M. 2020. Model of employee performance: ability, motivation, and opportunity in manufacturing company. Journal of Talent Development and Excellence 12(2s): 1019–1031.
Pak, K., Kooij, D.T., De Lange, A.H. and Van Veldhoven, M.J. 2019. Human Resource Management and the ability, motivation and opportunity to continue working: A review of quantitative studies. Human Resource Management Review 29(3): 336–352.
Paudel, T. and Yunho, J.I. 2020. A conceptual approach to green human resource management and corporate environmental responsibility in the hospitality industry. Journal of Asian Finance, Economics and Business 7(1): 195–203.
Pellegrini, C., Rizzi, F. and Frei, M. 2018. The role of sustainable human resource practices in influencing employee behavior for corporate sustainability. Business Strategy and the Environment.
Pinzone, M., Guerci, M., Lettieri, E. and Redman, T. 2016. Progressing in the change journey towards sustainability in healthcare: the role of 'Green' HRM, Journal of Cleaner Production 122: 201–211.
Pinzone, M., Guerci, M., Lettieri, E. and Huisingh, Do. 2019. Effects of 'green' training on pro-environmental behaviors and job satisfaction: Evidence from the Italian healthcare sector. Journal of Cleaner Production 226: 221–232.
Rajiani, I., Musa, H. and Hardjono, B. 2016. Ability, motivation and opportunity as determinants of green human resources management innovation. Research Journal of Business Management 10(1-3): 51–57.
Rashid, A. and Alam, W. 2020. The impact of green human resource management on organizational performance: a case of manufacturing industry. City University Research Journal 10(2).
Rayner, J. and Morgan, D. 2018. An empirical study of 'green' workplace behaviours: ability, motivation and opportunity. Asia Pacific Journal of Human Resources 56(1): 56–78.
Ribeiro, N., Gomes, D.R., Ortega, E., Gomes, G.P. and Semedo, A.S. 2022. The impact of green HRM on employees' eco-friendly behavior: the mediator role of organizational identification. Sustainability 14(5): 2897.
Richa Chaudhary. 2019. Green Human Resource Management and Employee Green Behavior: An Empirical Analysis Corporate Social Responsibility and Envinromental Management.
Roscoe, S., Subramanian, N., Jabbour, C.J.C. and Chong, T. 2019. Green human resource management and the enablers of green organisational culture: Enhancing a firm's environmental performance for sustainable development. Business Strategy and Environment 28(5): 737–749.
Rubel, M.R.B., Kee, D.M.H. and Rimi, N.N. 2021. Green human resource management and supervisor pro-environmental behavior: The role of green work climate perceptions. Journal of Cleaner Production 313: 127669.
Sabokro, M., Masud, M.M. and Kayedian, A. 2021. The effect of green human resources management on corporate social responsibility, green psychological climate and employees' green behavior. Journal of Cleaner Production 313.
Sadia, C., Farheen, J. and Tahir, N. 2017. The effects of corporate social responsibility towards green human resource management: The mediating role of sustainable environment. Cogent Business & Management 4: 1.
Saeed, B.B., Afsar, B., Hafeez, S., Khan, I., Tahir, M. and Afridi 2019. Promoting employee's proenvironmental behavior through green human resource management practices. Corporate Social Responsibility and Environmental Management 26(2): 424–438.

Saifulina, N., Carballo, P.A. and Ruzo-Sanmartín, E. 2020. Sustainable HRM and green HRM: The role of green HRM in influencing employee pro-environmental behavior at work. Journal of Sustainability Research 2.

Sarikwal, L. and Gupta, J. 2013. The impact of high performance, work practices and organisational citizenship behaviour on turnover intentions. Journal of Strategic Human Resource Management 2(3): 11–19. Retrieved from: http://search.proquest.com/openview/b723d547479f3c4705400d87ab29b703/1?pq-origsite=gscholar.

Schimansky, S. 2014. The Effect of a High-Commitment Work System on Innovative Behavior of Employees. Retrieved from: http://essay.utwente.nl/65249/1/Schimansky_BA_MB.pdf.

Shah Syed, M.A., Yang, J., Hao, W., Zahoor, A., Irfan, U. and Tomiwa Sunday, A. 2021. Linking green human resource practices and environmental economics performance: the role of green economic organizational culture and green psychological climate. International Journal of Environmental Research and Public Health 18(20): 10953.

Sharifa, K. and Mohammed, O. 2019. The impact of green human resource management practices on sustainable performance in healthcare organisations: A conceptual framework. Journal of Cleaner Production 234: 118595.

Sibian Adina-Raluca, Ispa, A. 2021. An approach to applying the ability-motivation-opportunity theory to identify the driving factors of green employee behavior in the hotel industry. Sustainability (Svizzera) 13(9).

Tay, L.-C., Tan, F.-Y. and Yahya, K.K. 2017. The power of ability-motivation-opportunity enhancing human resource management practices on organizational ethical climate. International Journal of Business and Society 18(3): 547–562. doi:10.33736/ijbs.3146.2017.

Ujma, M. and Ingram, T. 2019. Perception of ability-motivation-opportunity oriented HRM practices and organizational commitment: The role of task uncertainty. Journal of Entrepreneurship, Management and Innovation 15(4): 139–162.

Xuemei, X., Qiwei, Z. and Guoyou, Q. 2020. How can green training promote employee career growth? Journal of Cleaner Production 259.

Yafi, E., Tehseen, S. and Haider, S.A. 2021. Impact of green training on environmental performance through mediating role of competencies and motivation. Sustainability (Svizzera) 13(10): art. NO. 5624.

Zahrani, A.A. 2022. Team creativity and green human resource management practices' mediating roles in organizational sustainability. Sustainability 14(19): 12827.

Zenger, J. and Folkman, J. 2022. Quiet quitting is about bad bosses, not bad employees. Harvard Business Review. Retrieved October 24, from https://hbr.org/2022/08/quiet-quitting-is-about-bad-bosses-not-bad-employees.

Zhang, B., Yang, L., Cheng, X. and Chen, F. 2021. How does employee green behavior impact employee well-being? An empirical analysis. International Journal of Environmental Research and Public Health 18(4).

Zhao, F., Manita, K., Yun, C., Wei Hu. Fawad, A. and Dinesh, S. 2021. Influencing mechanism of green human resource management and corporate social responsibility on organizational sustainable performance. Sustainability 13(16): 8875.

Zubair Dr Syed, S. and Khan, M. 2019. Sustainable development: the role of green HRM. International Journal of Research in Human Resource Management 1(2): 1–6.

Appendix

Table 2. The list of selected articles.

1	Ababneh, O.M.A. 2021. How do green HRM practices affect employees' green behaviors? The role of employee engagement and personality attributes. Journal of Environmental Planning and Management 64(7): 1204–1226.
2	Aboradan, M. 2022. The effect of green HRM on employee green behaviors in higher education: the mediating mechanism of green work engagement. International Journal of Organizational Analysis 30(1): 7–23.
3	Abu Elnasr E. Sobaih, Ahmed Hasanein and Ibrahim Elshaer. 2020. Influences of green human resources management on environmental performance in small lodging enterprises: the role of green innovation. Sustainability 12(24): 10371.
4	Adeel, M., Mahmood, S., Khan, K.I. and Saleem, S. 2022. Green HR practices and environmental performance: The mediating mechanism of employee outcomes and moderating role of environmental values. Frontiers Environmental Sciences 10: 1001100.
5	Adjei-Bamfo, P., Bempong, B., Osei, J. and Kusi-Sarpong, S. 2020. Green candidate selection for organizational environmental management. International Journal of Manpower 41(7): 1081–1096.
6	Ahmed, M., Guo, Q., Qureshi, M.A., Raza, S.A., Khan, K.A. and Salam, J. 2021. Do green HR practices enhance green motivation and proactive environmental management maturity in hotel industry? International Journal of Hospitality Management 94: art. NO. 102852.
7	Alenzi Mohamad, A.S., Jaaffar Amar Hisham and Khudari Mohammed. 2022. The mediating effect of organisational sustainability and employee behaviour on the relationship between GHRM and sustainable performance in Qatar. WSEAS Transactions on Business and Economics 19: 1430–1442.
8	Ali Ababneh Omar Mohammed. 2021. How do green HRM practices affect employees' green behaviors? The role of employee engagement and personality attributes. Journal of Environmental Planning and Management 64(7): 1204–1226.
9	Aizgool Mahmoud Radwan Hussein. 2020. Nexus between green HRM and green management towards fostering green values. Management Science Letters 11.2.
10	Andjarwati Tri, Budiarti Endah, Audah Abdul Kadir, Khouri Samer and Rębilas, R. 2019. The impact of green human resource management to gain enterprise sustainability. Polish Journal of Management Studies.
11	Anwar Nosheen, Mahmood Nik Hasnaa, Yusoff Yusliza and Khalid Waqas. 2018. Review of green human resource management: from the lens of ability-motivation-opportunity framework. Advanced Science Letters 24(4): 2507–2510.
12	Asghar Afshar Jahanshahi, Tahereh Maghsoudi and Najla Shafighi. 2021. Employees' environmentally responsible behavior: the critical role of environmental justice perception. Sustainability: Science, Practice and Policy 17(1): 1–14.
13	Awan, F.H., Dunnan, L., Jamil, K. et al. 2022. Stimulating environmental performance via green human resource management, green transformational leadership, and green innovation: a mediation-moderation model. Enviromental Science and Pollution Research 30: 2958–2976.
14	Aykan, E. 2017. Gaining a competitive advantage through green human resource management. Corporate Governance and Strategic Decision Making.
15	Bano, S., Aijaz, U. and Athar, A. 2022. High Performance Work System (HPWS) in the IT Sector of Pakistan: An application of ability-motivation-opportunity model. Human Nature Journal of Social Sciences 3(3): 361–387.

16	Bombiak Edyta and Anna Marciniuk-Kluska. 2018. Green human resource management as a tool for the sustainable development of enterprises: polish young company experience. Sustainability 10(6): 1739.
17	Bos-Nehles, A., Townsend, K., Cafferkey, K. and Trullen, J. 2023. Examining the Ability, Motivation and Opportunity (AMO) framework in HRM research: Conceptualization, measurement and interactions. International Journal of Management Reviews.
18	Bahrami, L., Safaie, N. and Hamidi, H. 2021. Effect of motivation, opportunity and ability on human resources information security management considering the roles of attitudinal, behavioral and organizational factors. International Journal of Engineering 34(12): 2624–2635.
19	Chen Silu, Wanxing Jiang, Xin Li and Han Gao. 2021. Effect of employees' perceived green HRM on their workplace green behaviors in oil and mining industries: based on cognitive-affective system theory. International Journal of Environmental Research and Public Health 18(8): 4056.
20	Dahlin, K.B., Chuang, Y.T. and Roulet, T.J. 2018. Opportunity, motivation, and ability to learn from failures and errors: Review, synthesis, and ways to move forward. Academy of Management Annals 12(1): 252–277.
21	Dasí, À., Pedersen, T., Barakat, L.L. and Alves, T.R. 2021. Teams and project performance: An ability, motivation, and opportunity approach. Project Management Journal 52(1): 75–89.
22	Dumont, J., Shen, J. and Deng, X. 2017. Effects of green HRM practices on employee workplace green behavior: the role of psychological green climate and employee green values. Human Resources Management 56(4): 613–627.
23	Edgar, F., Blaker, N.M. and Everett, A.M. 2021. Gender and job performance: linking the high performance work system with the ability–motivation–opportunity framework. Personnel Review 50(1): 47–63.
24	Elshaer Ibrahim, A., Abu Elnasr, E. Sobaih, Meqbel Aliedan and Alaa MS Azazz. 2021. The effect of green human resource management on environmental performance in small tourism enterprises: mediating role of pro-environmental behaviors. Sustainability 13(4): 1956.
25	Engin Ari, Osman M. Karatepe, Hamed Rezapouraghdam and Turgay Avci. 2020. A conceptual model for green human resource management: indicators, differential pathways, and multiple pro-environmental outcomes. Sustainability 12(17): 7089.
26	Ehnert Ina, Parsa Sepideh, Roper Ianc, Wagner Marco and Muller-Camen Michael. 2016. Reporting on sustainability and HRM: a comparative study of sustainability reporting practices by the world's largest companies. The International Journal of Human Resource Management 27(1).
27	Ercantan, O. and Eyupoglu, S. 2022. How do green human resource management practices encourage employees to engage in green behavior? Perceptions of university students as prospective employees. Sustainability 14(3): art. N.1718.
28	Faezah Juhari Noor, Yusliza Mohd Yusoff, Maometto Zikri and Fawehinmi Olawole. 2022. Promoting employee ecological behavior through green initiatives. International Journal of Sustainable Development and Planning 17(1): 41–49.
29	Fang, L., Shi, S., Gao, J. and Li, X. 2022. The mediating role of green innovation and green culture in the relationship between green human resource management and environmental performance. Plos One 17(9).
30	Fiza Amjad et al. 2021. Effect of green human resource management practices on organizational sustainability: the mediating role of environmental and employee performance. Environmental Science and Pollution Research 28: 28191–28206.

31	Garavan Tommaso, Ullah Irfan, O'Brien Fergal, Darcy Colette, Wisetsri Worakamol, Afshan Gul et al. 2022. Employee perceptions of individual green HRM practices and voluntary green work behaviour: a signalling theory perspective. Asian Pacific Journal of Human Resources.
32	Guerci Marco, Montanari Fabrizio, Scapolan Annachiara and Epifanio Antonella. 2016. Green and nongreen recruitment practices for attracting job applicants: exploring independent and interactive effects. The International Journal of Human Resource Management 27(2): 129–150.
33	Gull, S. and Idrees, H. 2022. Green training and organizational efficiency: mediating role of green competencies. European Journal of Training and Development 46(½): 105–119.
34	He Jie, Alastair M. Morrison and Hao Zhang. 2021. Being sustainable: The three-way interactive effects of CSR, green human resource management, and responsible leadership on employee green behavior and task performance. Corporate Social Responsibility and Environmental Management 28.3: 1043–1054.
35	Hu Xiao, Khan Shumaila Mazar, Huang Shijiao, Abbas Jawad, Matei Mirabela Constanta and Badulescu Daniele. 2022. Employees' green enterprise motivation and green creative process engagement and their impact on green creative performance. International Journal of Environmental Research and Public Health 10(19).
36	Huo Xiaoyan, Arooj Azhar, Nabeel Rehman and Nauman Majeed. 2022. The role of green human resource management practices in driving green performance in the context of manufacturing SMEs. Sustainability 14(24): 16776.
37	Iftikar Taber, Hussein Saddam, Malik Muhammad Imran, Hyder Shabir, Kalem Maometto and Saqib Adel. 2021. Green human resource management and pro-environmental behaviour nexus with the lens of AMO theory. Cogent Business and Management 9.
38	Irani, F. and Kilic, H. 2022. An assessment of implementing green HRM practices on environmental performance: The moderating role of green process innovation. Journal of Global Hospitality and Tourism 1(1): 16–30.
39	Jia Jianfeng, Huanxin Liu, Tachia Chin and Dongqing Hu. 2018. The continuous mediating effects of GHRM on employees' green passion through transformational leadership and green creativity. Sustainability 10(9).
40	Kalimullah Khan, Muhammad Shahid Shams, Qaisar Khan Sher Akbar and Murtaza Masud Niazi. 2022. Organizational Psychology, Frontiers in Psychology Relationship Among Green Human Resource Management, Green Knowledge Sharing, Green Commitment, and Green Behavior: A Moderated Mediation Model. Original Research.
41	Kang Ya Chin, Hsiao Hsien-Sheng and Ni Jia Yi. 2022. The role of sustainable training and reward in influencing employee accountability perception and behavior for corporate sustainability. Sustainability (Svizzera) 14(18).
42	Kanika Sharma. 2016. Conceptualization of green HRM and green HRM practices: commitment to environment sustainability. International Journal of Advanced Scientific Research and Management 1(8), August.
43	Kaur Simranjeetun, Sehgal Jagdish Kumar and Grima Simone. 2022. Virtual hiring: an effective green human resource management practice. International Journal of Sustainable Development and Planning 17: 1699–1704.
44	Khan, A.J., Ul Hameed, W., Iqbal, J., Shah, A.A., Tariq, M.A.U.R. and Bashir, F. 2022. Green HRM and employee efficiency: The mediating role of employee motivation in emerging small businesses. Frontiers Enviromental Sciences 10: 1044629.
45	Khan Rasli, Qureshi. 2017. Greening human resource management: a review policies and practices. Advanced Science Letters 23(9): 8934–8938.

46	Kim, Taiuk. 2022. Assessing the impacts of individual and organizational factors on south korea hotels' green performance using the AMO model. International Journal of Environmental Research and Public Health 19(16): 10440.
47	Kim, Y.J., Kim, W.G., Choi, H.-M. and Phetvaroon, K. 2019. The effect of green human resource management on hotel employees' eco-friendly behavior and environmental performance. International Journal of Hospitality Management, Parte A 76: 83–93.
48	Krapež Trošt, J., Škerlavaj, M. and Anzengruber, J. 2016. The ability–motivation–opportunity framework for team innovation: efficacy beliefs, proactive personalities, supportive supervision and team innovation. Economic and Business Review 18(1): 4.
49	Kundu, S.C. and Gahlawat, N. 2018. Ability–motivation–opportunity enhancing human resource practices and firm performance: Evidence from India. Journal of Management & Organization 24(5): 730–747.
50	Lee-Chin Tay, Fee-Yean Tan and Khulida Kirana Yahya. 2017. The power of ability-motivation-opportunity enhancing human resource management practices on organizational ethical climate. International Journal of Business and Society 18(3): 547–562.
51	Cuifang, L. and Rui, W. 2019, March. Research on the influencing factors of employees' green behavior from the perspective of AMO. In 4th International Social Sciences and Education Conference (ISSEC 2019), China.
52	Lu Ying, Zhang Mingqiong Mike, Yang Miles M. and Wang Yu. 2023. Sustainable human resource management practices, employee resilience, and employee outcomes: Toward common good values. Human Resources Management 62(3).
53	Malik Saqib Yaqoob, Yasir Hayat Mughal, Tamoor Azam, Yukun Cao, Zhifang Wan, Hongge Zhu et al. 2021. Corporate social responsibility, green human resources management, and sustainable performance: is organizational citizenship behavior towards environment the missing link? Sustainability 13(3): 1044.
54	Malik Saqib Yaqoob, Yukun Cao, Yasir Hayat Mughal, Ghulam Muhammad Kundi, Mudassir Hayat Mughal e Ramayah, T. 2020. Pathways towards sustainability in organizations: empirical evidence on the role of green human resource management practices and green intellectual capital. Sustainability 12(8): 3228.
55	Manzoor Faiza, Longbao Wei, Tamás Bányai, Mohammad Nurunnabi e Qazi Abdul Subhan. 2019. An examination of sustainable HRM practices on job performance: an application of training as a moderator. Sustainability 11(8): 2263.
56	Marin-Garcia, J.A. and Martinez Tomas, J. 2016. Deconstructing AMO framework: A systematica review. Intangible Capital 12(4): 1040–1087 – Online ISSN: 1697-9818 – Print ISSN: 2014-3214 http://dx.doi.org/10.3926/ic.838.
57	Martins José Moleiro, Hira Aftab, Mário Nuno Mata, Muhammad Ussama Majeed, Sumaira Aslam, Anabela Batista Correia et al. 2021. Assessing the impact of green hiring on sustainable performance: mediating role of green performance management and compensation. International Journal of Environmental Research and Public Health 18(11): 5654.
58	Mateus Jerónimo Helena, de Lacerda Teresa Correia and Henriques Paulo Lopes. 2020. From sustainable HRM to employee performance: a complex and intertwined road. European Management Review 17(4).
59	McCarthy, G. and Milner, J. 2020. Ability, motivation and opportunity: managerial coaching in practice. Asia Pacific Journal of Human Resources 58(1): 149–170.
60	Mirčetić, V., Ivanović, T., Knežević, S., Arsić, V.B., Obradović, T., Karabašević, D. et al. 2022. The innovative human resource management framework: impact of green competencies on organisational performance. Sustainability 14(5): 2713.

61	Mousa, S.K. and Othmann, M. 2020. The impact of green human resource management practices on sustainable performance in healthcare organisations: A conceptual framework. Journal of Cleaner Production 243: art. N.118595.
62	Mwita Kelvin. 2019. Conceptual review of green human resource management practices. East African Journal of Social and Applied Sciences 1(2): 13–20.
63	Mwita Kelvin, M. and Stella Malangalila Kinemo. 2018. The role of green recruitment and selection on performance of processing industries in tanzania: a case of tanzania tobacco processors limited (TTPL). International Journal of Human Resource Studies 8(4).
64	Nauman Majeed, Arooj Azhar, Huo Xiaoyan e Nabeel Rehman. 2022. The role of green human resource management practices in driving green performance in the context of manufacturing SMEs. Sustainability 14(24): 16776.
65	Obaid, S., Ahmad, S.F. and Mumtaz, F. 2022. Ability-motivation-opportunity framework: An analysis of interrelated effects of HRM practice and leadership style on organizational outcomes. International Journal of Asian Business and Information Management (IJABIM) 13(1): 1–26.
66	Fawehinmi, O., Yusliza, M.Y., Wan Kasim, W.Z., Mohamad, Z. and Sofian Abdul Halim, M.A. 2020. Exploring the interplay of green human resource management, employee green behavior, and personal moral norms. Sage Open 10(4): 2158244020982292.
67	Ong, J.O. and Mahazan, M. 2020. Model of employee performance: ability, motivation, and opportunity in manufacturing company. Journal of Talent Development and Excellence 12(2s): 1019–1031.
68	Pak, K., Kooij, D.T., De Lange, A.H. and Van Veldhoven, M.J. 2019. Human Resource Management and the ability, motivation and opportunity to continue working: A review of quantitative studies. Human Resource Management Review 29(3): 336–352.
69	Paudel TULSI and Yunho, J.I. 2020. A conceptual approach to green human resource management and corporate environmental responsibility in the hospitality industry. Journal of Asian Finance, Economics and Business 7(1): 195–203.
70	Pellegrini, C., Rizzi, F. and Frey, M. 2018. The role of sustainable human resource practices in influencing employee behavior for corporate sustainability. Business Strategy and the Environment 27(8): 1221–1232.
71	Pinzone Marta, Guerci Marco, Lettieri Emanuele and Huisingh Donald. 2019. Effects of 'green' training on pro-environmental behaviors and job satisfaction: Evidence from the Italian healthcare sector. Journal of Cleaner Production 226: 221–232.
72	Rajiani Ismi, Musa Haslinda and Hardjono Budono. 2016. Ability, motivation and opportunity as determinants of green human resources management innovation. Research Journal of Business Management 10(1-3): 51–57.
73	Rashid Abdul and Alam Waqar. 2020. The impact of green human resource management on organizational performance: a case of manufacturing industry. Archives 10(2).
74	Rayner, J. and Morgan, D. 2018. An empirical study of 'green' workplace behaviours: ability, motivation and opportunity. Asia Pacific Journal of Human Resources 56(1): 56–78.
75	Ribeiro Neuza, Daniel Roque Gomes, Eduardo Ortega, Gabriela Pedro Gomes and Ana Suzete Semedo. 2022. The impact of green HRM on employees' eco-friendly behavior: the mediator role of organizational identification. Sustainability 14(5): 2897.
76	Richa Chaudhary. 2019. Green human resource management and employee green behavior: an empirical analysis. Corporate Social Responsibility and Environmental Management.

77	Roscoe, S., Subramanian, N., Jabbour, C.J.C. and Chong, T. 2019. Green human resource management and the enablers of green organisational culture: Enhancing a firm's environmental performance for sustainable development. Business Strategy and Environment 28(5): 737–749.
78	Rubel Mohammad Rabiul Basher, Kee Daisy Mui Hung and Rimi Nadia Newaz. 2021. Green human resource management and supervisor pro-environmental behavior: The role of green work climate perceptions. Journal of Cleaner Production 313.
79	Sabokro Mahdi, Masud Muhammad Mehedi and Kayedian Azin. 2021. The effect of green human resources management on corporate social responsibility, green psychological climate and employees' green behavior. Journal of Cleaner Production 313.
80	Sadia Cheema e Farheen Javed and Tahir Nisar. 2017. The effects of corporate social responsibility towards green human resource management: The mediating role of sustainable environment. Cogent Business & Management 4: 1.
81	Saeed, B.B., Afsar, B., Hafeez, S., Khan, I., Tahir, M. and Afridi. 2019. Promoting employee's proenvironmental behavior through green human resource management practiccs. Corporate Social Responsibility and Environmental Management 26(2): 424–438.
82	Saifulina Nailya, Carballo Penela Adolfo and Ruzo-Sanmartín Emilio. 2020. Sustainable HRM and green HRM: The role of green HRM in influencing employee pro-environmental behavior at work. Journal of Sustainability Research 2.
83	Shah Syed Mehmood Ali, Yang Jiang, Hao Wu, Zahoor Ahmed, Irfan Ullah and Tomiwa Sunday Adebayo. 2021. Linking green human resource practices and environmental economics performance: the role of green economic organizational culture and green psychological climate. International Journal of Environmental Research and Public Health 18(20): 10953.
84	Sharifa, K. and Mohammed, O. 2019. The impact of green human resource management practices on sustainable performance in healthcare organisations: A conceptual framework. Journal of Cleaner Production 234: 118595.
85	Sibian Adina-Raluca and Ispa Ana. 2021. An approach to applying the ability-motivation-opportunity theory to identify the driving factors of green employee behavior in the hotel industry. Sustainability (Svizzera) 13(9).
86	Tay, L.-C., Tan, F.-Y. and Yahya, K.K. 2017. The power of ability-motivation-opportunity enhancing human resource management practices on organizational ethical climate. International Journal of Business and Society 18(3): 547–562. doi:10.33736/ijbs.3146.2017.
87	Ujma, M. and Ingram, T. 2019. Perception of ability-motivation-opportunity oriented HRM practices and organizational commitment: The role of task uncertainty. Journal of Entrepreneurship, Management and Innovation 15(4): 139–162.
88	Xuemei Xie, Qiwei Zhu and Guoyou Qi. 2020. How can green training promote employee career growth? Journal of Cleaner Production 259.
89	Yafi, E., Tehseen, S. and Haider, S.A. 2021. Impact of green training on environmental performance through mediating role of competencies and motivation. Sustainability (Svizzera) 13(10): art. NO. 5624.
90	Zahrani Aida Ahmed. 2022. Team creativity and green human resource management practices' mediating roles in organizational sustainability. Sustainability 14(19): 12827.
91	Zhang Bajie, Yang Lifeng, Cheng Xiangyang and Chen Feyu. 2021. How does employee green behavior impact employee well-being? an empirical analysis. International Journal of Environmental Research and Public Health 18(4).

92	Zhao Fuqiang, Manita Kusi, Yun Chen, Wei Hu, Fawad Ahmed and Dinesh Sukamani. 2021. Influencing mechanism of green human resource management and corporate social responsibility on organizational sustainable performance. Sustainability 13(16): 8875.
93	Zubair, Dr Syed Sohaib and Khan Mukaram. 2019. Sustainable development: the role of green HRM. International Journal of Research in Human Resource Management 1(2): 1–6.
94	Abbas, Z., Gabbiano Khan, Afshan, Smaliukienė, Rasa Zámečník, Romano Hussein, Kanwal and Mubarik, Shujaat. 2022. Green HRM pursuit of social sustainability in the hotels: AMO theoretical perspective. Quality - Access to success.

CHAPTER 9

Organisations, Entrepreneurship and Crowdfunding

A Means of Bridging the Entrepreneurship Funding Gap in Nigeria

Ekene Okwechime,[1,*] *Osikwemhe Damisah*[1] and *Kefas Thomas*[2]

1. Introduction

Crowdfunding has gained popularity for its potential to provide funding for charitable and entrepreneurial initiatives in the last decade (Meyskens and Birds 2015, Singnori and Vismara 2018). This development is traceable to the impact of the global financial meltdown of 2008 on the lending patterns of banks. The financial crisis collapsed the global banking system, especially banks that were exposed to the American subprime mortgage crisis. Consequently, banks became reluctant to lend to start-up companies and small and medium scale enterprises (SME's) after the financial crash (Naiki and Ogene 2019). This made it difficult for entrepreneurs to access funds to facilitate their business operations. This situation resulted to the creation of crowdfunding—an online payment platform that facilitates the pooling of funds from individual donors to support entrepreneurs (Meyskens and Bird 2015).

Despite its growing popularity, the literature on crowdfunding is still evolving and this is evidenced by the shortage of research on the subject (Bellafalamme

[1] Anglia Ruskin University, East Rd, Cambridge, UK, CB1 1PT.
[2] Adamawa State College of Education, P.M.B. 044 Hong, Adamawa State, Nigeria.
* Corresponding author: ekene.okwechime@aru.ac.uk

et al. 2014, Signori and Vismara 2018). This gap in literature is particularly evident in developing countries such as Nigeria where there is scarcity of research on crowdfunding. Research has explored the relationship between crowdfunding and factors such as project features, the entrepreneur's self-belief and its potential to fund scientific research (Skinevskjy et al. 2017). Findings from this study provide valuable insights on crowdfunding; however, most studies on this subject were conducted in developed countries. On the contrary, research on crowdfunding in Nigeria is still relatively scarce (e.g., Okoyeuzu et al. 2019, Aladejebi 2020). Though, these studies did not explore the potential of crowdfunding to provide funding for entrepreneurial initiatives in the technology sector in Nigeria.

Context of Study

Nigeria is Africa's largest economy and a key centre of commerce and entrepreneurship in the continent. Nigeria's financial hub, Lagos, is the country's economic nerve centre (Egbejule 2020). The state plays host to a teaming population of technology experts and entrepreneurs (Pilling 2018, Osho and Adishi 2019). However, poor access to finance from private and public sector, affects the scaling up of technological innovations in Nigeria. In addition, technology (Information, Communication and Technology broadly) has been identified as the catalyst for solving Nigeria's socio-economic problems such as inadequate electricity supply, lack of rail transportation infrastructure and insecurity (Lawal et al. 2018). Consequently, such technological innovations struggle to scale up due to lack of finance for infrastructural development.

Studies on crowdfunding in Nigeria point to a need and willingness to embrace an alternative method of funding, aside from the traditional lending instruments and methods that are available (Ekpe et al. 2017, Okoyeuzu et al. 2019). Despite the fast growth of the crowdfunding landscape, policymakers and funders in Nigeria have shown little signs of expanding its reach. Theoretically, this perhaps, explains the lack of studies on crowdfunding in Nigeria, and consequently, our limited understanding of its operational dynamics, especially its potential to fund entrepreneurship. In practice, this implies that entrepreneurs, who intend to fund their businesses using crowdfunding, may not have sufficient information to make informed decisions.

Given the scheme of things, there is a need to explore crowdfunding as a means of bridging the funding gap in technology entrepreneurship in the context of interest. Therefore, we seek to achieve three objectives in this study. The objectives include: (a) explore the prospects of using crowdfunding for raising funds to finance technology entrepreneurship in Lagos State, Nigeria; (b) identify and explore the potential challenges of crowdfunding in Nigeria, in relation to funding technology entrepreneurs in Lagos State, Nigeria; and (c) ascertain if the relevant regulatory framework and mechanisms are in place to regulate crowdfunding in Nigeria.

The subsequent sections of the paper are structured as follows: we begin with a review of the literature on crowdfunding to ascertain the current state of the field, and then proceed to highlight and discuss the methodology for the study. Subsequently, we present the results and discussion, and then provide the summary, conclusion and implications of the study.

2. Literature Review

Crowdfunding has become popular for its ability to provide funding for charitable initiatives and entrepreneurial ventures (Signori and Vismara 2018). Consequently, some measure of research attention has been accorded to the concept, thus resulting to a developing body of literature. This section of the paper reviews the extant literature on crowdfunding and its theoretical origins.

2.1 Theoretical Foundations of Crowdfunding

The origins of the concept of crowdfunding can be traced to microfinance and crowdsourcing (Morduch 1999, Poetz and Schreirer 2012). Crowdfunding is intricately linked with micro lending, also known as micro finance, because both concepts focus on democratizing access to finance. However, crowdfunding provides a flexible approach to lending by removing the strict requirements such as interest rates and established business track record, for accessing credit facilities from financial institutions and venture capitalists. In contrast, micro finance reduces these requirements and provide small loans for individuals who are unable to access credit facilities from financial institutions, to execute personal, social or entrepreneurial initiatives (Armendariz and Morduch 2010).

Research shows that crowdfunding represents a dimension of crowdsourcing, in addition to crowd creation and crowd voting (Leimeister 2012, Richter et al. 2014). 'Crowdsourcing' comprises of two words—'crowd' and 'outsourcing'; the latter means to contract (outsource) part or an aspect of a process to an external organization (Kleeman et al. 2008). The idea of crowdsourcing emanates from the 'wisdom of a crowd' (Surowiecki 2004). Simply put, crowdsourcing is based on the view that capability can be sourced from the crowd. A succinct definition is provided by Howe (2006) who defined crowdsourcing as: 'the act of taking a job traditionally performed by a designated agent (usually an employee) and outsourcing it to an undefined, generally large number of people in the form of an open call' (Howe 2006, p. 1). This definition captures the dynamics and underlying premise of crowdfunding.

To illustrate further, the link between crowdsourcing and crowdfunding is hinged on the view that the latter draws the capacity to fund initiatives from the crowd, usually on internet-based platforms. This perspective indicates that crowdfunding is a subset of crowdsourcing since the latter provides the broad platform, i.e., 'resort to the crowd', from which capacity is drawn (also see Leimeister 2012, Richter et al. 2014). This illustration demonstrates that the roots of crowdfunding are embedded in the concept of crowdsourcing.

The conception of crowdfunding is still evolving due to the emerging nature of the field and the various disciplines it currently covers, and may likely cover going forward (Freedman 2015). According to Mollick (2014), 'the conception of crowdfunding is currently in an evolutionary flux'. Consequently, attempts to define crowdfunding from a broad perspective appears limited and elusive. However, scholars have made constructive attempts to define crowdfunding from different perspectives. Table 1 below outlines some notable definitions for crowdfunding.

Table 1. Definitions of crowdfunding.

Author(s) and Year	Definitions
Schwienbacher and Larralde (2010)	"An open call, essentially through the Internet, for the provision of financial resources either in form of donation or in exchange for some form of reward and/or voting rights to support initiatives for specific purposes."
Voorbraak (2011, p. 1)	"The process of one party requesting and receiving money and other resources from many individuals for financing a project, in exchange for monetary or non-monetary return on investment."
Tomczak and Brem (2013, p. 338)	"The act of taking a loan/funding traditionally performed by a designated agent and outsourcing it to an undefined, generally large group of people in the form of an open call."
Belleflamme et al. (2013)	"An open call, mostly through the Internet, for the provision of financial resources either in the form of donation or in exchange for the future product or some form of reward to support initiatives for specific purposes."
Wicks (2013)	"Crowdfunding is where many people (a crowd) financially support a project by giving a relatively small amount of money either in return for a reward, as a donation, or potentially in return for equity."
Mollick (2014)	"Efforts by entrepreneurial individuals and groups – cultural, social, and for-profit – to fund their ventures by drawing on relatively small contributions from a relatively large number of individuals using the internet, without standard financial intermediaries."
Friedman (2015)	"A method that is used to pool funds together from various people, often referred to as donors or sponsors, through internet-based platforms."

Source: Please refer to the authors' studies listed in the table and the corresponding entries in the References section.

Table 1 above outlines some definitions for crowdfunding. A review of these definitions reveals a consensus view of the meaning of crowdfunding in literature. That is, crowdfunding provides a novel approach to raising funds for various projects including, charitable, social, and entrepreneurial initiatives, from donors on internet-based platforms that are dedicated to specific causes (Mollick 2014, Freedman 2015). This perspective highlights the components in the operational mechanism of crowdfunding. These components include: (a) a flexible approach to raising money which excludes intermediaries such as banks and their rigid requirements to access funding; (b) from the public, i.e., online donors or sponsors; (c) to fund a range of projects or initiatives, i.e., social, entrepreneurial or environmental; (d) from dedicated internet-based platforms—web 2.0 (Friedman 2015). Therefore, it is expected that any meaningful definition of crowdfunding should integrate these components. However, some definitions in literature often omit one or more of these components of crowdfunding. For example, the definition provided by Schwienbacher and Larralde (2010) excludes other forms of crowdfunding such as internet-based peer lending (Lin and Viswanathan 2013), and fundraising campaigns that are driven by fans of a music group (Burkett 2011), amongst others (see Table 1 above). Similarly, Belleflamme et al. (2013), in their definition, failed to consider some elements of crowdfunding such as peer to peer lending and fundraising by individuals in diverse areas. Also, the definitions of Voorbraak (2011) and Wicks (2013) omitted the role of the internet and social media in facilitating crowdfunding.

Furthermore, Freidman (2015) defines crowdfunding as a method that is used to pool funds together from various people (donors or sponsors), through internet-based platforms. Though concise and clear, this definition does not take context into consideration. Contextual perspective is necessary when defining crowdfunding because the concept covers various subject areas and is also projected to cover other areas in the future. The omissions on scope that is, the type/forms of crowdfunding, and lack of context, are evident in other definitions of crowdfunding for example, Tomczak and Brem (2013). Consequently, attempts to provide a broad definition for crowdfunding remains elusive, a situation that reflects the evolutionary state of the literature. Therefore, it may be more practical to provide a narrower definition for crowdfunding that reflects its context of usage. This approach will not only ensure clarity in contextual interpretation but also accommodate the evolutionary nature of crowdfunding.

Taking the above perspective into consideration, it is therefore safe to define crowdfunding in this study from an entrepreneurial context. This approach aligns with the aim of this study which is to explore the concept of crowdfunding as an alternative means of funding technology entrepreneurs in Lagos, Nigeria. Accordingly, we adopt Mollick's definition of crowdfunding for this study. According to Mollick (2014), crowdfunding is defined as:

> "*the efforts by entrepreneurial individuals and groups – cultural, social, and for-profit – to fund their ventures by drawing on relatively small contributions from a relatively large number of individuals using the internet, without standard financial intermediaries.*"

In addition to its alignment with the aim of this study, Mollick's definition is also appealing because it takes the critical elements of crowdfunding into consideration. However, defining crowdfunding from a contextual perspective does not undermine the credibility of other broad definitions. Instead, it ensures that alignment and clarity which are critical for conceptual clarifications, are present in the definition that is adopted for this study.

2.2 Types of Crowdfunding

Courtney (2015) outlines four types of crowdfunding namely: donation-based, reward-based, equity-based and debit or credit-based crowdfunding. A brief overview of the types of crowdfunding is provided below (see Table 2 below).

Donation-based Crowdfunding

Donation-based crowdfunding provides funding for initiatives that benefit the community and society via internet platforms. These include charitable, environmental and entrepreneurial projects. Donation-based crowdfunding is premised on 'the doctrine of giving without expecting in return' (Courtney 2015). Therefore, donors do not expect profit or incentives for their donations. Instead, donors focus on the greater good for the society (Kuti and Madarász 2014). Also, beneficiaries using

Table 2. The dominant models of crowdfunding in the industry.

	Types of Crowdfunding	Definitions
1.	Donation-based Crowdfunding	Funders donate funds to facilitate initiatives (e.g., charitable, environmental, and entrepreneurial) that benefit the` community and society. Donors do not get any reward because donation-based crowdfunding is premised on the doctrine of giving without expecting in return (Courtney 2015).
2.	Reward-based Crowdfunding	Individual donors contribute funds to finance business initiatives and projects, in return for non-financial rewards such as acknowledgement, goods or services for their donations.
3.	Equity-based Crowdfunding	A method used by companies or entrepreneurs to raise funds from investors (funders or backers), via the internet (stock market) to finance creative entrepreneurial ideas or projects (Courtney 2015). Investors, in return, demand for ownership stake as a reward for their financial investments.
4.	Debit- or Credit-based Crowdfunding	Facilitated by individual lenders or funders who contribute funds together and disburse to borrowers on internet-based platforms (Stasik and Wilkczynska 2018). Loans do not require collateral or intermediaries, but a fixed amount is agreed by both parties until the loan expires.

Source: Authors.

donation-based crowdfunding methods are not obliged to their sponsors. Some examples of internet-based platforms for donation-based crowdfunding include *GoFundMe* and *Kopernik,* etc.

Reward-based Crowdfunding

Reward-based crowdfunding is facilitated by individual donors who support a business or project and expect to get some non-financial rewards such as acknowledgement, goods or services, for their donations (Courtney 2015). This method of crowdfunding comprises of the earlier and later levels. At the earlier level, the fundraiser, entrepreneur soliciting for funds, compensates donors with non-physical or physical rewards, an appreciation letter or souvenirs, e.g., branded t shirts, based on their level of contribution (Mitra 2012).

A review of reward-based platforms for crowdfunding such as *Indiegogo* and *Kickstarter*, reveals certain themes that characterise this method. For example, such platforms (companies), although profit driven, mainly support entrepreneurial and creative initiatives. Also, the objectives of such platforms are not driven by maximizing financial benefits. Their emphasis is to redefine entrepreneurship and the method of bringing new ideas to reality, as well as empowering people (Mitra 2012).

Equity-based Crowdfunding

Equity-based crowdfunding is a method used by companies or entrepreneurs with creative ideas, to raise funds from investors via the internet (stock market), with investors having claim over the future cash flow of such companies (Courtney 2015).

This method of crowdfunding requires a company to issue and sell shares at a cheap price on the internet (stock market) for investors to acquire. Unlike donation and reward-based crowdfunding, equity-based crowdfunding allows companies that are unable to access funding from angel investors, friends or family to access funds from investors who purchased their shares. In return, investors become equitable partners of the organization, and share from their profit and loss (Kuti and Madarász 2014). The underlying theme of equity-based crowdfunding is to democratize access to funds and inclusion of investment for the entrepreneur and investors.

Debit- or Credit-based Crowdfunding

Debit- or credit-based crowdfunding, also called peer-to-peer (P2P) lending, is facilitated by individual lenders who contribute funds together and disburse to borrowers on internet platforms (Stasik and Wilczyńska 2018). The loans do not require financial intermediaries or collateral. However, some credit-based platforms such as *Zopa* and *Upstart*, do offer peer-to-business (P2B) lending, with the condition that the borrowing organization must undergo pre-screening before accessing funds from private creditors (Kuti and Madarász 2014). The credit-based method of crowdfunding is focused on eliminating intermediaries between creditors and borrowers, and offer fast, direct and simple services that benefits both parties.

Crowdfunding in Nigeria

The literature on crowdfunding in Nigeria is still evolving as reflected in the scarcity of studies on the subject. This situation is not surprising because crowdfunding was unregulated until January 2021, when the Securities and Exchange Commission (SEC) issued the Rules for crowdfunding (Olowogboyega 2021). It is important to note that, in 2016, the Securities and Exchange Commission (SEC) banned all activities relating to equity crowdfunding in Nigeria (Egene 2016). The ban was predicated on the following concerns:

- The absence of an effective regulatory framework to monitor crowdfunding activities in Nigeria, and its associated risks.
- The legal barriers resulting from the provisions of the Investment and Securities Act, section 67 (1) & (2) and the Companies and Allied Matters Act, section 22 (3) & (5).

However, prior to January 2021, there were indications that crowdfunding may soon gain full regulatory acceptance in Nigeria. In March 2020, the SEC, in exercising the powers conferred on it by Section 313 of the Investment and Securities Act (ISA), released a document titled 'Exposure of Proposed New Rules to the Rules and Regulations of the Commission' (Olowogboyega and Edalere 2020). The new rules highlight the SEC's plans to provide a safe, conducive and profitable market for crowdfunding activities in Nigeria. It identifies the categories of companies that are permitted to raise funds through crowdfunding, the criteria for participation and other details.

Despite the previous ban of crowdfunding activities in Nigeria, some studies had explored the potential of crowdfunding to fund entrepreneurship in the country. Eniola and Entebeng (2015) examined the performance of SMEs from the perspective of funding deficit and the financial innovations available, as well as the challenges. Their findings suggest that SMEs in Nigeria can bridge the funding gap through crowdfunding. The study concluded that the Federal Government, through its regulatory institutions, should provide a conducive environment to accommodate crowdfunding in Nigeria. Ekpe et al. (2017) surveyed 217 lecturers to ascertain the effect of crowdfunding on entrepreneurial intentions amongst academic staff in three Universities, in the Northeast and western regions in Nigeria. Their findings showed a positive relationship between crowdfunding and entrepreneurial intentions. It was also discovered that majority of the lecturers were ignorant of crowdfunding as a new means of financing enterprises.

Moreover, Soreh (2017) surveyed three cities–Lagos, Port Harcourt and Yenagoa–to explore the awareness and attitudes towards crowdfunding in Nigeria. A hundred and fifty respondents participated in this study, and the findings indicated that the participants awareness of crowdfunding was exceptionally low at 24%. It was also reported that most donors usually donate for social and humanitarian causes, for example, to help the sick in Nigeria. The study concluded that crowdfunding could fund entrepreneurial activities in Nigeria if the people are well informed of the concept. Soreh (2017b), in a subsequent study, explored the potential of crowdfunding to finance entrepreneurship ideas in Nigeria, using a review-based methodology and secondary data. Findings revealed that constraints and risks such as the legal and regulatory framework, may hinder the implementation of crowdfunding in Nigeria. The study concluded that the time is right to introduce crowdfunding, specifically, donation or pre-order models, to facilitate entrepreneurship in Nigeria.

Furthermore, Okoyeuzu et al. (2019) explored crowdfunding as an alternative mechanism for funding women entrepreneurs in Enugu State, Nigeria. A mixed methodology was used for the study and data was obtained from 402 small and medium enterprise (SME) owners in the state. Interviews were also conducted amongst bankers, legislators and industrialists, to sample various opinions on crowdfunding. Their findings indicate that crowdfunding may provide an alternative mechanism for financing women entrepreneurs in Nigeria. Findings also reveal that gender is not significant for understanding crowdfunding. This revelation is indicative of the strong cultural barriers' women face when accessing finance for business.

The Gap in the Literature

There is a growing perception that crowdfunding could provide an alternative source of funding for entrepreneurs (Soreh 2017b, Okoyeuzu et al. 2019). However, findings from the literature review reveals some gaps which limit our understanding of crowdfunding and its potential to fund entrepreneurs in Lagos state and Nigeria in general. This section discusses the gaps in literature.

One of the gaps in literature is the lack of studies on crowdfunding in Nigeria. Undoubtedly, there are studies on crowdfunding in Nigeria (e.g., Soreh 2017b, Okoyeuzu et al. 2019). However, these studies did not consider the potential of crowdfunding to fund entrepreneurs in Nigeria, especially in Lagos State. This is worrying because technology is identified as a catalyst for solving Nigeria's socio-economic and infrastructural challenges such as insecurity, corruption, inadequate power (electricity) supply and rail transportation (Ogidan et al. 2017, Lawal et al. 2018). However, due to the lack of funding from the public and private sectors, technological innovations from Nigeria's technology hub have not been adequately financed (NIDTA 2019). This funding deficit makes it important and timely to explore crowdfunding as an alternative source of funding for entrepreneurs in Nigeria. Thus, if entrepreneurs take full advantage of alternative methods of funding, instead of loans and other credit facilities from banks, the challenges that clog the wheel of entrepreneurial development can be minimised.

Another gap in literature is that which focuses on crowdfunding in Nigeria. A review of these studies shows that they focused more on asserting the potential of crowdfunding to fund entrepreneurial initiatives in Nigeria. For example, Soreh (2017b) explored the potentials of crowdfunding to finance entrepreneurship ideas in Nigeria, using a review-based methodology. Okoyeuzu et al. (2019) explored crowdfunding as an alternative mechanism for funding women entrepreneurs in Enugu State, Nigeria. These studies, however, do not substantiate their findings with practical and procedural discourse on how crowdfunding can provide opportunities for entrepreneurship. This pattern is also observed in other studies such as Eniola and Entenbang (2015) and Soreh (2017a), though some evidence is provided by Ekpe et al. (2017) to support the assertions.

Furthermore, the review of crowdfunding in Nigeria also reveals that studies in this context often take a broad scope instead of focusing on a specific context. Soreh (2017a), for instance, surveyed three cities, Lagos, Port Harcourt and Yenagoa, to explore the awareness and attitudes towards crowdfunding in Nigeria. Okoyeuzu et al. (2019) explored crowdfunding as an alternative mechanism for funding women entrepreneurs operating in SMEs in Enugu State, Nigeria. The broad scope of both studies makes it difficult to quantify their findings within a specific context. For example, 150 participants took part in the survey conducted by Soreh (2017a) in highly populated cities in Nigeria. Taking the sample size into consideration, it is difficult to draw a valid inference from 150 participants in highly populated cities in Nigeria such as Lagos. Moreover, Okoyeuzu et al. (2019) made no reference to any specific sector in their study. This makes it difficult to ascertain the contextual factors that may have influenced the results from the study. Since crowdfunding is a novel method of financing entrepreneurship in Nigeria, these observations limit our understanding of its behavioural pattern.

Having explored the literature around crowdfunding and entrepreneurship in Nigeria, we highlight gaps and issues that need to be addressed in the literature. Therefore, there is a need to explore how crowdfunding provides funding for entrepreneurs in Nigeria, and beyond.

3. Methodology

Given the fast-moving nature of crowding in Nigeria, it was important to contextualize the research problem and, ultimately, answering the research questions. The research has been designed primarily by consulting with the literature on crowdfunding and designing a longitudinal in-depth case on the topic under review. Data was obtained from secondary sources, that is, journal articles, books and relevant websites on crowdfunding. We conducted independent literature searches from 2000 to the present, using databases such as *Google Scholar* and *Ebsco*. A general web search was conducted on Google. The result from these searches were compared amongst the three authors. The inclusion criteria centred on contributions that addressed crowdfunding in Nigeria and Africa at large. The contributions were thus selected multilaterally based on relevancy upon reading the abstract.

3.1 Analysis

The case analysis was in twofold: (a) reviewing the collected data; (b) triangulating different sources. For methodological quality and rigour, we coded the different sources of data. We carried out our coding based on the identified constructs and relationships that emerged from the data. We identified thematic units from the secondary data collected. Following an iterative process of coding between the three authors, we coded the data until we arrived at a satisfactory level of inter-coder reliability.

For transparency and rigour, we tracked the first round of our individual findings in a shared folder. We then started analysing our data by open coding the constructs in the data. Afterwards, we carried out axial coding, that is, searching for relationships between these constructs. This analytic and recursive process is consistent with Vanpoucke et al. (2014), as we continued the open and axial coding until we identified consistent themes and relationships. Moreover, the nebulous details, divergent views and inconsistent results were further explored for consistency and rigour. The following section presents our findings and explains our results.

4. Findings and Discussions

4.1 Research Context: Crowdfunding for Technology-based Entrepreneurship in Nigeria

Crowdfunding has gained rapid popularity globally for its potential to provide funding for entrepreneurial initiatives (Singnori and Vismara 2018). In recent times, crowdfunding has begun to get a footing in Nigeria, specifically in Lagos state. For example, *Naijafund*, the biggest and fastest growing crowd funder in Nigeria, is a crowdfunding online platform for Nigerian entrepreneurs to raise money, especially to fund technology initiatives (Africa Business Communities 2018, Africa Press List 2018). The platform is a donation-based website that functions as "a keep all you raise model" and proscribes offerings of rewards in return for contributions. Registration and creation of platforms is free, and operations are subjected to a fee when a donation is made. The *Naijafund* platform has about twenty-five campaign categories for entrepreneurs, ranging from medical to education (www.naijafund.com). This sub-section unpacks the phenomenal growth of crowdfunding as an alternative source of funding for entrepreneurs in Nigeria.

Certainly, the growth of crowdfunding has provided funding opportunities for entrepreneurs seeking to raise funds for their initiatives (Moed 2018). Crowdfunding has increased the group of potential idea-backers from Nigeria and beyond. In essence, donors with experience and funds can provide adequate backing to facilitate entrepreneurial initiatives.

Given the complexity of crowdfunding in a fast-moving environment such as Nigeria, the crux of this context examines the changing regulatory environment in the crowdfunding space (Techpoint 2018). From 2010 till date, various rigorous compliance requirements have been introduced to protect the economic interests of funders (backers) in Nigeria. Therefore, each pitching entrepreneur is subject to the due diligence process. The implication of this changing environment is that funders are well informed of the risks of backing entrepreneurial initiatives in the technology sector.

The regulatory changes became necessary because of the growing appeal of crowdfunding as a method of funding entrepreneurial initiatives in the technology sector (Disrupt Africa 2017). The perceived benefits of crowdfunding have been particularly amplified in emerging markets. Nigeria is well placed within the emerging markets, mainly because the country has the largest market (i.e., GDP) on the continent (Techpoint 2018). The size of Nigeria's economy also correlates with the total funding by country in the continent (see Figure 1). Moed (2018) is of the opinion that there has been a primary growth in access to capital. In 2017, technology start-ups and entrepreneurs raised up to US$195 million (see Figure 1). In 2017, to put the amount raised into perspective, funds raised in the United States of America (USA) reached the amount of US$84 billion (Disrupt Africa 2017).

As shown in Figure 1, crowdfunding is gradually making inroads into Africa, especially into Nigeria (Moed 2018). The inflow of capital is necessary given the size of the target market and the wide scale of its developmental needs. This is because there has been an over reliance on foreign direct investments (FDIs). Therefore, finding alternative sources of funding for entrepreneurs in Nigeria has become imperative. Reliance on FDIs will not be adequate to propel the fast growth that will scale up entrepreneurial initiatives in the technology sector. To put this point into perspective, in USA, despite the abundance of capital in the form of venture funds, the funds raised are not adequately distributed (Disrupt Africa 2017). This situation indicates that crowdfunding is a suitable alternative source of funding

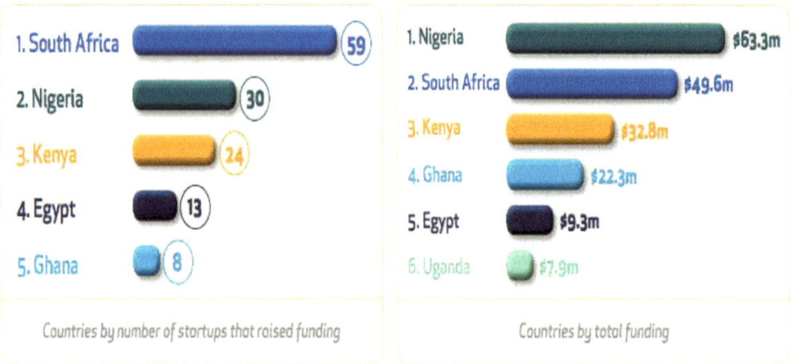

Figure 1. Total of funding by country. Source: Moed (2018).

for technology-entrepreneurs because foreign investors might have unrealistic anticipations for the timeframe needed to scale up businesses; also, local investors might be less risk averse. Overall, crowdfunding has provided an alternative source of funding for entrepreneurs by allowing local and sometimes international residents, to fund and invest in locally registered businesses. Most importantly, crowdfunding platforms need to comply with financial and legal requirements.

4.2 Exploring the Prospects of Using Crowdfunding for Raising Funds to Finance Technology-Entrepreneurs in Nigeria

Our findings show that there has been a substantial uptake in crowdfunding for entrepreneurial endeavours. A report by Financial Nigeria (2016) revealed that $83.3 million was raised in Africa via crowdfunding in 2015 and Nigeria accounted for $7–$8 million. Meanwhile, in 2018, the amount raised in Africa via crowdfunding was US$195 million (Disrupt Africa 2018). These figures show that the amount raised in 2018 doubled that of 2015. Most importantly, the amount raised in Lagos, the economic capital of Nigeria, was $63.3 million in 2018. This implies that Nigeria accounts for up to half of funds raised via crowdfunding in Africa.

On a micro-level, the entrepreneurial initiatives in the technology sector seems to be a lucrative business venture that attracts funding to get kick-started. In other words, crowdfunding has become an increasingly common method for entrepreneurs and founders to finance their business ventures. However, the reality for founders and entrepreneurs is that not all ventures get access to grants, bank loans or venture capital funds, to get kickstarted (Disrupt 2017). Consequently, crowdfunding facilitates the democratization of access to capital to fund projects or businesses. The data shows that a lot of projects in Lagos State, and in Nigeria at large, have taken off due to the robust backing from the crowd.

Given the scheme of things, whether an entrepreneur is funding a breakthrough, radical innovation or mission-based social innovation, there are various crowdfunding platforms that help with entrepreneurs in Nigeria. It is free to create a project on most crowdfunding platforms. For example, the platform *Kickstarter* is used to fund creative projects in technology, such as software design or producing creative work that is cloud-based. Such projects entice funders to buy into the products, benefits and fun experiences. Founders and entrepreneurs must account for the funds that they have been afforded. This means that entrepreneurs are expected to meet the set-out objective or goal within the allotted time or everyone gets their money back.

Similarly, *NaijaFund*, another crowdfunding platform, allows business founders to raise funds by removing the obstacles—rigid requirements that hinder access to funding—by allowing entrepreneurs to connect their platform accounts with their social media account and networks. This method allows entrepreneurs to easily solicit for funds from their network of connections, such as friends, friends of friends, community leaders, family, and others. Most platforms, however, charge a processing fee that could range from 3–10% (Disrupt Africa 2018). For example, even though it is free to create on *NaijaFund*, there is a deductible fee of 10% from each donation received. On the contrary, businesses that are focused on building consumer brands use *CircleUp*, another crowdfunding platform. Entrepreneurs that are working towards getting their product into the market are offered various services, including the possibility to connect with 'accredited' funders and high-level investors who draw insights using artificial intelligence (AI), machine learning technology and have access to unique lines of credit for new start-ups (Schwienbacher and Laralde 2010, Covington 2017).

Moreover, there is opportunity for international platforms to provide crowdfunding as a mechanism for raising funds to finance entrepreneurs. For example, Indiegogo, is a crowdfunding platform that empowers entrepreneurs globally to fund projects and ventures. The Indiegogo platform enables start-ups to generate pre-sales input and feedback from initial adopters prior to their manufacture. Indiegogo has offered crowdfunding opportunities and an avenue for innovative products to emanate. Since its inception, in 2010, Indiegogo has helped entrepreneurs globally to raise $1 billion for about 700,000 projects (Wierzbicka 2018).

4.3 Challenges Limiting Crowdfunding for Entrepreneurs in Nigeria

From the data analysis, numerous challenges that could limit crowdfunding as an alternative source of funding for entrepreneurs in Nigeria were highlighted. Findings from the data analysis specifically highlights that lack of financial innovation, in the form of avenues of alternative funding, could pose a huge burden on the growing crowdfunding eco system in the country. Research indicates that financial innovation, for example, an alternative method of funding, will help entrepreneurs struggling with funding in developing countries such as Nigeria. For example, Eniola and Entebeng (2015) explored the difficulties entrepreneurs in developing countries face when trying to access funds. They noted that crowdfunding is a form of financial innovation, which entails the creating of alternative sources of finances to ameliorate difficulties faced by entrepreneurs.

The gap in funding for entrepreneurial initiatives is coupled with multiple challenges for entrepreneurs. Overall, inventive forms of financing for entrepreneurial endeavours are crucial prerequisites for bridging existing funding gaps in technology sector. Traditional bank loans whether commercial or microfinance, are insufficient to meet the soaring demand for funds by entrepreneurs in Nigeria. This is not surprising because Nigeria has the biggest economy in Africa (Naido 2020), while Lagos State has the seventh-largest economy in the continent (Egbejule 2020). Most specifically, entrepreneurs may struggle to cope with the interest rates offered by traditional financial institutions. Thus, crowdfunding provides an innovative means of financing entrepreneurial ventures.

Our findings reveal that the absence of an effective regulatory framework poses a huge challenge to the smooth operation of crowdfunding in Nigeria. Funders and entrepreneurs in the crowdfunding domain were originally operating in a loosely unregulated industry (Egene 2016). The lack of regulation posed a challenge to crowdfunding as an alternative source of financing entrepreneurial initiatives in the technology sector in Nigeria. The lack of laws meant that crowdfunding investors were inadequately protected in terms of privacy, mandated disclosures, and opportunities for legal redress. This may have been the reason for the lack of trust in the crowdfunding and financial ecosystem. In comparison with developed countries such as USA, crowdfunding platforms are required by law to issue securities for potential crowd funders to make disclosures to investors. Thus, the lack of disclosure in Nigeria meant that investors would have been deprived of relevant information to make sound financial judgments—this would have affected investor confidence.

Moreover, the uncertainty surrounding the effectiveness of the recently introduced regulatory framework for crowdfunding in Nigeria, is another potential challenge that affects its operations in entrepreneurship. In January 2021, the SEC issued the Rules for crowdfunding (Olowogboyega 2021). Given its early days, players in the sector, including funders and investors, may be sceptical of the effectiveness of the rules, particularly in its implementation. The uncertainty, if not effectively managed by the regulators, could result to a lack of investor confidence, and consequently, a slow pace of activities in the crowdfunding eco system. Investors would be particularly concerned about flouting laws when contributing funds, and the likelihood of getting speedy legal redress if they are defrauded.

Furthermore, our findings also revealed that the mechanism for transferring funds between funders and entrepreneurs on the platform is ineffective. This has been a complex regulatory barrier in Nigeria because most payments go through traditional financial institutions that trade in non-convertible currencies, that is, the companies cannot be traded or exchanged internationally in currencies such as dollars or euros (Wierzbicka 2018). The implication of this barrier, caused by the lack of payment platforms, indicates a lack of digital payment opportunities. This highlights a critical challenge that impedes the potential of crowdfunding to provide funding for entrepreneurs in Nigeria. Lastly, as the literature demonstrates, insufficient information provided by entrepreneurs to their target audience might also hinder crowdfunding efforts. Research suggests that the more information on a project that is available for donors, the higher the project's chances of funding success (Parhankangas and Renko 2017).

4.4 Frameworks and Mechanisms for Regulating Crowdfunding in Nigeria

Crowdfunding is still at the early stages of its development in Nigeria and Africa in general. Before January 2021, when the Securities and Exchange Commission (SEC) released the new rules for crowdfunding called 'the rules' in Nigeria, there was no regulation governing its operations in the country. This is due to the ban on crowdfunding activities in Nigeria by the SEC in 2016 (Egene 2016). However, a proposed version of the new rules for crowdfunding was released in March 2020 (Olowogboyega and Edalere 2020). Certainly, the regulatory framework is a catalyst for growth in the crowdfunding domain. However, it is difficult to ascertain the robustness of the new rules for crowdfunding in Nigeria because it is still relatively new, having been introduced in January 2021.

Contrary to the Nigerian situation, there is established legislation that governs all aspects of crowdfunding in the developed world, that is, in USA. These include fundraising limits, corporate filings, financial disclosures and customer due diligence. Under the Securities and Exchange Commission (SEC) regulations, the public could invest in start-ups looking to raise funds. The regulation is designed to support the public in understanding crowdfunding rules and procedures that would enable them to make educated decisions concerning the risks and rewards of making investments in technology start-ups.

Moreover, in the USA, a law was established for crowdfunding that allowed early-stage ventures to offer and sell equities. The SEC adopted a policy to regulate crowdfunding by implementing crowdfunding JOBS Act in 2017 (FINRA 2017). Consequently, the Financial Industry Regulatory Authority (FINRA) was established in 2017. The role of FINRA is to administer the registering of crowdfunding platforms and to make sure that platforms obey with the laws and FINRA rules. Therefore, funding portals need to be registered with the SEC; as such, FINRA laws allow funders and entrepreneurs to offer and sell equity to the public leveraging crowdfunding.

Currently, in Nigeria, there is no similar legislation to that which is obtainable in developed economies such as USA. As earlier mentioned, the Nigerian SEC banned crowdfunding operations in 2016 (Egene 2016), proposed new rules in 2020 (Olowogboyega and Edale 2020), and eventually published new rules in January 2021 (Olowogboyega 2021). The ban was issued because the SEC noted that the lack of rules hindered the effective regulation of crowdfunding, as a source of funding for entrepreneurial initiatives, in Nigeria. Moreover, the crowdfunding rules did not cover non-reward-based campaigns.

The current cost structure and the legal requirements involved in setting up and managing an equity crowdfunding platform are prohibitive for many would-be platforms. Wierzbicka (2018) noted that on platforms such as *CircleUp*, which was launched in 2017, takes the costs of dealing with specific categories of licensing. For example, in South Africa, it adheres to the Financial Services Board (FSB), the regulatory body's rules even though most platforms do not fall under its regulatory remit. In other words, some platforms regulate themselves. Regulation could also benefit investors and funders by protecting them, while providing them with further benefits. For instance, in the United Kingdom, investors and funders are incentivized to invest through equity or ownership crowdfunding platforms by receiving tax cuts on the investments they make.

Based on this, it is evident that there is currently no effective regulatory framework for regulating crowdfunding in Nigeria. This could hinder the growth of the crowdfunding eco system in Nigeria. Crowdfunding platforms could struggle to grow on a large scale because their survival and effectiveness, especially in terms of providing funding for entrepreneurial initiatives in the IC technology sector, is dependent on the development of robust regulatory framework. Nevertheless, the new rules proposed by the SEC, to regulate crowdfunding in Nigeria, are timely, and a step in the right direction.

4.5 Prospects and Barriers to Crowdfunding in Nigeria

This section discusses the prospects of crowdfunding for entrepreneurs in Nigeria. The use of dedicated online platforms to raise funds for entrepreneurial ventures is a rapidly growing phenomenon globally (Poetz and Schreirer 2012, Wardrop et al. 2015). This phenomenon has begun to get a footing in Nigeria. Nevertheless, crowdfunding in Nigeria remains limited as compared to other parts of the world. In 2015, the Nigerian crowdfunding market was valued at 70 million USD, which translates to about 1% of the global market of crowdfunding (World Bank 2015). However, the World Bank projects that crowdfunding could grow globally to reach $96 billion USD by 2025.

Based on the data collection and analysis in this research, the business model for crowdfunding platform is as follows: the entrepreneur posts their business idea on to a platform such as *NaijaFund* (Schwienbacher and Larralde 2010). The pitching of ideas includes fundraising targeted to the people the entrepreneur wants to reach. The participants can range from all over the world—that is, non-Nigerian entrepreneurs can pitch their ideas and raise funds from investors globally. However, some foreign platforms may use different payment techniques that curb contributions coming in from lower-income nations. Generally, funders are part of the social network of entrepreneurs; in some cases, investors may be part of the public (including institutional investors). Therefore, most crowdfunding endeavours in Nigeria are donation-based, but there are some activities around equity-based and debt-based platforms.

Crowdfunding provides some unique opportunities for entrepreneurs in Nigeria. Firstly, crowdfunding enables entrepreneurs to access capital via creative means. Traditionally, entrepreneurs, when possible, can either borrow at variable or fixed rates from banks or investments venture capital firms. However, access to credit for Nigerian entrepreneurs' is often constrained (Ovat 2013, Afolayan 2016). In turn, financial institutions are highly risk-averse and potential borrowers have scalable businesses but lack credit history to qualify for financial instruments. Therefore, crowdfunding empowers entrepreneurs to be attractive to potential donors/investors without worrying much about creditworthiness, credit history or incomes.

Secondly, since crowdfunding operates mainly on digital platforms, entrepreneurs in Nigeria could leverage the amplified use of mobile devices/networks to transact (Ziegler et al. 2018). Despite the lack of trust and familiarity associated with online fundraising, the widespread use of phones has been critical in fostering activities in the crowdfunding domain. In addition, crowdfunding platforms subsidize the costs of doing business that is, marketing, by allowing entrepreneurs to use the platform with an in-built user base. Specifically, listing an entrepreneurial venture on a platform exposes such venture to investors.

Beyond opportunities, the rise of crowdfunding in Nigeria also comes with its challenges. Practitioners must realize that crowdfunding could deepen the urban-rural divisions with the reliance on social connections and individual rewards depending on the strength of their network. Also, there is uncertainty on the robustness of the new rules for crowdfunding operations in Nigeria, which was published by the SEC in January 2021. Although, the rules have been applauded in some quarters, funders in the crowdfunding ecosystem may watch closely for some time to ascertain its effectiveness. This could slowdown activities in the crowdfunding ecosystem in the meantime. Therefore, to encourage crowdfunding, policy makers should take deliberate steps to mitigate the concerns around money laundering. In addition, research shows that insufficient information provided by the founders to their target audience (donors) might hinder campaign efforts (Parhankangas and Renko 2017).

Trust is another factor that affects crowdfunding operations in Nigeria. The issue of trust management must be emphasised within crowdfunding platforms. For example, Pekmezovic and Walker (2015) argue that "lack of trust could hinder the adoption of e-commerce service" and for internet-related transactions, an individual's perception of the institutional environment is critical. Therefore, trust is the panacea to reducing uncertainty in crowdfunding. Establishing trust also provides confidence between two parties, and this improves the reliability and integrity of business. This cognitive and social behaviour reduces complexity and provides a coping mechanism for uncertainty and risk (Nwolisa 2017). Also, in crowdfunding campaigns, investors and stakeholders may not have sufficient information to reduce uncertainty because of the complexity of e-commerce transactions. Hence, they are likely to apply shortcuts mentally, that is, rely on their trust instincts (Ziegler et al. 2018).

On the positive side, crowdfunding could be impactful in Nigeria because it provides an alternative source of funding for entrepreneurs in Nigeria (Mollick 2014, Covington 2017). Crowdfunding addresses the gap created by the difficulty in accessing funds from banks and other financial institutions (Eniola and Entebang 2015, Wardrop et al. 2015). This could facilitate the development of a supplementary and inclusive finance model that offers increased control to early-stage entrepreneurs.

5. Summary and Conclusion

Based on our findings, we conclude that crowdfunding could provide an alternative method of funding for entrepreneurs in Nigeria. However, the effectiveness of the new rules for crowdfunding is yet to be ascertained since it was only introduced by the SEC in January 2021. This could hinder the potential for crowdfunding to bridge the funding gap in the technology sector in the short term.

In line with this conclusion, we proffer the following recommendations for stakeholders, for example, policymakers, investors and entrepreneurs, to create an enabling economic environment for crowdfunding operations in Nigeria. First, the security and effectiveness of crowdfunding platforms should be strengthened to foster trust among investors and entrepreneurs. Trust reduces uncertainty in crowdfunding and enhances confidence amongst stakeholders in the crowdfunding ecosystem. Second, the new rules should be clear and made easy for investors to maximize the opportunities offered by crowdfunding. The regulation should stipulate to what extent investors can invest and own equity on ventures with regards to their investment. Lastly, payment systems should be developed and harnessed to ease transactions for stakeholders within the crowdfunding ecosystem.

6. Contribution to Knowledge

Theoretically, this study contributes to the literature by providing fresh insights to fill the gap in our knowledge and understanding of crowdfunding. As previously mentioned, the literature on crowdfunding is still evolving and this is evidenced by the general shortage of studies on the subject (Singori and Vismara 2018). Besides, most of the available studies on crowdfunding were conducted in western countries. Consequently, little is known about its the operational dynamics in Nigeria. Therefore, this study and its findings, provides useful insight on crowdfunding in a typical non-western country.

This study also contributes to the literature by demonstrating that with an effective regulatory framework, crowdfunding could provide funding for entrepreneurial initiatives in the technology sector in Nigeria. Studies on crowdfunding in Nigeria have mainly focused on the awareness and attitudes towards the concept (Soreh 2017a), and its potential as a mechanism for funding entrepreneurship in southeast Nigeria (Okoyeuzu et al. 2019). This contribution to knowledge has theoretical and practical implications. Theoretically, it advances the literature on crowdfunding as past studies have not explored the potential of crowdfunding for entrepreneurs in Nigeria.

To practice and policy, the findings from this study highlight the need to provide adequate funding for the technology sector in Nigeria. Research has identified technology as a catalyst for solving Nigeria's socio-economic problems such as inadequate power (electricity) supply, lack of rail transportation infrastructure and insecurity, etc. (Bubou et al. 2011, Ogidan et al. 2017). However, the lack of funding from government and private sector continues to hinder laudable technological innovations from solving Nigeria's socio-economic challenges. The provision of funding should be supported with a strict and robust regulatory framework to protect funders and entrepreneurs alike.

7. Direction for Future Studies

Before providing the direction for future studies, it is imperative to highlight the limitation of this study since it informs the directions for future studies. Due to the reliance on secondary data, our findings did not capture the views of entrepreneurs in Nigeria, who may have funded their businesses via crowdfunding. We also do not specify any aspect of entrepreneurship in the paper. Based on this limitation, we hereby offer the following directions for future studies on crowdfunding in Nigeria.

Future studies exploring the potential of crowdfunding to fund entrepreneurial initiatives in the technology sector in Nigeria, should use both primary and secondary data. Data should be obtained from entrepreneurs that have, or otherwise, benefited from crowdfunding or similar initiatives, in the technology sector. This will enable entrepreneurs in the technology sector to share their firsthand experience and understanding of crowdfunding in Nigeria. Consequently, researchers will ascertain the operational dynamics and behavioural pattern of crowdfunding in the Nigerian context.

Future studies should explore the potential of crowdfunding to fund entrepreneurial initiatives in other sectors of the economy. Emphasis should be given to the power and healthcare services sectors which are critical to leapfrogging Nigeria's economic growth. The power sector is critical for driving industrialisation and local production in the country. Researchers should critically explore the effectiveness of the new legislation governing crowdfunding operations in Nigeria. For crowdfunding to be effective in Nigeria, the regulatory framework must be effective and suitable for the current economic climate and social realities that characterise the Nigerian environment.

References

Afolayan, O.T. 2016. Inadequate access to finance: a bottleneck for entrepreneurial vibrancy in Ilaro, Ogun State, Nigeria. International Journal of Academic Research in Business and Social Sciences 6(10): 2222–6990.

Africa Business Communities. 2018. Naijafund crowdfunding platform makes service globally accessible to Nigerians. Retrieved 1st August 2020, from: https://africabusinesscommunities.com/news/naijafund-crowdfunding-platform-makes-service-globally-accessible-to-nigerians/.

Africa Press List. 2018. Crowdfunding platform makes service globally accessible to Nigerians. Rertrieved 1st August 2020, from https://africapresslist.com/en/pressreleases/naijafund-crowdfunding-platform-makes-crowdfunding-globally-accessible-to-nigerians-02-08-2018-17-57-59.

Aladejebi, O. 2020. Crowdfunding: An emerging source of funds in Nigeria. Archives of Business Review 8(7).

Armendariz, B. and Morduch, J. 2010. The Economics of Microfinance. Cambridge, MIT Press.

Belleflamme, P., Lambert, T. and Schwienbacher, A. 2013. Individual crowdfunding practices. Venture Capital 15(4): 313–333.

Block, J., Hornuf, L. and Moritz, A. 2018. Which updates during an equity crowdfunding campaign increase crowd participation? Small Business Economics 50: 3–27.

Bubou, Gordon Monday and Festa Okrigwe. 2011. Fostering technological entrepreneurship for socioeconomic development: a case for technology incubation in Bayelsa State, Nigeria. Journal of Sustainable Development 4.6: 138–149.

Business Day. 2020. CACOVID has been Nigeria's COVID-19 response hero, and more. Retrieved 3rd September, 2020, from: https://businessday.ng/features/article/cacovid-has-been-nigerias-covid-19-response-hero-and-more/.

Butticè, V., Colombo, M. and Wright, M. 2017. Serial crowdfunding, social capital and project success. Entrepreneurship Theory and Practice 1(2): 183–207.

Chan, C. and Parhankangas, A. 2017. Crowdfunding innovative ideas: how incremental and radical innovativeness influence funding outcomes. Entrepreneurship Theory and Practice 41(2): 237–263.

Colombo, M.G., Franzoni, C. and Rossi-Lamastra, C. 2015. Internal social capital and the attraction of early contributions in crowdfunding. Entrepreneurship Theory and Practice 39(1): 75–100.

Courtney, V. 2015. Crowdfunding brings new opportunities for CPAs. Journal of Accountancy 220(4): 38–42.

Covington. 2017. Crowdfunding in Africa: Opportunities and Challenges. Retrieved 1st August 2020 from: https://www.covafrica.com/2017/02/crowdfunding-in-africa-opportunities-and-challenges/.

Detert, J.R. and Treviño, L.K. 2010. Speaking up to higher-ups: How supervisors and skip-level leaders influence employee voice. Organization Science 21(1): 249–270.

Disrupt Africa. 2017. African Tech Start-ups Funding Report 2019. Disrupt Africa 1(1): 1.

Egbejule, E. 2020. Lagos is a country. Retrieved 2nd September 2020, from https://www.theafricareport.com/28089/lagos-is-a-country/.

Egene, G. 2016. SEC Rules out Crowdfunding in Nigeria for now. Retrieved 2nd September, 2020, from: https://www.thisdaylive.com/index.php/2016/08/15/sec-rules-out-crowdfunding-in-nigeria-for-now/.

Ekpe, I., Mat, N., Ahmad, A. and Kura, K.M. 2017. Effect of crowdfunding on entrepreneurial intentions among academic staff of Nigerian Universities. International Journal of Management in Education 11(4).

Eniola, A.A. and Entebang, H. 2015. SME Firm Performance - Financial Innovation and Challenges. Procedia - Social and Behavioral Sciences 195: 334–342.

Financial Nigeria. 2016. New report reveals huge crowdfunding potential in Nigeria. Available: http://www.financialnigeria.com/new-report-reveals-huge-crowdfunding-potential-in-nigeria-sustainable-photovideo-details-809.html. Last accessed 8 July 2021.
FINRA. 2017. Crowdfunding and the JOBS Act: What Investors Should Know. Retrieved 1st August 2020, from: https://www.finra.org/investors/alerts/crowdfunding-and-jobs-act.
Freedman, D. 2015. The Growth of Equity Crowdfunding. Value Examiner 6–10.
Greenberg, J. and Mollick, E. 2017. Activist choice homophily and the crowdfunding of female founders. Administrative Science Quarterly 62(2): 341–374.
Horvat, E.A., Wachs, J., Wang, R, Hanna, K.A. 2018. The role of novelty in securing investors for equity crowdfunding campaigns. HCOMP.
Howe, J. 2006. The rise of crowdsourcing. Wired Magazine 14(6): 1–4.
Kleeman, F., Vob, G. and Rieder, K. 2008. Under paid innovators: The commercial utillization of consumer work through crowdsourcing. Science, Technology and Innovation Studies 4(1): 5–26.
Kuti, M. and Madarász, G. 2015. Crowdfunding. Public Finance Quarterly 355–366.
Lawal, Lasisi, S., Chatwin, C.R. and Hasan, R. 2018. The communications satellite industry as an element in Nigeria's attempt to modernise its economy and society. International Journal of African and Asian Studies 51: 30–39. ISSN 2409-6938.
Leimeister, J.M. 2012. Crowdsourcing: Crowdfunding, Crowd voting, Crowd creation. Zeitschrift für Controlling und Management (56): 388–392.
Lin, M., Phrabala, N.R. and Viswanathan, P.S. 2012. Judging borrowers by the company they keep: friendship networks and information asymmetry in online peer-to-peer lending. Management Science 59(1): 17–35. https://doi.org/10.1287/mnsc.1120.1560.
McKenny, A., Allison, T., Ketchen, D., Short, J. and Ireland, R. 2017. How should crowdfunding research evolve? A survey of the entrepreneurship theory and practice editorial board. Entrepreneurship Theory and Practice 41(2): 291–304.
Meyskens, M. and Bird, L. 2015. Crowdfunding and value creation. Entrepreneurship Research Journal 5(2): 155–166.
Mitra, S. 2012. A review of service quality research in India. IMS Management Journal, The Journal of IMS Kolkata 4: 54–66.
Moed, J. 2018. Equity crowdfunding: a new model for investing in Africa. Forbes 1(1).
Mollick, E. 2014. The dynamics of crowdfunding: An exploratory study. Journal of Business Venturing 29(1): 1–16.
Morduch, J. 1999. The microfinance promise. Journal of Economic Literature 37(4): 1569–1614.
Naido, P. 2020. Nigeria Tops South Africa as the Continents biggest economy. Retrieved 30th August, 2020 from: https://www.bloomberg.com/news/articles/2020-03-03/nigeria-now-tops-south-africa-as-the-continent-s-biggest-economy.
Naiki, E. and Ogane, Y. 2019. Bank soundness and bank lending to new firms during the global financial crisis. Review of Financial Economics.
NITDA. 2019. Nigeria ICT Innovation and Entrepreneurship Vision. Retrieved 27th August 2020, from https://nitda.gov.ng/wp-content/uploads/2019/04/NIIEV-2019.pdf.
Nwolisa, C.A.C. 2017. Financial Innovation and Entrepreneurship Development in Lagos State of Nigeria: Challenges and Prospects for Small and Medium Scale Enterprises. Proceedings: 5th International Conference on Innovation Management, Entrepreneurship and Sustainability (IMES). Retrieved 2nd August, 2020, from: http://paper.researchbib.com/view/paper/127851.
Ogidan, J., Adekola O., Emmanuel, G. and Okogun, O. 2017. ICT for good governance and socio-economic development in Nigeria. World Scientific News 72: 522–534.
Okoyeuzu, C., Nwakoby, I. and Onwujekwe, O. 2019. Crowdfunding: An alternative to funding women entrepreneurs. South Asian Journal of Social Studies and Economics 5(2): 1–10.
Olowogboyega, A. and Edalere, I. 2020. Equity Crowdfunding in Nigeria. Available at: https://www.lawyard.ng/2020/04/22/equity-crowdfunding-in-nigeria/ (Accessed 3rd, June, 2020).
Olowogboyega, O. 2021. Crowdfunding intermediaries will need ₦100 million capital per SEC's new rules. Retrieved 23rd June 2021, from https://techcabal.com/2021/02/15/crowdfunding-regulations/.

Osho, G.S. and Adishi, O. 2019. The effects of macroeconomic variables on Lagos state economy: as Lagos economy goes, so goes the economy of Nigeria? Journal of Economics and Development Studies 7(1): 1–9.

Ovat, O.O. 2013. Liquidity constraints and entrepreneurial financing in Nigeria: The fate of fresh graduate entrepreneurs. Global Journal of Management and Business Research Finance 13(9).

Parhankangas, A. and Renko, A, 2017. Linguistic style and crowdfunding success among social and commercial entrepreneurs. Journal of Business Venturing 32(2): 215–236.

Pekmezovic, A. and Walker, G. 2015. Crowdfunding: Solving the SME Funding Problem and Democratising Access to Capital. Retrieved 1st August, 2020, from: http://works.bepress.com/context/alma_pekmezovic/article/1000/type/native/view content.

Pilling, D. 2018. Nigerian economy: Why Lagos works. The Financial Times. Retrieved 17th August, 2020, from https://www.ft.com/content/ff0595e4-26de-11e8-b27e-cc62a39d57a0.

Pitschner, S. and Pitschner-Finn, S. 2014. Non-profit differentials in crowd-based financing: Evidence from 50,000 campaigns. Economics Letters 123(3): 391–394.

Poetz, M. and Schreier, M. 2012. The value of crowdsourcing: can users really compete with professionals in generating new product ideas? Journal of Product Innovation Management 29(2): 245–256.

Richter, C., Seidler-de Alwis, R. and Jötten, M. 2014. Crowdsourcing als Chance fürmittelständische Unternehmen. Zeitschrift für KMU und Entrepreneurship (1): 1–30.

Schwienbacher, A. and Larralde, B. 2010. Crowdfunding of small entrepreneurial ventures. Handbook of Entrepreneurial Finance. Oxford University Press.

Signori, A., Vismara, S. 2018. Does success bring success? The post-offering lives of equity-crowdfunded firms. Journal of Corporate Finance 50: 575–591.

Skirnevskiy, V., Bendig, D. and Brettel, M. 2017. The influence of Internal social capital on serial creators' success in crowdfunding. Entrepreneurship Theory and Practice 1(2): 209–236.

Soreh, W.C. 2017a. Awareness and attitudes towards crowdfunding in Nigeria. International Journal of African and Asian Studies 36.

Soreh, W.C. 2017b. Tapping the potentials of crowdfunding as a financing mechanism for entrepreneurship ideas in Nigeria. Research Journal of Finance and Accounting (8): 14.

Sorenson, O., Assenova, V., Cheng Li, G., Boada, J. and Fleming, L. 2016. Expanding innovation via crowdfunding. Science 354(6319): 1526–1528.

Stasik, A. and Wilczyńska, E. 2018. How do we study crowdfunding? An overview of methods and introduction to new research agenda. Journal of Management and Business Administration. Central Europe 26(1): 49–78, ISSN 2450-7814; e-ISSN 2450-8829.

Surowiecki, J. 2004. The Wisdom of Crowds. New York: Anchor Books.

Techpoint. 2018. How will the SEC's new regulations shape crowdfunding in Nigeria? Retrieved 1st August, 2020, from: https://techpoint.africa/2020/03/31/sec-regulations-crowdfunding-nigeria/.

Tomczak, A. and Brem, A. 2013. A conceptualized investment model of crowdfunding. Venture Capital 15(4): 335–359.

Vanpoucke, E., Vereecke, A. and Wetzels, M. 2014. Developing supplier integration capabilities for sustainable competitive advantage: A dynamic capabilities approach. Journal of Operations Management 32(7-8): 446–461.

Voorbraak, K.J.M. 2011. Crowdfunding for Financing New Ventures: Consequences of the Financial Model on Operational Decisions. Eindhoven, Eindhoven University of Technology.

Walton, J. and Whicker, L. 1996. Virtual Enterprise: Myth & Reality. J. Control, Oct. 96.

Wardrop, R., Zhang, B., Rau, R. and Gray, M. 2015. Moving Mainstream. The European Alternative Finance. University of Cambridge and EY, Benchmarking Report, University of Cambridge and EY.

Wierzbicka, K. 2018. Crowdfunding as an alternative method of raising capital. Financial Internet Quarterly 1(1): 22.

Wicks, M. 2013. Crowdfunding - An Introduction. Victoria Blue: Beetle Books.

World Bank. 2015. Crowdfunding in Emerging Markets: Lessons from East African Startups. Retrieved 21st August 2020, from: https://www.infodev.org/infodev-files/crowdfunding-in-east-africa.pdf.

Zhang, B., Ziegler, T., Burton, J., Garvey, K., Wardrop, R., Lui, A. et al. 2016. Sustaining momentum, The 2nd European Alternative Finance Industry Report. University of Cambridge. Retrieved 25th

August, 2020 from https://www.jbs.cam. ac.uk/fileadmin/user_upload/research/centres/alternative-finance/downloads/2016-european-alternativefinance-report-sustaining-momentum.pdf, access 12.11.2018.

Zheng, H., Li, D., Wu, J. and Xu, Y. 2014. The role of multidimensional social capital in crowdfunding: A comparative study in China and US. Information & Management 51(4): 488–496.

Ziegler, T., Shneor, R., Garvey, K., Wenzlaff, K, Yerolemou, N., Zhang, B. et al. 2018. Expanding horizon, The 2nd European Alternative Finance Industry Report. University of Cambridge, 2017. Retrieved 25th August, 2020, from https://www.jbs.cam.ac.uk/fileadmin/user_upload/research/centres/alternative-finance/downloads/2018-02-ccaf-exp-horizons.pdf, access 12.11.2018.

Index

M

N

O

P

Q

R

S

T

U

W